UNDER FIRE
with the
Tenth U.S. Cavalry

UNDER FIRE
with the
Tenth U.S. Cavalry

———

by

HERSCHEL V. CASHIN, Rec'r U.S. Land Office, Huntsville, Ala.;
CHARLES ALEXANDER, General Newspaper Correspondent;
WILLIAM T. ANDERSON, Chaplain Tenth U.S. Cav., Fort McIntosh,
Texas; ARTHUR M. BROWN, A. A. Surgeon Tenth U.S. Cav., Fort
McIntosh, Texas; HORACE W. BIVINS, Sergeant Tenth U.S. Cav.,
Fort Sam Houston, Texas

Introduction by RICHARD N. ELLIS

UNIVERSITY PRESS OF COLORADO

Copyright © 1993 by the University Press of Colorado
P.O. Box 849
Niwot, Colorado 80544

All rights reserved.

The University Press of Colorado is a cooperative publishing enterprise supported, in part, by Adams State College, Colorado State University, Fort Lewis College, Mesa State College, Metropolitan State College of Denver, University of Colorado, University of Northern Colorado, University of Southern Colorado, and Western State College.

Library of Congress Cataloging-in-Publication Data

Under fire with the Tenth U.S. Cavalry / by Herschel V. Cashin ... [et al.]; introduction by Richard N. Ellis.
    p. cm.
    Originally published: London; New York: F.T. Neely, c1899.
    ISBN 0-87081-280-7; ISBN 0-87081-270-x (pbk.) (alk. paper)
    1. United States. Army. Cavalry, 10th. 2. Spanish-American War, 1898 — Regimental histories. 3. Spanish-American War, 1898 — Participation, Afro-American. 4. Afro-American soldiers — History — 19th century. I. Cashin, Herschel V.
E725.45 10th.U53 1993
973.8'9 — dc20   92-40171
                                                                       CIP

The paper used in this publication meets the minimum requirements of the American National Standard for Information Sciences—Permanence of Paper for Printed Library Materials. ANSI Z39.48–1984

∞

10 9 8 7 6 5 4 3 2 1

INTRODUCTION

When *Under Fire with the Tenth U.S. Cavalry* was published in 1899, the contribution of Blacks to American military history had been largely ignored. Blacks had, however, served with distinction in all American wars. In the American Revolution individuals such as Crispus Attucks and Salem Poor earned recognition while at least one Negro unit, the so-called Black Regiment from Rhode Island, was in service from 1778 to 1783. Blacks served in both the navy and the army during the War of 1812, and two Negro battalions participated in the Battle of New Orleans. Thousands of Blacks served in the Civil War, and in 1866 legislation was passed that authorized Black regiments in the regular army.

The act of July 28, 1866, provided for two Black cavalry regiments, the Ninth and Tenth, and four infantry regiments. In 1869 when the army was reduced in size, the four infantry regiments were reduced to two, the Twenty-fourth and the Twenty-fifth.

While some army officers discriminated against and mistreated Black soldiers in these regiments and other officers declined the opportunity to serve in such units, a number of distinguished soldiers accepted such assignments. Among them were Ranald S. Mackenzie and Abner Doubleday of the Twenty-fourth Infantry, Benjamin Grierson of the Tenth Cavalry, Wesley Merritt of the Ninth Cavalry, and Nelson Miles of the Fortieth Infantry, which was merged into the Twenty-fifth Infantry in 1869.

During most of the remainder of the century, units of these four regiments were scattered across the West on frontier duty. They were stationed from Texas and New Mexico on the south to the Dakotas and Montana in the north and from Minnesota to Arizona. They fought warriors of the Western Sioux, Cheyennes, Comanches, and various Apache groups, and some participated in Mackenzie's Raid across the Rio Grande in 1878. Frontier duty meant isolation, harsh working conditions, disagreeable living conditions, boredom, and occasional danger. Frontier service also meant familiarity with racism, particularly in small towns on the Texas frontier, but discrimination also existed within the army. Prejudice was evident in other regiments, in some of the officers who commanded the Black troops, and in the command structure of the army, which frequently provided the Black regiments with castoff equipment.

Despite such problems, the Negro regiments established excellent records, particularly the Ninth and Tenth Cavalry, which acquired the nickname "Buffalo Soldiers" from Plains Indians. It was troopers from the Tenth Cavalry who rescued Major George Forsyth and his group of scouts at Beecher's Island in 1868, and it was troopers from the Ninth Cavalry who rescued troops pinned down by Northern Utes after the Meeker uprising in Colorado in 1879. It was in honor of the meritorious service of the Buffalo Soldiers that a troop of the Ninth Cavalry was stationed at Fort Myers, Virginia, in 1891, but this assignment caused such an outcry locally that the troop was quickly returned to the West.

The declaration of war against Spain in April 1898 caught the United States Army unprepared. During much of the late nineteenth century the army had been limited in size to twenty-five thousand men, a limit that had been increased slightly following the sinking of the *Maine*. The declaration of war brought further enlargement of the regular army, but the United States relied heavily upon volunteer regiments to fight the Spanish-American War. It was no surprise that the four Black regiments were ordered to the South in preparation of the invasion of Cuba.

American planning for the invasion of Cuba was marked by the lack of preparedness and by confusion. There were shortages of virtually everything, and many soldiers went to Cuba wearing woolen uniforms. While the regular army was armed with the Krag-Jorgensen bolt-action rifle, which fired a smokeless powder cartridge, most of the volunteer units were armed with old black powder single-shot Springfields. This placed the volunteer units at a distinct disadvantage to the Spanish army, which was armed with the smokeless powder Mauser rifle. Even regular regiments still used black powder artillery, which was notoriously deficient by comparison to the smokeless powder artillery of the Spanish army, and which left the United States without effective artillery support when it went into battle. When transport vessels reached Cuba, they were unprepared to land the horses, and as a result, the animals were simply dumped into the water to swim ashore. When some, in confusion, swam out to sea, an alert bugler from one of the regiments blew assembly and successfully attracted the animals to shore. Correspondent Richard Harding Davis, who watched the landing at Daiquiri, commented, "God takes care of drunkards, sailors and the United States." Happily the small Spanish force at Daiquiri had retreated, and the American landing was unopposed.

On June 24, several days after the landing, a division of dismounted cavalry led by former Confederate cavalry commander, General Joseph Wheeler, confronted the Spanish at Las Guasimas. Wheeler's command, which included the Tenth Cavalry and the Rough Riders, pushed the Spanish back. In the excitement of battle, Wheeler shouted, "We've got the damn Yankees on the run!"

On July 1, American forces, including the four Black regiments, attacked well-entrenched Spanish troops at the village of El Caney and the heights, or hills, of San Juan. American forces ascending San Juan Hill did so without much overall direction, and, as Theodore Roosevelt of the Rough Riders said, "The battle simply fought itself." Artist Frederick Remington, commenting on the disparity between Spanish and United States artillery, observed that smokey powder belonged with stone axes in museums.

As the Tenth Cavalry moved into position, an American observation balloon that flew directly above the regiment attracted Spanish fire, which Sergeant Horace Bivins described as galling. Lieutenant John Pershing of the Tenth described the converging fire from all Spanish troops within range, which caused the Seventy-first New York to nearly stampede. The Tenth, however, moved through the jungle, through barbwire, and then came out into the open where it was under direct fire from Spanish troops. Author and observer Stephen Crane wrote, "The front had burst out with a roar like a brush fire." At the front, he noted, "The battle-sound, as if it were simply music, was beginning to swell until the volleys rolled like surf." Theodore Roosevelt, who was impressed with the Spanish Mauser rifles and smokeless powder, commented, "the Mauser bullets were singing through the trees over our heads, making a noise like the humming of telephone lines."

The ascent up San Juan Hill was more of a scramble and a crawl than a charge, and foreign military observers called the attack gallant but foolish and observed that the Americans would be unable to take the hill against well-entrenched defenders. In the confusion of the assault, many American units became intermingled with each other. Black and White fought side by side, and Roosevelt watched Sergeant George Barry of the Tenth, the regimental color bearer, grab the colors of the Third Cavalry as that regiment's color bearer fell. Barry continued on up the hill, serving as color bearer for two regiments. Rough Rider Frank Knox, who later became secretary of the navy, became separated from his comrades, "but I joined a troop of the Tenth Cavalry, colored, and for a time fought with them shoulder to shoulder, and in justice to the colored race I must say that I never saw braver men anywhere. Some of those who rushed up the hill will live in my memory forever."

Roosevelt heaped praise on the Black soldiers when he wrote in his book *The Rough Riders*, "No troops could have behaved better than the colored soldiers had behaved so far." He also noted that his Rough Riders "were entirely willing, in their own phrase, 'to drink out of the same canteen'" with the Black cavalrymen. Reflecting the prejudice of the day, however, he also concluded that the Black troopers were dependent on their White officers. As an officer in the Tenth Cavalry, Lieutenant John Pershing was perhaps a less biased observer. He commented, "White regiments, Black regiments, regulars and Rough Riders, representing the young manhood of the North and South, fought shoulder to shoulder, unmindful of race or color, unmindful of whether commanded by an ex-Confederate or not, and mindful only of their common duty as Americans."

The attack on the heights of San Juan was gallant and successful but also costly, for American forces suffered more than a thousand casualties. It was an assault in which junior officers, noncommissioned officers, and enlisted men provided inspired leadership and example, and it set the stage for the ultimate surrender of Santiago because it gave the American army control of the heights and thus forced the Spanish fleet into battle and defeat.

The American press and public recognized the heroism of the Black soldiers. Writing about the "gallant Tenth," the New York *Mail and Express* stated, "The War has not shown greater heroism. The men whose own freedom was baptized in blood have proved themselves capable of giving up their lives that others may be free." And the *Washington Post* concluded that the Rough Riders would have been exterminated had it not been for the Negro cavalry. Theodore Roosevelt described the Black cavalrymen as "an excellent breed of Yankees," and the Tenth Cavalry passed in review before President William McKinley in the nation's capitol. When the City of Philadelphia held a peace jubilee, it requested that all four of the Black regiments be permitted to attend although only several companies of the Tenth Cavalry received such permission.

Unfortunately the fame of the Black soldiers was fleeting. Sergeant Carter Smith of the Tenth Cavalry perhaps best stated the attitude of Black soldiers when he said, "I notice that both White and colored soldiers had a brotherly affection for each other while on the way to Cuba, in Cuba and on our way back to the United States. Why can't it be so at home?"

As things returned to normal, the Black soldiers returned to stations in the western part of the United States while some saw continued combat in the Philippines. Black soldiers expected to be recognized for their contributions in Cuba, but unfortunately only a few received commissions for meritorious service, and those commissions were in volunteer regiments rather than in the regular army. As historian Marvin Fletcher aptly notes, the army judged Black soldiers by a racial standard rather than by a military standard. The status of Blacks in the American army failed to improve in the early part of the twentieth century. Fletcher concludes that the army enforced segregation and prevailing racial mores. The army specifically prohibited Black noncommissioned officers from drilling White recruits, and when a White woman married a soldier of the Twenty-fifth Infantry in 1911, the army found cause to discharge the soldier. Blacks were also excluded from artillery units until United States entry into World War I.

It was to call attention to the contribution of Black soldiers and particularly to the Tenth Cavalry that a group of men compiled *Under Fire with the Tenth U.S. Cavalry*. The men who compiled the book included Herschel V. Cashin, a receiver of the United States Land Office, newspaper correspondent Charles Alexander, Tenth Cavalry Chaplain William T. Anderson, Tenth Cavalry surgeon Arthur M. Brown, and Tenth Cavalry Sergeant Horace W. Bivins. The book is a collection of military reports, historical narratives, writings of Black soldiers, and oral testimony by those who served in the campaign.

While the book is not particularly well organized, it did achieve its purpose. It has become a commonly used source for the history of Blacks in the military, and it has become an important part of that body of literature about Black Americans. As a result, it has been reprinted several times.

This book is dedicated to the memory of Sara Dunlap Jackson of the National Archives. I first met Sara when I went to Washington, D.C., in 1966 to begin work on a doctoral dissertation. My mentor at the University of Colorado, Bob Athearn, sent me specifically to Sara because she had assisted him in his work in the past. That summer I met a number of other graduate students who also had been sent specifically to Sara Jackson. Sara treated me as she did so many other graduate students. She took me under her wing, and I became part of her professional family. In subsequent years I sent my own doctoral students to Sara for assistance, and even after she moved from Old Military Records to the National Historical Publications and Records Commission, Sara always looked after those of my students who worked in the National Archives.

Sara Jackson's impact on historical scholarship was great and her professional family was large. That family included scholars working in western history, military history, Civil War history, southern history, and Black history. It also included a host of people in historical agencies across the country. Scholars always appreciate the assistance of archivists and librarians, but there was something special about Sara Jackson because the people who knew her came to love her. She was, I know, the most loved individual in the National Archives.

I shared that love and admiration for Sara Jackson but was also privileged to get to know Sara better than those who simply knew her professionally. Sara became part of my family, or perhaps we became part of hers, and she spent every Christmas with us for some twenty years. When my daughter was born, it seemed only natural that we name her for her extra grandmother, and Sara Jackson became known as "Big Sara" in our family. And so for Luann, David, and Sara Ellis, and all of those who knew and loved her, we dedicate this book to Sara Dunlap Jackson.

UNDER FIRE.

WITH THE TENTH U. S. CAVALRY.

BEING A BRIEF, COMPREHENSIVE REVIEW OF THE NEGRO'S PARTICI-
PATION IN THE WARS OF

THE UNITED STATES.

Especially Showing the Valor and Heroism of the Negro Soldiers of the Ninth and
Tenth Cavalries, and the Twenty-fourth and Twenty-fifth Infantries of the
Regular Army; as Demonstrated in the Decisive Campaign Around
Santiago de Cuba, 1898, when these Soldiers Crowned
Themselves with a Halo of Unfading Glory.

THRILLING EPISODES INTERESTINGLY NARRATED BY OFFICERS AND MEN. FAMOUS
INDIAN CAMPAIGNS AND THEIR RESULTS.

A PURELY MILITARY HISTORY OF THE NEGRO.

WITH INTRODUCTION BY
MAJOR-GENERAL JOSEPH WHEELER,
Commanding Cavalry Div. U S Army, Santiago Campaign.

BY

HERSCHEL V. CASHIN, Rec'r U. S. Land Office, Huntsville, Ala.; CHARLES ALEXAN-
DER General Newspaper Correspondent; WILLIAM T. ANDERSON, Chaplain 10th
U. S. Cav., Fort McIntosh, Texas; ARTHUR M. BROWN, A. A. Surgeon
10th U. S. Cav., Fort McIntosh, Texas; HORACE W. BIVINS,
Sergeant 10th U S. Cav., Fort Sam Houston, Texas.

*Beautifully Illustrated with over One Hundred Fine Engravings from Original
Photographs made for this Work Exclusively.*

F. TENNYSON NEELY,
PUBLISHER,
LONDON.　　　NEW YORK.　　　CHICAGO.

Copyright, 1899,
by
CASHIN AND ANDERSON.

PREFACE.

CONTEMPLATING the great inequalities of men, the tendency of the average historian to either entirely ignore or very grudgingly acknowledge the courage, valor, and patriotism of a so-called *alien race*, in their efforts to court the favor and patronage of the influential and popular; appreciating the fact that some men are almost imperceptibly raised to the very summit of human glory without apparent effort on their part, while others are depressed to the lowest level of humiliation; some have powerful and brilliant intellects, while others slowly drag out a miserable existence of imbecility and helplessness; some enjoy perfect health and are happy, while others are afflicted from their birth with every ill that flesh is heir to; some are made rich by a sudden turn of fortune, while others are doomed to a life of dire poverty and distress; and that some classes and races meet special impediments — peculiar obstructions to fame, justice and progress; because of the fact that the Negro race belongs to such a class and is already the subject of slight, parsimonious notice in the histories which were largely made by its deeds of valor, this work is presented to the reading public.

There are no charms in the unspeakable horrors of war. Even the mentally and morally depraved being of that type dignified by the term mediocrity feels the sensation as of a chill creeping over him when the melancholy scene of devastation and crime is adequately presented. But history demands that all events in human affairs shall be carefully recorded; and, as some historians allow their narrow prejudices to enter into the execution of their intellectual tasks, it is to be seriously regretted that great injustice is often done to the most worthy.

The diffusion of general knowledge concerning the war so recently ended between the United States and Spain has taxed the book-making machinery of this country to its utmost capacity. It is therefore important that if another book is to be presented to the public, it should have a special mission, and be designed to fill a place in the records of races peculiarly its own.

"Under Fire with the Tenth U. S. Cavalry," a purely military narrative, was written for the purpose of telling the Negro's story of the Cuban campaign. It is, therefore, made up of testimony which has come directly from the lips of those Negro soldiers who actually participated in the struggle for humanity in the Island of Cuba.

General Joseph Wheeler was invited to furnish the introduction for this work because of his close identification with the campaign, his manly attitude toward the Negro soldier, and because the reading public has an abiding faith in his nobility of heart and integrity of character and will properly regard what he has to say as the whole truth.

THE AUTHORS.

SERGEANT HORACE W. BIVINS.
Of the 10th U. S. Cavalry and his dog Booth.

BRIG.-GENERAL T. A. BALDWIN,
Late Lieut.-Col. 10th Cavalry.

BRIG.-GENERAL GUY V. HENRY.
Late Col. 10th Cavalry.

CONTENTS.

CHAPTER I.
THE NEGRO AND LIBERTY.
                                                                        PAGE

The Negro's Introduction Into North America—His Suffering—Crispus Attucks in 1770—The Battle of Bunker Hill—Salem Poor—The Battle of Long Island—The War of 1812—What Secretary Stanton Said Concerning the Negro in the Civil War—General Benjamin F. Butler—Change of Sentiment in Favor of Negro Heroism and Valor.. 17

CHAPTER II.
WORK IN INDIAN CAMPAIGNS.

The First Regular Negro Regiment—Fort Wagner—Sergeant William H. Carney Planting the Colors of His Regiment—Organization of Regiments of Colored Cavalry in 1866—Brevet Major-General B. H. Grierson—Exciting Indian Campaigns and Their Results.................... 24

CHAPTER III.
THE WARS OF THE UNITED STATES.

Governmental Responsibilities—Obligations of Men in Office—Spanish Cruelty and Injustice—Destruction of the Maine—Some Facts Concerning the Discovery of the West India Islands...................................... 46

CHAPTER IV.
THE ATTITUDE OF THE NEGRO.

Prejudice Resulting from the Condition of Servitude from Which the Negro but Recently Emerged in His Way—The Intelligence of the Negro Soldier—A Remarkable Character—Horace W. Bivins—An Ex-Slave—a Great Observer of Men and Deeds—His Life.................... 57

CONTENTS.

CHAPTER V.

SOME EXPERIENCES IN CUBA.   PAGE

Important Narrative—Tenth Cavalry Ordered East—Delay in Florida Causes Uneasiness among Regulars—Men Excited at Sea—Landing of the Tenth Cavalry Marked by the Loss of Two Men—Personal Letter Written on the Battlefield.. 67

CHAPTER VI.

CONTINUATION OF SERGEANT BIVINS' NARRATIVE.

General Garcia—General Joseph Wheeler—Progress of the Tenth United States Cavalry—Captain Grimes—The Part Played by the Balloon—Spanish Become Confused—The Great Charge Up San Juan Hill—The Tenth Win Unfading Glory.. 89

CHAPTER VII.

THE NINTH UNITED STATES CAVALRY.

The Part Taken by the Ninth Regiment of Cavalry—A Famous Regiment of Great Fighters—Road Building in Times of War—Echoes from San Juan Hill—Troop C Initiates the Assault on San Juan Hill................... 109

CHAPTER VIII.

THE TWENTY-FOURTH INFANTRY.

The Story of the Twenty-fourth Infantry—What Her Men Accomplished on the Battlefields in Cuba—Great Victories Won—General Kent's Appeal to seventy-first N. Y. Volunteers—His Joy at Sight of His Colored Boys—"Liscum, Turn to Your Right, Ford the Stream and Fight Everything Before You"—Their Worst Night in Cuba—Nursing Yellow Fever Patients Without a Murmur—Last Regiment to Leave Cuba................................. 120

CHAPTER IX.

THE TWENTY-FIFTH INFANTRY.

A Private Letter Reproduced—How the Battles were Won—Troop Commander Lieutenant W. H. Smith Killed—Lieutenant Robertson Wounded—Troop Commanded by Sergeant Saint Foster—Sergeant Foster Promoted—Chaplain T. G. Steward of the Twenty-fifth Infantry gives Account of the Negro Soldier—General Reports are Quoted 135

CONTENTS. ix

CHAPTER X.
THE NINTH AND TENTH CAVALRY.

What Colonel Theodore Roosevelt, Governor of New York, has to Say of the Ninth and Tenth Cavalry—Major-General Nelson A. Miles—General Field Orders—General Wheeler's Testimony—Major-General Shafter—Lieutenant-Colonel T. A. Baldwin—Captain Woodward Announces the Retirement of Sergeant George Berry, Who Spent Thirty years in the Service...................... 147

CHAPTER XI.
THE CONDUCT OF THE NEGRO TROOPS.

The Powerful Press—Spontaneous Outburst of Splendid Commendation of the Negro's Right to Share in the Glory Won by American Arms—Report of Captain John Bigelow, Jr., of Troop D, Tenth Cavalry—Evidences of Negro Heroism—Death of Lieutenant J. G. Ord, Sixth Infantry, Avenged by Corporal Walker, Tenth Cavalry, who Narrates Particulars.............................. 159

CHAPTER XII.
TENTH CAVALRY OFFICERS' REPORT.

Daring Expedition of Lieutenant Carter P. Johnson, Carrying Supplies to General Maximo Gomez's Army—Words of Praise from President William McKinley — Commissioned and Non-Commissioned Officers Make Reports—Statements Made for this Work Only—Strong Arguments Offered for the Negro Troops—Captains and Lieutenants Pleased with Results—The Close of Hostilities—Blanco's Cunning Letter—General Maximo Gomez Replies....... 175

CHAPTER XIII.
THE CAMPAIGN OF SANTIAGO.

Lieutenant John J. Pershing Gives His View of the Great Campaign—What the Tenth Cavalry and other Negro Troops Accomplished................................... 195

CHAPTER XIV.
GREAT SUFFERING ENDURED.

Predictions Among Enlisted Men as to the Outcome of the War—Sergeants Peter McCown, David T. Brown, and

CONTENTS.

PAGE

other Noncommissioned Officers give Personal Accounts of Cuban Campaign—Splendid Words from Captain Charles G. Ayres.. 217

CHAPTER XV.
THRILLING STORY OF GALANTRY.

Sergeant Presly Holliday, of Troop B, Tenth United States Cavalry, Tells What He Saw—Graphically Describes Ascent up San Juan Hill—Generals Wheeler and Young Leading the Way—Sergeant Douglass—Hospital Corps Complimented—Horrible Scenes on the Battlefield—Coincidences in the Lives of Lieutenants Wm. E. Shipp and Wm. H. Smith—Lieutenant H. C. Whitehead...... 231

CHAPTER XVI.
EXULTANT SONGS OF PRAISE.

Corporals and Sergeants Relate Personal Experiences—The Negro's Heroism Clearly Demonstrated—Seven Days at Sea—Engagement of June 24th—Night Spent Digging Trenches—Camp Hamilton—Ironclad Determination of the Tenth to Win... 252

CHAPTER XVII.
SOME THRILLING EPISODES.

Corporal John Walker of D Troop, Tenth Cavalry, Gives Dramatic Account of Death of Lieutenant Ord—Captain Bigelow—Capture of Spaniards—The Death of a Hero—Sketch of one of Uncle Sam's Noted Musical Organizations, the Tenth Cavalry Band......................... 267

CHAPTER XVIII.
PORTFOLIO OF WAR POEMS.

Wheeler at Santiago—The Fighting Tenth—The Negro Soldier—The Rough Rider's Remarks—Sergeant George Berry Who Served His Country for Thirty years—Poem on Sergeant Berry, by Rev. B. A. Imes................ 274

CHAPTER XIX.
PERSONNEL OF OFFICERS AND MEN.

Biographical Sketches... 285

CONTENTS.

CHAPTER XX.

GENERAL MILES WARNS AGAINST ALCOHOL.

Intoxicating Drinks a Dangerous Element in War—Booth, the Faithful Dog Messenger—How He Passed His Examination for Service in Cuba—Arthur Thompkins, the Regimental Mascot—"I Don't See What them Spaniards Wanted to Shoot Me for, I Wasn't Doing Nothing to Them"—The Fighting Tenth in Philadelphia............ 322

CHAPTER XXI.

THE OFFICIAL ROLL OF HONOR.

The True Aim of the American Soldier, Service, Not Gain—Roll of Honor from Each Troop of the Tenth United States Cavalry—Troops A, B, C, D, E, F, G, H, I, K, L, M—Full List of Names............................... 335

Second colored graduate from West Point Military Academy.

INTRODUCTION.

"Under Fire with the Tenth U. S. Cavalry" needs no words of introduction or commendation from me. The title page speaks for itself and sets forth a most inviting narrative, giving an epitome of the history of the Negro in this country and a thrilling account of his courage and heroism on the field of battle.

Beginning with the introduction of the blacks into America, the book mentions the Negro patriots who fought with our forefathers in their great struggle for liberty in 1776. Continuing the military history of the race in America, it notes the formation of regiments which did good service in some of the bloodiest battles of the great Civil War, later in the Indian outbreaks in the Western territories; and leading the reader on to the outbreak of hostilities between Spain and America in the spring of 1898, it describes the enthusiasm with which the troops hurried to the mobilizing centers, their embarkation at Tampa, their momentous voyage, their landing in Cuba, and their participation in the bloody fights at Las Guasimas and San Juan.

With unfaltering courage and devotion they took part in the heroic charge of the cavalry at Las Guasimas, and after that gallant fight moved steadily forward with the cavalry division, forded the San Juan River, and under a murderous fire gained the crest of San Juan Hill and captured the formidable intrenchments of the Spaniards, driving back the astonished enemy, fighting by day and working by night until glorious victory crowned their efforts and peace once more dawned upon our beloved country.

The reports of all their commanders unite in commending the Negro soldier. Captains Watson, Beck, and Ayres, Major Norvell and others, all speak of their brave and good conduct, their obedience, efficiency and coolness under a galling fire. A detachment of Troop B under Captain Watson were for a time in charge of a Hotchkiss gun with which they did good service, and although the gun was a special target for the enemy, the men of the troop stood by it with steady coolness and heroism.

Lieutenant-Colonel Baldwin, in his report of the ba - tle of San Juan, says: "They exhibited great bravery, obeying orders with unflinching alacrity," and l e recommends a number of the men for special bravery.

Those who see in the future of the colored race in America a difficult and perplexing problem will find encouragement in this book, the product of Negro intelligence and the record of Negro patriotism, and be brought to the conclusion that the more enlightened men of the race are solving the problem by teaching their disciples, both by precept and example, to elevate themselves through the only safe and sure method, that of education. In the unchanging natural law of growth and development will be found the answer to the problem. By education, discipline, and judicious training, the peculiar characteristics and virtues of the race will be developed; and with enlightened judgment they will learn the great truth that a man is worthy of respect in proportion to his intrinsic mental and moral worth.

The men of the South know that the prominent characteristic of the old Negro slave was loyalty—a loyalty touching in its beauty and simplicity. How few examples we have of treachery compared with the many instances of unselfish devotion exhibited by the slave in his loyalty to a loved master or mistress. Who has not seen a thousand times the counterpart of Sam in "Mars' Chan," a story so touchingly true to life that one can scarcely read it with dry eyes. Is it then any wonder or any matter of surprise that the colored troops true to their inborn spirit of loyalty, went forth full of martial enthusiasm to battle with a foreign foe, and returned from Cuba's bloodstained fields covered with glory?

JOSEPH WHEELER.

Major-General Commanding Cavalry Division, Santiago Campaign.

Initiation of the Assault on San Juan Hill by Troops C and D, Ninth Cavalry.

UNDER FIRE.

CHAPTER I.

THE NEGRO AND LIBERTY.

The Negro's Introduction Into North America—His Sufferings—Crispus Attucks in 1770—The Battle of Bunker Hill—Salem Poor—The Battle of Long Island—The War of 1812—What Secretary Stanton Said Concerning the Negro in the Civil War—General Benjamin F. Butler—Change of Sentiment in Favor of Negro Heroism and Valor.

It seems like a paradox to speak to the modern reader of history of the Negro as efficiently related to the cause of popular freedom, and with the solution of those grave and tremendous political, social, and economic problems which have taxed the wisdom of the people of the United States of America for so many years. For his ignorance, illiteracy, and seeming moral weakness, coupled with his extreme poverty and impecuniosity have been anything but propitious and encouraging to him, and to those who have manifested sympathy for him in his inferior condition. Proscription and an appalling prejudice have each conspired to embarrass him and to impede his onward and upward progress.

He was brought to this country when it was an infant in civilization and was forced into slavery, in which condition he was held most of the time since the country was settled. He was not treated as a human being, but as property to be used only for the advantage of his oppressors. In 1863 he was set free, but at the North as well as at the South, he was largely shut out of remunerative avenues of industry and of opportunities to improve his mental, moral and material condition. He was kept under a social ban and was not recognized as being equal in any respect to his fellow-man of a different complexion. After thus suffering for generations it could hardly be expected that he would feel much enthusiasm in the cause of popular liberty, restricted to the enjoyment of the tyrant race.

But notwithstanding this the Negro accepted the situation in silence, and, with an intense religious fervor, displayed a love for freedom, a willingness to fight and make sacrifice for the common cause of liberty, a valor and intrepidity, even when his own prospect of sharing in it was not promising, that have not been paralleled by any race, under similar conditions, in the history of the world.

From the 5th day of March, 1770, when Crispus Attucks, a Negro, led the American patriots into the main guard of the British line on King Street, Boston, Massachusetts, the Negro has been conspicuous in every movement in which patriotism and courage are essential requisites.

At the battle of Bunker Hill, Major Pitcairn was killed, which proved to be a very serious loss to the British. It was he who was the chief commander of the forces that went out to Lexington and Concord at the time of the famous fight there. He fell at the hands of Private Peter Salem of Colonel Nixon's regiment of the Continental army. This Negro soldier's claim to this honor could not be disputed. There was another Negro soldier who distinguished himself, named Salem Poor, who demonstrated such great courage that fourteen American officers called the attention of Congress to his merits. The memorial was dated at Cambridge,

December 5, 1775, and stated "that under our own observation, we declare that a Negro man called Salem Poor, of Colonel Frye's regiment, Captain Ames' company, in the late battle at Charlestown, behaved like an experienced officer as well as an excellent soldier. The reward due to so great and distinguished a character we submit to the Congress."

The army organized at Cambridge under General Washington had from the start Negroes in it. The historian Bancroft states that free Negroes stood in the ranks by the side of white men.

At the battle of Long Island, in 1776, Negroes fought bravely. Theodore Parker, once alluding to the discovery of the remains of these, remarked: "Now after seventy-five years have passed by, the bones of the forgotten victims of the Revolution are shovelled up, carted off, and shot into the sea, as rubbish of the town. Had they been white men's bones, how they would have been honored with sumptuous burial anew, and the purchased prayers and preaching of Christian divines! Now such relics are but rubbish of the streets."

In the War of 1812 the Negro performed heroic service on land and sea. Commodore Perry said the Negroes in the navy seemed to be absolutely insensible to danger. He solicited and welcomed them into the service of their country. In September, 1814, he issued a proclamation, which contained the words: "As sons of freedom, you are now called upon to defend our most inestimable blessing. As Americans your country looks with confidence to her adopted children for valorous support."

In the War of the Rebellion the Negro performed a very prominent and heroic part. This furnished on a large scale an opportunity to show his loyalty and courage, and he met the highest expectations of his friends. For two years the war had been carried on by the North on the principle of saving the Union without interfering with the institution of slavery, which was really at the bottom of the whole trouble, and while that policy was pursued the prospect of success was dark; but after the proclamation of emancipation was issued, victory seemed almost at once to turn on the side of the Union forces.

By the North, Negroes were not allowed for some time to shoulder the musket in behalf of the cause of freedom. Some predicted that if so allowed they would not begin to compare in efficiency with the white man. But the experiment proved a grand success.

Generally the Negro troops acquitted themselves most creditably as soldiers. Mr. Stanton, then Secretary of War, said of them at Petersburg, Virginia: "The hardest fighting was done by the black troops. The parts they stormed were the worst of all. After the affair was over General Smith went to thank them, and tell them he was proud of their courage and dash. He says that they cannot be exceeded as soldiers."

In the War of the Rebellion there were in all 178,975 Negro soldiers in the United States Volunteers, and of these 38,847 were killed, wounded and missing. They took part in 449 battles. Besides the large military force there were 150,000 Negro laborers in other departments. Of the brilliant achievements of Robert Small, of whom the New York *Tribune* said:

"To this colored man was the nation indebted for the first vindication of its honor on the sea," much might be said. General Benjamin F. Butler, who at first opposed the idea of admitting Negroes into the army, took occasion to say on the floor of Congress: "It became my painful duty to follow in the track of the charging column, and there, in a space not wider than the clerk's desk, and three hundred yards long, lay the dead bodies of three hundred and fifty-three of my colored comrades, slain in the defense of their country, who laid down their lives to uphold its flag and its honor as a willing sacrifice; and as I rode along among them, guiding my horse this way and that way lest he should profane with his hoofs what seemed to me the sacred dead, and as I looked on their bronzed faces upturned in the shining sun as if in mute appeal against the wrongs of the country for which they had given their lives, and whose flag had only been to them a flag of stripes on which no stars of glory had shone for them —feeling I had wronged them in the past, and believing what was the future of my country to them—among my dead comrades there I swore myself a solemn oath: 'May my right hand forget its cunning, and my tongue cleave to the roof of my mouth, if I ever fail to defend the rights of those men who have given their blood for me and my country this day, and for their race forever,' and God helping me, I will keep this oath."

A radical change of sentiment has taken place in recent years as regards the capabilities and possibilities of the Negro. This sentiment is favorable to him and this is largely due to his honorable record as a soldier and his very successful exploits in the far West in conflict with the hostile Indians and his enviable record made at San Juan Hill and El Caney in Cuba.

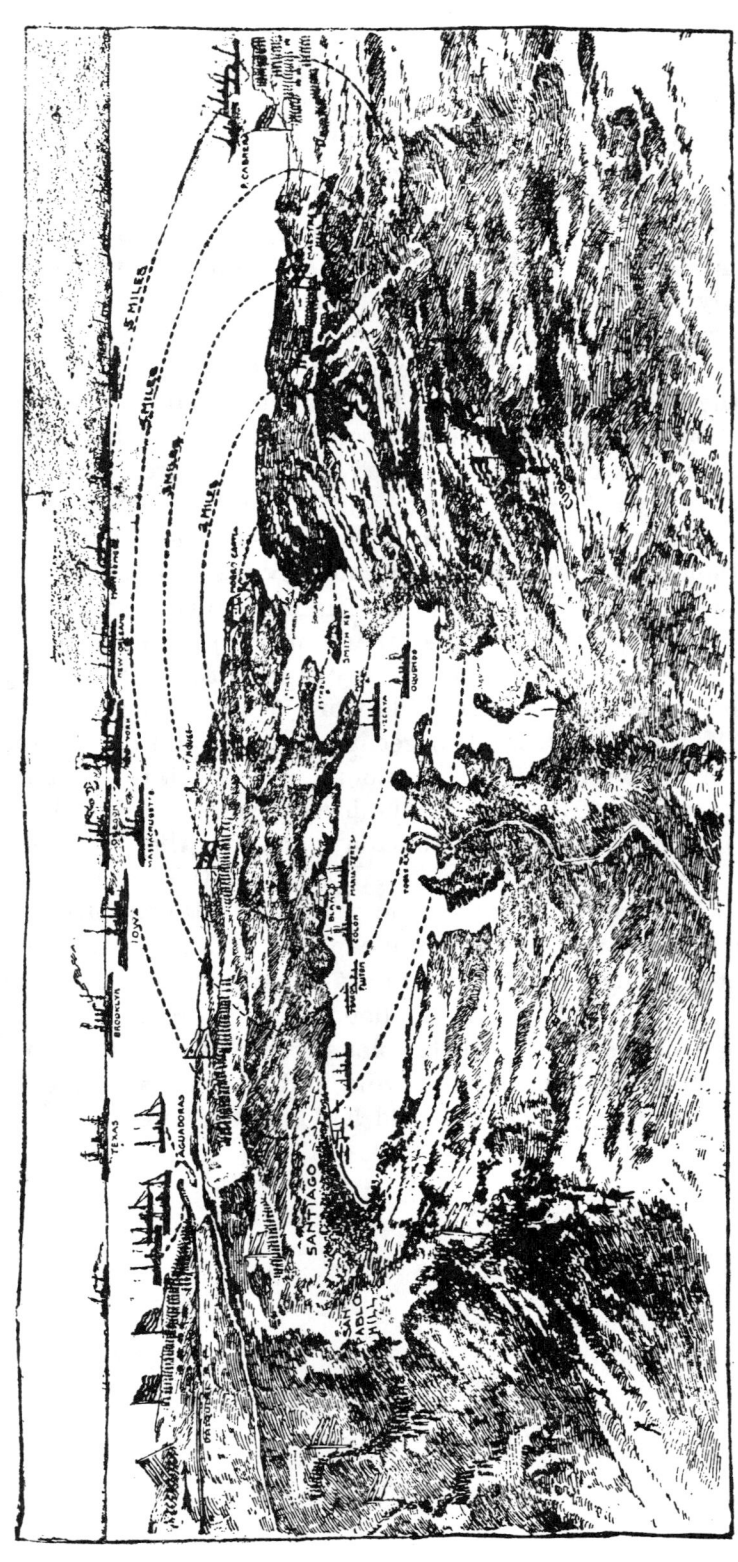

GEN. SHAFTER'S FORCES LANDING. SANTIAGO HARBOR AND SPANISH ARMY. GEN. G. V. HENRY'S FORCES LANDING.
View from North.

SITTING BULL—ONE OF THE FAMOUS FIGHTERS.

CHAPTER II.

WORK IN INDIAN CAMPAIGNS.

The First Regular Negro Regiment—Fort Wagner—Sergeant William H. Carney Planting the Colors of His Regiment—Organization of Regiments of Colored Cavalry in 1866—Brevet Major-General B. H. Grierson—Exciting Indian Campaigns and Their Results.

MASSACHUSETTS is entitled to credit for the organization of the first regular Negro regiment in the United States. This regiment was known as the Fifty-Fourth Massachusetts. This regiment took a very conspicuous part in the effort to capture Fort Wagner, near Charleston, South Carolina. The men composing the regiment marched two days and nights through marshy fields, swampy woodland and drenching rains to be on hand in time to make the assault. Soaking wet, covered with mud, hungry and greatly fatigued, these irresistibly brave men reached the battlefield in time and gladly took the front rank.

After five minutes' rest they double-quicked a half-mile to the fort, where after a most gallant and desperate fight, Sergeant William H. Carney planted the regimental flag on the works. While Sergeant Carney received a very severe wound, and was so weakened that he fell to his knees, he continued to advance until he had reached the outer slope of the fort; there he remained for over an hour till the second brigade came up. He kept his colors flying until the end of the second conflict. When the forces retired, he followed, creeping on one knee and one hand, still holding the flag. When he entered the hospital, bleeding from a wound in the head and one in his left thigh, amid the cheers of his wounded comrades, he said: "Boys, the old flag never touched the ground."

While the Negro possesses in a large degree that altruistic sympathy admired by the noblest and best men in the world, he is nevertheless relentless and unsympathetic when called on to defend his country's honor.

The conduct of the Negro soldier during the entire Civil War was such as to make a profound impression on all who observed it, and while there were many who were slow to acknowledge his worthiness to participate in the battle for freedom and to practice the right of citizenship, still they would gladly grant that he possessed the qualities of which heroes are made, and would exhibit as much courage, when the occasion required, as any other class of citizens. The government therefore deemed it wise and expedient to form permanent organizations of all Negroes whose healthy physical development and manifest power for physical endurance of hardships, such as attend the career of a soldier, would insure the government efficient service.

In 1866 the Ninth and Tenth United States Cavalries were organized, with Brevet Major-General B. H. Grierson as colonel of the Tenth; and in 1868-9 the Twenty-fourth and Twenty-fifth Regiments of Infantry, all Negroes, were organized.

General Grierson, on taking leave of the Tenth Cavalry at Santa Fe, New Mexico, being assigned to command of the Department of Arizona, December 1, 1888, alludes in orders No. 51 to the services rendered by officers and men as follows:

"Always in the vanguard of civilization and in contact with the most warlike and savage Indians of the Plains, the officers and men have cheerfully endured many hardships and privations, and in the midst of great dangers steadfastly maintained a most gallant and zealous devotion to duty, and they may well be proud of the record made, and rest assured that the hard work undergone in the accomplishment of such important and valuable service to their country, is well understood and appreciated, and that it cannot fail, sooner or later, to meet with due recognition and reward."

Perhaps no incidents in American history present a greater number of brilliant achievements, more thrilling experiences, more daring deeds, dramatic episodes, and bloody tragedies than those adventures which attended the pioneers of the Western plains—the maiden efforts of these organizations, and which characterized the conquests, development, and entire life of the United States army in the far West, in its attempts to subdue the wild, hostile and savage Indian, for the purpose of advancing the civilization of the Western World. The great success of the Negro soldiery in this respect sufficiently vindicates their worth as efficient defenders of the country's flag and honor.

These military operations embraced a vast territory, covering a large part of Kansas, Texas, Indian Territory, New Mexico and Arizona; and from the organization until coming to Montana in May, 1892, there was scarcely a month of idleness. Colonel Grierson was promoted to the grade of brigadier, April 15, 1890, and was succeeded in command of the regiment by Brevet Brigadier-General John Kemp Mizner. It has been the purpose to collect and set forth an account of some of the exploits of officers and men who have borne conspicuous part in the actions, toils and sufferings of

AN INDIAN CAMP.

tne regiment. These sketches intentionally make prominent the work of enlisted men. It is impossible to enlarge upon these stories. They are therefore given in few words with no attempt at ornament. They have been gathered from records in the shape of letters or regimental returns, or from the lips of veterans now living, who have told the tales with simplicity and earnest purpose to be accurate.

One of the earliest records of gallantry placed to the credit of enlisted men of the regiment is found in a letter written by Lieutenant W. B. Kennedy, under date of October 1, 1867. The substance of this letter is used without reference to exact language.

Private John Randall, Compa y G, Tenth Cavalry, was attacked in company with two civilians by a band of Cheyenne Indians numbering sixty or seventy, near a spring, about four miles distant from Colonel McGrath's camp, forty-five miles west from Fort Hays on the line of the Union Pacific Railroad, and in the fight which ensued the two citizens were killed, one of whom was scalped. Private Randall was shot in the hip and was given eleven lance thrusts in his shoulders and back. These wounds were received after Randall and one of the citizens named Parks had taken refuge in a hole under a cut bank. The Indians succeeded in caving large portions of the bank upon Mr. Parks and despatching him with their lances. The savages, weary with trying to get Randall out of the hole, disappeared, leaving thirteen braves dead; so effective had been the fire of Randall and his friend up to the time of the latter's end.

The Indians attacked the main camp on the railroad which was protected by Sergeant Charles H. Davis and eight men, and they were repulsed. Davis immediately gave orders to have his horses saddled, but after-

UNDER FIRE. 29

ward thought it best to force the fighting and attack the enemy on foot. As soon as the warriors saw the soldiers advancing they mounted their ponies and rode leisurely along the line of the railroad until they met an ox-team with two men. They at once fell upon the men. One escaped to the camp; the other remained and fought until his last cartridge was fired. Three of the warriors dismounted to lift his scalp. Just at this critical moment Sergeant Davis and his detachment arrived and opened fire upon the war-party with such success that the redskins abandoned their victim and broke into precipitate flight for the river bottoms. Returning to camp with the rescued teamster, Davis ordered his men to mount and at the head of the detachment rode with greatest speed toward the river to ascertain if possible the whereabouts of Private Randall, who was then lying under the bank bleeding and exhausted by the side of his dead companion, Mr. Parks.

On nearing the river and ascending a little rise of ground he discovered an Indian picket on the lookout. Dismounting his men, eight in number, as quietly and quickly as possible and leaving his horses to be held by two privates, he, with the remaining six, crept up to the top of a hillock and a single shot from a carbine put an end to the savage sentry. As soon as their man fell, the Indians, who had been secreted in two ravines on his right and left rear to the number of seventy-five or eighty, advanced in battle array. The sergeant finding himself partially surrounded, divided his little band so as to engage those in rear and front with, as he feared, little chance of success. The men who held the Indians off on the sergeant's left rear fired so rapidly that the warriors broke and concentrated on his right. At this juncture the ponies belonging to the braves which had been left in the ravines become frightened at the firing and stampeded in every direction. The hostiles finding themselves afoot fled in disorder from the scene. The sergeant followed in hot pursuit until close to the stream, when he concluded to return to his horses and to the brave fellows who stood at their post holding the animals in check. One of the horses had been killed. The men had not only been able to keep the horses together but defended themselves like heroes against overwhelming numbers.

The sergeant and the eight men were alive and without a scratch. The path of flight of the hostiles was strewn with war bonnets, quivers, arrows, skins, robes, belts and other paraphernalia. On returning toward camp Davis found a fresh scalp of a white man lying on the ground.

Concluding that this must tell the tale of the death of one of the brave citizens with Randall he began at once to make diligent search for the soldier and companions, dead or alive.

The detachment passed close to this bank under which Randall was lying. Seeing the evidences of struggle on every hand the closest investigation was made. The Indians killed by Randall and Mr. Parks had now been removed, but the marks of warfare were still visible. Randall recognized the voices of the soldiers and cried out until he made himself heard. He was dragged from his hiding-place nearly dead. The dead men were buried near the place where they fell and Randall was carried to camp where he rapidly revived. Considering the number of soldiers and the number of the foe, the amount of punishment inflicted upon the savages, the amount of war materials captured, and the success in bringing out of the fight all of the men Sergeant Davis took into it, this engagement must be regarded as among the most notable of the period to which it belongs.

UNDER FIRE.   31

First Sergeant of H Troop, Shelvin Shropshire, was a constituent member of C Company, organized at Fort

WEALTHY SIOUX INDIAN WOMAN.
(Cloak Decorated with Elk Teeth.)

Leavenworth, Kansas, May 16, 1867, and has been a conspicuous figure in regimental history since.

Shropshire was first in action against Indians at

Great Bend on the Arkansas River. The Cheyennes attacked a Mexican provision train and killed several of the teamsters. One man escaped into the cavalry camp twenty miles distant and gave the alarm. When the troop arrived on the scene of the butchery, dead oxen lay in their places under yoke where they had fallen pierced with arrows, while in some instances their mates were standing beside them in resolute determination not to die. One ox was noticed to have nearly or quite a dozen arrows bristling from his back while he was indifferently grazing as if nothing unusual had happened. Near the dead drivers lay three Indians so drunk upon liquor found in the wagons that they were utterly helpless.

The command was ordered north to the transcontinental railway line. For months thereafter the Indians attacked the camps of the troops on an average of three mornings out of every week.

In point of exciting interest these engagements were not comparable to an incident which occurred within the command itself.

While in camp at Galesteo, New Mexico, a second lieutenant with Troop C shot and killed two enlisted men of this company and was disarmed by Sergeant Shropshire, who by his great coolness and self-possession, prevented a mutiny and saved the officer from instant death. In those days on the frontier little was thought of taking human life and this officer seems to have been particularly handy on the trigger. Such practices, however, were uncommon in the army. He shot the first man squarely through the head as he stood on the ground; the second he shot as accurately from the saddle. Neither man had done anything so far as can be learned which was worthy of death. The lieutenant was tried by civil court of the territory and acquitted, but subsequently left the service.

UNDER FIRE.   33

Shropshire participated in the important action at Wichita Agency in August, 1874, and was mentioned in orders for his bravery.

Four troops, C, E, H and L, under General Davidson had arrived at the Agency from Fort Sill to arrest a noted renegade Kiowa sub-chief named Red Food. This Indian had been guilty of many crimes and depredations. His lodge was soon located near that of Toshwi, a friendly chief, with the manifest intention of involving him in any clash he might precipitate with the whites.

General Davidson drew up the command facing the Indian, and with backs to a stockade which inclosed the post trader's store and a well of most excellent water round which were seated many bucks and squaws. The day was a very hot one and at that hour growing hotter. Lieutenant S. L. Woodward, the adjutant, was sent among the tepees to ascertain if arms and ammunition were secreted in them.

The tepees were for the most part empty, the Indians had gone out and were either near the schoolhouse, which was guarded by a company of the Twenty-fifth Infantry, or were within the stockade at the store or hidden in the brush of the Wichita River nearby.

Red Food was invited to meet General Davidson and hold a council. He approached mounted upon a pony. Before the conference had resulted in any appreciable understanding Red Food turned his pony suddenly, and throwing his blanket over his head dashed through the native village and disappeared in the brushy bottom lands beyond. A volley from the troopers pursued him, and the wonder is that the adjutant was not killed. He had been forgotten for the moment and might have perished at the hands of his men. At this instant the Indians within the stockade rose *en masse* and rushing to the wooden wall, threw aside their blankets which had secreted their firearms, and through the loopholes poured a deadly fire into the backs of men and horses drawn up in line without.

This was an unexpected attack. The troops were wheeled away from the perilous position and rapidly sought and found shelter under the break of the river. From this place a fearless and successful charge was made upon the stockade and store now held by the Indians. The trader had fled from his premises and was with the frightened school-teachers and other employees gathered at the schoolhouse. Men who were in the fields in the act of procuring forage for the cavalry horses were killed and scalped by the furious red devils who sought to facilitate their work of destruction by firing the dry prairie grass. Now the fire reinforced the heat of that August sun. To save the buildings and haystacks was nothing short of a herculean task. The men behaved as only men do who know that duty well done is the only possible escape from the combination of the elements and the savages. Horses and men sank under the heat and toil. The wounded suffered and bled and famished for water. The flames were at length subdued, the agency was saved, and the Indians were scattered and many killed. Shropshire was in command of a squad who killed one Indian under peculiar circumstances. He had noticed that a shot at regular intervals came from a neighboring cornfield. Under slight cover he crept up to the edge of rising ground determined to locate the sharpshooter whose balls were coming closer with each discharge. Presently he discovered what looked like a shock of newly cut corn. He watched that shock; he saw it move; there was an Indian inside of it. The savage had inclosed himself with green cornstalks; he was well dis-

AN INDIAN WAR DANCE.

guised. Calling a corporal to him he pointed out the object and ordered a volley poured into the shock. The value of corn as clothing fell in that vicinity. The next day the Indian's remains were examined and his body was found to have been pierced by five bullets.

Shropshire has followed the fortunes of the regiment in many campaigns but recalls no engagement where men and animals suffered so much from heat of sun and fire.

He also rendered excellent service through the Geronimo campaign of 1885-6.

Sergeant Robert Kurney, H Troop, is one of the "old timers" in the history of the regiment. His first experience with hostile Indians was at Fort Sill, in May, 1871.

General Sherman, General Marcy, Colonel McCoy and Colonel Tourtelotte made a tour of inspection of Texas posts in the spring of that year. On that tour they went from Fort Griffin to Fort Richardson over a road which was infested with hostile Indians. At one point shortly after they had passed, a government provision train was attacked by a force of one hundred savages. Several teamsters were killed and wounded; some of the latter were bound to the wagon wheels and burned alive. Three men escaped and reached Fort Richardson, then commanded by Major J. K. Mizner, now colonel of the Tenth Cavalry.

General Sherman and party arrived at Fort Sill, and became guests of General Grierson. Fort Sill was within the reservation of the Kiowas and Comanches and the agency was near the post. On May 13th when a large number of Indians were at the latter place drawing rations Satanta boasted in an oration delivered to his assembled people that he was in command of the recent raiding party. He described the affair with such

UNDER FIRE. 37

graphic particularity as to leave no doubt in the minds of those who could understand him of his personal participation in the bloody transaction. The agent, Mr. Tatum, an intelligent and thoroughly conscientious Quaker, on learning of Satanta's defiant confession dispatched a messenger to General Grierson, commanding the garrison, requesting the arrest of the chief and any others he might apprehend as having been connected with the recent massacre.

He ventured to say that a good many of the guilty Indians were then present at the agency. General Grierson reported the matter to General Sherman and ordered his whole command, several troops of the Tenth Cavalry, to quietly saddle their horses inside of the high-walled stables preparatory to action; indicating to troop commanders his intention to surround all the Indians at the agency with a view to arresting the culprits. In the meantime Satanta and Satank hearing that General Sherman was at the post came up to have a talk with him. Indeed, they were on the stoop of General Grierson's quarters when the messenger from Mr. Tatum arrived. There was something said or done which aroused the suspicions of the Indians for Satanta cut the conference short and started to leave. Observing the movement General Grierson directed his orderly, a fearless and otherwise splendid specimen of the colored race named Murphy, then standing in front of the house with pistol at his belt, to stop the chief. The orderly with pistol drawn marched the wily savage back where he was again seated. Satank had not stirred. The warriors seemed to recognize the fact that they were prisoners. At this juncture another message from the agent arrived requesting the arrest of Big Tree as one of the active spirits in the murders. This Indian had only a few minutes before passed the house riding in the direction of the post trader's store. Accordingly the adjutant was ordered to take a small detachment and endeavor to secure him. As Lieutenant Woodward entered the store Big Tree divined the intention and throwing his blanket over his head he ran to the rear of the building and sprang through the window carrying with him sash and glass. He found himself surrounded by a tight board fence ten feet high over which he vaulted with the agility of an acrobat. Once clear of such trifling obstructions he started for a neighboring thicket. The soldiers ran around the inclosure and opened fire on the chieftain as he fled. The officer pursued on horseback and succeeded in bringing him to a halt near his coveted hiding-place. He thought his time had come and surrendered without resistance. Stirring events were in progress at the post commander's quarters. Lone Wolf, another Kiowa chief, had arrived. He dismounted and tied his pony to the fence, gathering his blanket about his body and head in characteristic fashion as he approached. Horace Jones, the interpreter, who knew all these Indians, remarked in a low tone: "Here comes Lone Wolf, there's going to be trouble." The guard posted in the house filed out and lined up facing the porch. Lone Wolf advanced with an exceedingly friendly smile, but the moment he stepped upon the floor he thrust aside his blanket disclosing a bow and a quiver full of arrows and two carbines. Two other Indians seized these weapons and endeavored to use them upon the group of officers. General Grierson, comprehending the crisis, sprang at the treacherous redskins and gripping both guns by the barrels, threw the muzzles upward and with superhuman strength seated the Indians. The soldiers brought their loaded pieces to a "ready" and "cocked" them. Had a single gun been discharged

An Indian Burial.

the Kiowa chiefs and their body guard would have lost their lives, but not until General Grierson and perhaps others had been sacrificed.

Some other Indians at this moment entered the post. They saw evidences of excitement at the post commander's quarters and whipped their ponies into a run and sought to escape at the farther end of the parade ground. One of them lost his life in the attempt and the others were captured.

At a given signal the troops rode out and encircled the post. This was a beautiful sight. Every horse and man was ready for action and preferred a necessary fight to a good dinner.

The thousands of Indians at the agency hearing shots at the post abandoned their tepees and scattered like frightened partridges and were not seen again for many days. Satanta, Satank, and Big Tree were informed that they would be taken to the Texas penitentiary at Huntsville. Some time after this when preparations were being made to transport them Satank sang the death song. At the moment of departure Big Tree used his best offices in getting Satank into the wagon. He explained afterward that Satank was intending to kill, if opportunity offered, Generals Grierson and Mackenzie. When about a mile from Fort Sill *en route*, Satank made a vicious attack upon a sick soldier who was riding in the wagon with him. The guard killed Satank at once. Satanta committed suicide in prison at Huntsville, Texas. Big Tree was subsequently pardoned and returned to his people over whom he exercised a beneficial influence for a number of years.

Among the hundreds of others who took part in the exciting dramas of savage warfare in the wild West are John Wiggins, First Sergeant Thomas A. Allsop,

Sergeant Washington Brown, Philip Jones, Sergeant Peter Clayborne, Sergeant William H. Givens, Chief Trumpeter James H. Thomas, Trumpeter Silas Jones, Charles H. Farrell, Sergeant Daniel Johnson, Joseph Clegget, Sergeant Daniel Brown, Levi Bradley, Madison Veile, E. Robinson, Henry Robinson, Zachaiah Pope, Andrew J. Smith, Robert Anderson, Benjamin F. Davis, First Sergeant David Haskins, Sergeant George Berry, John H. Jackson, Courteney Matthews, and Henry Allen.

The settlement and civilization of the West is largely due to the sacrifices, hardships, and arduous duties performed by these noble specimens of the Negro race.

Speaking of Indians, it is interesting to note the great change which has taken place in the life and character of Geronimo, who once gave the United States a great deal of trouble.

Geronimo preached an eloquent sermon to his people on learning that the Indians of Minnesota were attempting to go to war with the United States government.

Geronimo is an Apache who belongs to the Chirachia band, and who for many years was the most vexatious and troublesome Indian with whom the government had to deal. He is now an old man of probably seventy years. He was born in New Mexico, and for years served as a herder, working for Spaniards who owned ranches in the territory. When about twenty-one years of age he conceived the idea that he had been greatly wronged by the white man, and from that time until his final surrender to General Miles, in 1886, he was almost continually on the war-path.

Geronimo declares that it is a great mistake for the Indians to approach the whites in a warlike attitude:

"When I say that the Minnesota Indians have made a mistake I know whereof I speak. From long experience, in both war and peace, I know that it is better to submit to great wrongs than to fight the United States. Years ago the Indians made up a great nation, but now they have gone, never to return. We have got to give up our old ways and take on those of the whites. There are only a few of us left, and we are herded in like a lot of sheep, so that it is foolish to go to war. The young men of the tribes will never know anything of war, except as the tales are told by the old men.

"I have never been in Minnesota, but I hear that up there and for hundreds of miles beyond the white men are as many as the blades of grass. If that is so, what can a few poor Indians do in a fight? They are making a great mistake and are fools. For years I fought the white men, thinking that with my few braves I could kill them all off; and that we would again have the land that our Great Father gave us, and which he covered with game. I thought that the Great Spirit would be with us, and that after we had killed the white men, the buffalo, deer and antelope would come back. After I fought and lost, and after I traveled over the country in which the white man lived and saw his cities and the work that he had done, my old heart was ready to burst. I knew that the race of the Indians had run, and that there was nothing left but to submit."

Asked what he thought would eventually become of the North American Indians, Geronimo hesitated a moment and then, pointing to the west, replied:

"The sun rises and shines for a time and then it goes down, sinking out of sight and is lost; so it will be with the Indians. When I was a boy my old father told me that the Indians were as many as the leaves on the trees, and that way off in the North they had many horses and furs. I never saw them, but I know that if they were there they have gone now, and the white man has taken all they had.

"Schools are good things for the Indians, but it takes many years to change the nature of the Indian. If an Indian boy goes to school and learns to be like a white boy he comes back to the agency and there is nothing for him to do but to put on a blanket and be like an Indian again. This is where the government is to blame. When it takes our children away and educates them it should give them something to do, not turn them loose to run wild upon the agency. Until that time comes educating the Indians is throwing money away. What can an educated Indian do out in the sage brush and cactus?

"I am an old man and can't live many years, so that this don't trouble me much, but before I die I would like to see the Indians have the same chance as the colored people or the poor whites. Then there will be no more big Indian wars. The Indian's fighting days are over, and there is nothing left for him to do but to be a beggar and live on charity around the agency."

MAJ.-GEN. NELSON A. MILES.

MAJ.-GEN. WM. R. SHAFTER.

MAJ.-GEN. JOSEPH WHEELER.

GENERAL ANTONIO MACEO.

CHAPTER III.

THE WARS OF THE UNITED STATES.

Governmental Responsibilities—Obligations of Men in Office—Spanish Cruelty and Injustice—Destruction of the Maine—Some Facts Concerning the Discovery of the West India Islands.

AFTER all that may be said, a nation is but a composite of its people. More especially must this be inevitably and invariably true of a nation like ours, where the people make their laws, engraft their sympathies and purposes upon the public acts—where their opinion is *lex suprema.*

Individuals owe their duties to societies of men; nations owe solemn obligations to their associate nations in the world's galaxy of combined masses of mankind; hence, just as the individual, who acknowledges his duty to his fellows, listens to the calls of Christian charity in its broad sense and strives to shape his deeds for the good of the many as well as for himself, so must a nation live its relative life, that all the world beside, as well as its own people, are better conditioned and happier for its being. This surely is not a mere poetic fancy, but rather a serious pledge each nationality should make with itself. At any rate, this is a controlling thought in these United States, and the inception of the war for the liberation of Cuba is a pointed demonstration that the national momentum which this sense imparts cannot be withstood.

The obligations of men lifted into power by their fellows enhance with their increased strength and enlarged capacity for doing good; so, too, with the nations of the earth. Their moral exactions increase as they grow in strength. When Washington, in his Farewell Address, spoke of "our detached and distant situation," we were young and insecure and there were no railroads and ocean steamers and cables to tell us promptly of such things as Spanish oppressions and Cuban suffering and starvation. Moreover, while he warned his country against participating in the political vicissitudes of Europe, it may be safely assumed that one so imbued with liberty and a sense of right would not have faltered when humanity's ear was pierced with those woeful cries that came up from a close neighbor. The later history of our country, exemplified in the Heaven-inspired deeds of the matchless Lincoln, more fully proclaimed to the world that cruelties and atrocities, like those of Spain, would not be tolerated on or near these shores. Since the Great Liberator we have neither retrograded nor retarded in the onward march. The great majority of the people of the United States may always be trusted in the great outcome. There is deeply resident a transcendant spirit of humanity and justice. While there have been sporadic cruelties and gross injustice to the colored citizen, it does not have its basis in the grand national sense of right which permeates the great masses of the people all over the land; and the same strong spirit and quickened conscience which took up the cause of Cuba will surely secure justice to the American Negro.

Spain had for centuries planted herself upon the effete idea that antiquity is supreme wisdom; that devastation is progress; that cruelty to her colonial subjects is a divine right she might always enjoy. She had forgotten how her haughty and harsh bearing had driven her numerous South American dependencies to strike for freedom more than fifty years before.

She was using Cuba to enrich Madrid. The unhappy isle had filed her many protests—in the insurrections of 1850, of 1851, of 1854, notably in the ten years' war from 1868 to 1878; and the last rebellion 1895, which gave to the Valhalla the name of Antonio Maceo, the Negro, was the most formidable of them all. Spanish arms had illustrated their utter incapacity to suppress the struggle for freedom; the starvation of the reconcentrados had been invoked in vain. To revert; filibustering had long been practiced around Cuba's extensive, advantageous coast.

Years dragged on and many times an international collision was imminent. There were innumerable plans discussed to buy the island, while its annexation had long been a topic for discussion among American statesmen and journalists. The entire trouble, though acute, was by no means new. American commerce had suffered greatly, although be it truthfully said, this was least spoken of and commanded a minimum of public consideration. The public thought dwelt on a higher plane. The tension had grown in severity, and, a busy people though we were, we had abundant time to listen unto, and to keep thoroughly informed about, the afflictions of our ill-fated little neighbor.

What wonder with these extreme contrasts between Spain and the United States—these conflicts of incentive—and with an administration at Washington prompt to respond to that exalted public purpose which its own keen sympathy so unerringly taught it to fully comprehend, what wonder that the conflict of arms should speedily come?

Spanish rule in Cuba had become an abomination—

UNDER FIRE. 49

a reproach. The destruction of the Maine, whether from accident or design, acted as a mere precipitant not as a cause. The pent-up indignation of a great, humane, liberty-loving people forced the issue from that fateful day. The day before we were alert but peaceful, serene. The day after, so to speak, we were in arms, and the people applauded wherever the martial tread of our soldiery was heard in their mobilization toward Cuba. Instantaneously there was no North, no South, no black, no white. We were at once a compact national force marching forward on a high mission.

What a splendid coronation was accorded our efforts.

STATEMENT OF THE NUMBER OF UNITED STATES TROOPS ENGAGED.

Wars.	From.	To.	Regulars.	Militia and Vol't'rs.	Total.
War of the Revolution	Apr. 19, 1775	Apr. 11, 1783	130,711	164,080	294,791
Northw't'n Indian wars.	Sept. 19, 1790	Aug. 3, 1795	....	....	8,983
War with France	July 9, 1798	Sept. 30, 1800	....	....	*4,593
War with Tripoli	June 10, 1801	June 4, 1805	....	....	*3,330
Creek Indian war	July 27, 1813	Aug. 9, 1814	600	13,181	13,781
War 1812 with Great Britain	June 18, 1812	Feb. 17, 1815	85,000	471,622	556,622
Seminole Indian war	Nov. 20, 1817	Oct. 21, 1818	1,000	6,911	7,911
Black Hawk Indian war	Apr. 21, 1831	Sept. 31, 1832	1,339	5,126	6,465
Cherokee disturbance or removal	1836	1837	....	9,494	9,494
Creek Indian war or disturbance	May 5, 1836	Sept. 30, 1837	935	12,483	13,418
Florida Indian war	Dec. 23, 1835	Aug. 14, 1843	11,169	29,953	41,122
Aroostook disturbance.	1838	1839	....	1,500	1,500
War with Mexico	Apr. 24, 1846	July 4, 1848	30,954	73,776	104,730
Apache, Navajo and Utah war	1849	1855	1,500	1,061	2,561
Seminole Indian war	1856	1858	....	3,687	3,687
Civil war †	1861	1856	....	....	2,772,408

* Naval forces engaged.
† The number of troops on the Confederate side was about 600,000.

The number of casualties in the volunteer and regular armies of the United States during the war of 1861-65 was reported by the Provost Marshal General in 1866; Killed in battle, 61,362; died of wounds, 34,727;

died of disease, 183,287; total died, 279,376; total deserted, 199,105. Number of soldiers in the Confederate service who died of wounds or disease (partial statement), 133,821. Deserted (partial statement), 104,428. Number of United States troops captured during the war, 212,608; Confederate troops captured, 476,169. Number of United States troops paroled on the field, 16,431; Confederate troops paroled on the field, 248,599. Number of United States troops who died while prisoners, 29,725; Confederate troops who died while prisoners, 26,774.

ADDRESS OF THE QUEEN OF SPAIN.

April 20, 1898, the Queen Regent of Spain delivered the following address to the Spanish Cortes or Congress.

"The grave anxieties which saddened my mind the last time I addressed you have increased and are heightened by public uneasiness, conveying the presentment of fresh and greater complications as a result of the turn which events in Cuba have taken.

"These complications were brought about by a section of the people of the United States, which seeing that the autonomy previously offered in my message was about to be put in force, foresaw that the free manifestation of the Cuban people, through its chambers, would frustrate forever the schemes against Spanish sovereignty which have been plotted by those who, with resources and hopes sent from the neighboring coast, have fettered the suppression of the insurrection in that unhappy island.

"Should the government of the United States yield to this blind current, menaces and insult, which we have hitherto been able to regard with indifference, for they were not an expression of the sentiments of the true American nation, would become intolerable provocations, which would compel my government, in defense of the national dignity, to sever relations with the government of the United States.

"In this supreme crisis the sacred voice of Him who represents human justice on earth was raised in counsels of peace and prudence, to which my government had no difficulty in hearkening, strong in the consciousness of its right and calm in the strict performance of its duties.

"Spain's gratitude is due to the Pope and also to the great powers, whose action strengthens my conviction that Spain's cause deserves universal sympathy, and that her conduct merits unanimous approval. It is possible, however, that an act of aggression is imminent, and that not the sanctity of our rights, nor the moderation of our conduct, nor the expressed wish of the Cuban people, freely manifested, may serve to restrain the passions and hatred let loose against the Spanish fatherland.

"In anticipation of this critical moment when reason and justice will have for their support only Spanish courage and the traditional energy of our people, I have hastened the assembling of the Cortes, and the supreme decision of Parliament will doubtless sanction the unalterable purpose of my government to defend our rights, whatsoever sacrifices may be imposed upon us in accomplishing this task.

"Thus identifying myself with the nation, I not only fulfill the oath I swore in accepting the regency, but I follow the dictates of a mother's heart, trusting to the Spanish people to gather behind my son's throne and to defend it until he is old enough to defend it himself, as well as trusting to the Spanish people to defend the honor and the territory of the nation.

"Although a dark and gloomy future is before us the difficulties are not beyond our powers, with our glorious army, navy, and the united nation, before foreign aggression. We trust in God that we shall overcome without stain on our honor the baseless and unjust attacks made upon us."

Cuba is the largest of the West India Islands; it was discovered by Christopher Columbus, October, 1492, and first colonized by his son Diego, who founded Santiago and Trinidad in 1514, and Havana in 1519.

In forty years the aborigines, who numbered three hundred thousand, were blotted out by Spain. Havana quickly grew into importance, and was destroyed by a French privateer in 1538, and again in 1554, and in 1624 the Dutch captured it, but gave it back to Spain.

In 1762 a British force captured Havana, under Lord Albemarle, and restored to Spain under the Treaty of Paris of 1763. The French deposed the reigning family in Spain in 1808, Cuba declared war against Napoleon; Spain lost all her American possessions but kept Cuba. Because of government by a foreign captain-general as far back as 1810, and also of the heavy taxation, a discontent was breeding, which gradually hardened into opposition, hatred and defiance after 1836, when Cuba was denied a share in the benefits of the new constitution granted the mother country.

In 1873 occurred the tragic Virginius incident, when Captain Fry, of that ill-fated vessel, and fifty-two other Americans were shot at Santiago as "pirates." In 1889 Premier Sagasta, told the United States Minister there was not gold enough in the world to buy Cuba.

The year 1868 inaugurated an effort for Cuban independence, under the leadership of Maximo Gomez, a native West Indian. The war lasted ten years, being limited to the eastern third of the island. It was finally terminated by the treaty of El Zanjon, between Gomez and Capt.-General Martinez Campos, providing for important concessions of Cuban autonomy, and the early abolishment of slavery. This war cost Spain 100,000 men and about $60,000,000 and this expense was taxed on the Cubans. Taxation without the knowledge of the Cubans themselves was, as ever, the core of the whole fiscal system, and every native Cuban was excluded from every office which could give him influence in public affairs, and to make the most out of the colonists' labor for the benefit of Spain. The government at Madrid continually issued decrees, whose effect would be to cheapen sugar and tobacco, the two great Cuban products. Spain practically confiscated the product of the Cubans' labor without giving them in return either safety, prosperity or education. She systematically improverished Cuba, while demoralizing its people by condemning them to political inferiority. The Cuban deputies were never able to accomplish anything in the Cortes of Madrid, the majority owing their places to distinctly Spanish influence. The vast sums amassed by taxes, multitudinous, searching, grasping, were raised and spent, not for roads, schools, improvements, or for developing internal resources, but for the enrichment and indulgence of a swarm of overbearing foreigners. Spain had fastened a debt on Cuba of $200,000,000, in addition to a system of taxation which wrung annually $39,000,000 from them.

The disturbance, which gave rise to the difference between Spain and the United States, has already called forth Marshal Campos in 1895, General Weyler in 1896, and General Blanco in October, 1897, and about 200,000 Spanish troops. The uprising began on February 24, 1895.

Cuba is divided into six provinces, each with a capital of the same name, viz:

PROVINCE.	CAPITAL.	POPULATION.
Havana	Havana	451,928
Matanzas	Matanzas	225,891
Pinar del Rio	Pinar del Rio	259,570
Puerto Principe	Puerto Principe	354,122
Santa Clara	Santa Clara	67,789
Santiago de Cuba	Santiago de Cuba	272,319
	Total	1,631,619

Cuba is long and narrow, 750 miles long and an average breadth of 60 to 70 miles; the area is 41,655 square miles. The population is now estimated at 1,723,000, composed of Spaniards, Creoles, and mulattoes and Negroes.

The governor-general is assisted by a council of administration, and the island is represented in the Spanish Cortes by 16 senators and 30 deputies.

Havana has an estimated population of 250,000; the other important towns are: Matanzas, 87,760; Santiago de Cuba, 71,307; Cienfuegos, 65,067; Puerto Principe, 46,641; Holguin, 34,767; Santa Clara, 34,635; Sancti Spiritus, 32,608; Cardenas, 20,505; Guanabacoa, 16,402. There are 843 public schools and a university at Havana.

The revenue is about $22,632,143; expenditures, $24,061,505; total debt about $341,737,333; total exports, $82,018,228; imports, $52,101,862; the principal products are sugar, coffee and tobacco. There are 1,000 miles of railway in operation and the larger sugar estates have private lines connecting with the main lines, making a total of 1,200 miles. There are 2,300 miles of telegraph lines.

Admiral George Dewey.

Admiral Wm. T. Sampson.

Admiral W. S. Schley.

HORACE W. BIVINS EQUIPPED FOR SERVICE.

CHAPTER IV.

THE ATTITUDE OF THE NEGRO.

Prejudice Resulting from the Condition of Servitude from Which the Negro but Recently Emerged in His Way—The Intelligence of the Negro Soldier—A Remarkable Character—Horace W. Bivins— An Ex-Slave—a Great Observer of Men and Deeds—His Life.

WHILE the Negro soldier found that he had to face hostilities in his own land due to the foolish prejudice resultant from the condition of slavery from which he so recently emerged, and while he paid little or no attention to the insults heaped upon him by the people of a certain section of the United States, he felt very keenly the gravity of the situation, and so earnestly did he conduct himself in the war that the most commendable achievement was registered in his favor, and there are few to be found to-day who would deny his ability to fight.

To those who recall the soldierly bearing of the Negro volunteers during the Civil War, after their first baptism of fire in the heroic charge but lately commemorated in St. Gaudens' magnificent monument to Robert Gould Shaw, in Boston, and their subsequent faithful service in numberless Indian campaigns as the last of the line, no vindication is needed by the Negro soldier. But there has always been a tendency on the part of some to belittle the value of his service in the past, or to admit it very grudgingly; and realizing this the negro attempted to justify the government's reliance upon him.

It is fortunate that the average Negro in the regular army is intelligent and fairly well educated.

Horace Wayman Bivins, son of Severn S. and Elizabeth Bivins, was born in Pungoteague, Accomack County, Virginia, May 8, 1862. He spent his early childhood on his father's farm. At the age of fifteen he was put in charge of an eight-horse farm one mile from Keller Station, Va. His father is a farmer, but has spent much of his time in religious and educational work. He advanced money in 1862 to build a church and schoolhouse at Pungoteague. These were the first buildings erected on the eastern shore of Virginia, for that purpose. Prejudice was so great in that section that the day that the schoolhouse was completed it was reduced to ashes before 10 o'clock that night, and a notice was placed upon his father's door notifying him to leave the country within five days or else he would be hanged by his d——d neck until dead. The following day the old gentleman received information that the Yankees were at Drummondtown, but twelves miles away. He rode to headquarters and reported the transaction to the division commander. He at once sent a part of his staff to investigate the matter. The result was in Mr. Bivins' favor, and he was successful in establishing a school and had it opened the following Monday.

The following narrative was written by Sergeant Bivins while in the Cuban campaign, and it shows that he is a careful observer and faithful historian:

"I entered Hampton School, June 13, 1885, at which place I received my first military training. Having a very great desire for adventure and to see the wild West, I enlisted in the United States army, November 7, 1887, at Washington, D. C. Ten days later I was sent to Jefferson Barracks, Missouri. After receiving a few lessons in mounted and dismounted drill I was assigned to Troop E, Tenth Cavalry. Major Kelley was then captain of the troop. I joined my troop at Fort Grant, Arizona Territory, June 19, 1888. In a few days my troop was ordered to take the field. It was reported that some Indians had left the San Carlos Reservation and were *en route* to Old Mexico.

"We scouted along St. Pedro River east and west. For thirty days we were searching for Indian trails, but found none. We then returned to the post. On February 22, 1889, my troop was ordered to San Carlos, Arizona Territory. We arrived there after four days' hard march. Our camp was established on the north side and along the Gila River. I was detailed as lineman. I had to ride and keep the telegraph line in good repair between Camp Carlos and Globe, a mining camp about thirty-five miles from San Carlos.

There were two troops of the Tenth Cavalry, F and E; G Troop of the Fourth Cavalry and companies C and G of the Twenty-fourth Infantry. There were several thousands of Indians on this reservation. I often had to ride the line alone, and had to pass within two miles of a band of hostile Indians who had intrenched themselves on the heights opposite Benson's Camp, within twelve miles of Carlos.

"Churchana, an Indian chief, had established his headquarters near Benson's Camp and defied the government to arrest him. We kept a detail of twelve men and one noncommissioned officer at Benson's Camp, two miles from the hostile intrenchment. It was a very unpleasant duty that I had to perform, as often I had to pass this camp in the night.

"April 9, 1889, Lieutenant (now Captain) Watson, Lieutenant Dade and Lieutenant Littebrant of the

Tenth, with three troops and sixty Indian scouts, surrounded the hostile camp and demanded their surrender, which was accepted on conditions. The Indian chief was to identify and turn over all the murderers and the government was not to prosecute him. When the fact became known among the Indians that the chief was going to surrender they mutinied, and in the fight four were killed, and the chief was stabbed in several places and was admitted in the government hospital. Lieutenant Watson at daybreak planted two Hotchkiss guns, six hundred yards east of their fortified position, and trained the guns on their works, and thus effected the surrender.

"These same guns helped to form our battery before Santiago, and of which I was gunner.

"After the surrender of the Indians my troop was ordered to change stations with troop I of our regiment. We arrived at Fort Apache, Arizona Territory, October 17, 1889, after a seven days' march over a rough and rocky road. I was detailed as clerk in the regimental adjutant's office, November 10, 1889, and served until made corporal, June 15, 1890. My first target practice with the rifle was at San Carlos. I stood No. 2 in the troop of sixty men although it was the first time that I had ever shot a rifle. I was made sharpshooter in that year, 1889, and have ever since led my troop in marksmanship. I represented my troop in 1892, '93, and '94, winning eight medals and badges at the department competition. I also in 1894 won three gold medals when I represented the Department of the Dakotas at the army competition at Fort Sheridan and carried off the first gold medal.

"Our regiment was ordered to Chickamauga, April 14, 1898. My troop, G, at this time, was in the field. First Lieutenant W. H. Smith and Second Lieutenant

Johnson and thirty-eight enlisted men had been ordered to do patrol duty in the Blackfeet Reservation, which the government had announced would be thrown open for settlement on the 15th of April, 1898.

"When the order came for us to go South, General Henry sent a telegram for the troop to report at the post as soon as possible. The troop arrived at post at 2:30 P.M. on the 18th, looking very much fatigued, having patroled the Canadian line, a portion of the Rocky Mountains and St. Marys Lake, a part of the time wading through mud and water from two to three feet deep and more than half of the time without anything to eat.

"We left Fort Assinniboine, Montana, April 19th. We were delayed near a little town in Wisconsin about twenty-two hours on account of the burning of a bridge just before we reached it. It was throught that it was burned on purpose to have us lie over there.

"We received great ovations all along the line. Thousands of people were thronged at the places where we would stop and we were treated royally; at Madison, Wisconsin, we were presented with enough flags to decorate our train and were given cigars and many other pleasantries. Our band would play in response to the ovations that were given us from time to time.

"After reaching Illinois we received both flags and flowers from the ladies and schoolgirls. I planted one of the flags given me on the crest of San Juan Hill, July 1, 1898. As we neared the South the great demonstrations became less fervent. There were no places that we entered in which we were courteously treated.

"The signs over the waiting room doors at the Southern depots were a revelation to us. Some read thus: 'White waiting room.' On the door of a lunch room we read: 'Niggers are not allowed inside.' We were traveling in palace cars and the people were much surprised that we did not occupy the 'Jim Crow' cars, *the curse of the South.*

"At Nashville, Tennessee, we were met by thousands of people, both white and colored. Our band played in respose to the cheers that went up from the great multitude. After leaving Nashville we were soon in Chickamauga, and our regiment, notwithstanding the fact that we had just come from the extreme cold of the Northwest began the routine duties of camp life and put in several hours at hard drill. We soon became well-seasoned warriors under the discipline required in war. Not a word of complaint was heard in the lines as our men were marched and countermarched under the hot sun in preparing them for the hardships of the campaign in Cuba. General Wheeler, when first visiting our regiment at Lakeland, Florida, was much impressed by the appearance of our men and said that we looked like fighters. And there were in our lines many Indian fighters who were anxious to get a whack at the Spaniards."

Full Corps of Officers of the Tenth U. S. Cavalry Just Before Going to Cuba.

Hurry and Bustle Boarding Transports.

Officers of the Tenth U. S. Cavalry after Battle.

TRUMPETERS OF THE TENTH U. S. CAVALRY.

CHAPTER V.

SOME EXPERIENCES IN CUBA.

Important Narrative—Tenth Cavalry Ordered East—Delay in Florida Causes Uneasiness among Regulars—Men Excited at Sea—Landing of the Tenth Cavalry Marked by the Loss of Two Men—Personal Letter Written on the Battlefield.

CONTINUING his narrative, which is one of the most reliable and straightforward ever given of the campaign in Cuba, and which, on account of the simplicity of the language, must attract a great deal of attention throughout the United States and in Europe, where the people are thirsting for reliable information concerning the grave questions involved in such a discussion, Sergeant Bivins relates further all that he saw, all the impressions made on him in Florida, on the transport, while landing in Cuba, and while in active participation in the battles.

"We arrived at Tampa, Florida, at 11 P.M. the same day. We loaded on property, horses, rations, ammunition, baggage, etc. My regiment went aboard of transport Leona, No. 21. Our gun detachment, 28 men, Lieutenant Hughes Tenth Cavalry in command, received orders to take his detachment on board the Comal, No. 7. We transferred our rations and baggage to No. 7. This transport was loaded with rations, ammunition, horses and mules, and had on board batteries E and K, Second Artillery, and the Tenth Cavalry gun detachment. Everything was in readiness by 5 A.M. We received orders to pull out into the bay. We anchored two miles from the dock.

"At 5:30 A.M. June 9, 1898, we received orders to return to dock, which we did, unloaded our stock and carried it down to the stockyard, two miles away. I was sent in charge of the stock. We were much disappointed as we were expecting to leave for Cuba on that day. The question was asked by thousands: 'What is the trouble?'

"Later we were informed that a phantom Spanish fleet had been discovered at sea, and a wait of seven days was the result. We could hear all kinds of tales. Some said that Sampson had had a fight with Cervera and had destroyed his fleet, while others said that our fleet had been destroyed by the Spaniards. June 12, 1898, I was at the stock yard in charge of stock when an order was handed me from our detacament commander to bring up the animals at 1 A.M. next day to be loaded on transport. At 12:15 I started up with the horses and mules. We had considerable trouble with them. They seemed so anxious to get to the transport that we could scarcely hold them back. We began to load on stock, and by sunrise the morning of June 13th we were ready for final orders. At 6 P.M. the order came for us to leave the dock. We anchored in the bay two miles from dock for the night.

"Next morning we arose early. The boys were singing: 'The Battleship Maine,' 'A Hot Time in Cuba,' etc. General Miles was there and witnessed the embarkation. We were all in readiness in Port Tampa Bay. Early on the morning of the 14th the officers and enlisted men were keyed up to a very high pitch of excitement at the flinging out of battle flags. At first the little Lyden hoisted a good-sized flag to her masthead, then a huge one at the stern which was quite as large if

Troop A Tenth Cavalry.

not larger than herself, which made it appear that she had her hands full. The Wasp then showed her two big flags. Then the Anne with three at her masthead, each of which looked as large as an acre of ground. Last of all the Topeka hoisted three, one at the foremast head, one at the main masthead and one at the stern, which were so large that they made her have the appearance of one huge American flag. It seemed as if no Spaniard, unless he were totally blind, could fail to see that we were Americans with warships.

"We left the bay and went as far as quarantine station (twenty-five miles), anchoerd and remained there until 3 P.M. Ten minutes before 3 P.M. the little revenue cutter came splitting through the water. As it neared us the officer on board, by the aid of a trumpet, said 'We will pull out at once, you (Comal, No. 7) will follow in rear of No. 19. We will sail in column of threes with the battleship Helena at the head of the column.' She went flitting through the water from transport to transport giving the order. When that final order was given to leave, the information ran through the ships like electricity. In a few minutes every man was on the upper deck. It required the strictest of army discipline to suppress the enthusiastic delight of the men. This was the case on each transport. A few minutes later every transport was in motion.

"June 14, 1898, will ever be a memorable day in the history of the American Republic, for on that day the advance guard of the military expedition sailed for Cuba pursuant to the orders of General N. A. Miles, commanding United States army.

"June 15th I arose just as the brilliant sun, the king of day, was to all appearance emerging from the bosom of the great ocean, and to my surprise I beheld thirty-six transports in columns of three, the battleship

Troop B, Tenth Cavalry.

Helena at the head of the columns and several gunboats as rear guard and flankers. No land could be seen as far as the eye could reach, nothing but the beautiful blue waters of the Gulf of Mexico. An escort consisting of several gun and torpedo boats joined us off Dry Tortugas about 11:45 P.M. At 12:30 A.M., June 16th, a mysterious light was sighted about eight miles west of us. Two of our gunboats went to examine it. It retreated. They chased it for several miles then abandoned the chase. "We sighted land east of us at 3:45 P.M. June 17th we saw land to the southwest. Several islands could be seen near Point Lookout lighthouse in Bahama Channel. A small sailboat came near us from the lighthouse. From its masthead was flying the American flag and under it the Cuban flag. The crew consisted of three Cubans (two of them very dark and one light). Cheer after cheer went up from our boys. The Cubans seemed to be overwhelmed with joy.

"June 18th and 19th we passed several high mountain peaks. We did not know where we were until on the 20th, about 9 A.M. We came in sight of Morro Castle at 11 A.M. and oh, what a beautiful spectacle!

"When we came within ten miles of our fleet our ships stopped, and about 5 P.M. Sampson's fleet began to shell the hills in the vicinity of the castle. Our bands began to play 'A Hot Time in Cuba.' (Never heard sweeter music.) June 21st I was up early and as soon as I could use my glasses I was looking in every direction and found that we were near our fleet and not many miles from Morro Castle. At 9 A.M. the order was signaled 'We will try to land.' At 10 A.M. we received orders to pull near the armored cruiser New York, which we did. A Cuban officer was transferred from the New York to our transport as pilot to go sixteen miles down the bay, west of Santiago, to deliver some

Troop C, Tenth Cavalry.

rations to the insurgent army, in camp along the shore, and in the mountainous region. We went within two miles of their camp (two miles of the shore), reaching that point at 4 P.M. Thirty crates of bacon, several sacks of coffee, sugar, and one hundred and fifty boxes of hard bread (hard-tack) were transferred to a small steam vessel. It was so late when the transfer was made that the captain decided that the rations would not be delivered until next morning, as at that time he was expecting to go up a narrow stream some six miles in the mountains. We moved around all night in order to give our horses some air. It was very hot. Next morning we were up very early and at 3:30 the morning of the 22d a detachment (fifteen men) was sent to deliver the rations. While they were being delivered I wrote this letter to a friend:

" 'DEAR FRIEND: We have just delivered rations to the starving insurgent army. I have seen a piteous sight. The men ate dry hard-tacks as if they were almost starved. We are expecting to land to-day at Daiquiri. Probably we will have to land under a heavy fire from the Spanish battery. I send you this letter by the first transport and will destroy my diary for it might fall into the hands of the enemy, though I am not afraid of such. We have had a safe voyage so far. The sea has been calm and we scarcely had a case of seasickness on board. We are in good shape and are ready to do our duty. We are not afraid to fight for our country's honor and for this cause; for we believe that it is a just one. *Tyranny*, tyranny is what Spain has kept imposing upon the Cubans for the last century. Spain will lose. Spanish tryanny can no longer be tolerated by the civilized world. Every foot of the island I believe is marked with sad evidences of cruelty. Oh, God! at last we have taken up the sword to enforce the divine rights of a people who have long been unjustly treated. I believe that God will

Troop D, Tenth Cavalry.

strengthen the hand of all of those who are fighting for humanity; and as we march on that fortified city, Santiago, we go forth to defend that emblem of eternal liberty and justice, the Stars and Stripes, the flag of our great republic.

" 'There is no people on earth more loyal and devoted to their country than the Negro. I believe in the doctrine of peace taught by the lowly Nazarene, but men must have liberty before abiding peace can come. Force saved the Union, kept the stars in the flag and made Negroes free. The time for God's force has come to free Cuba and avenge the Maine. I am sorry to say that we were not treated with much courtesy while coming through the South. God grant the time will soon come when this country will have power to enforce the teaching of the heavenly doctrine that all men are created free and equal. If I die on the shores of Cuba my earnest prayer to God is that when death comes to end all, I may meet it calmly and fearlessly.

" 'Your soldier friend,
" 'HORACE W. BIVINS,
" 'Sgt. Troop G, 10th Cavalry,
" 'Second Cavalry Brigade, Fifth Army Corps, Gun Detachment.
" 'Off Santiago de Cuba.'

"We found the coast of Cuba in the vicinity of Santiago Bay steep and rocky, with few good landing places. At Daiquiri we found an iron pier used by a railroad company for unloading iron ore, etc. Part of it was still standing. The beach was rocky and the surf rough. It looked too rough to permit the landing of horses and mules by swimming ashore. We returned and rejoined the other transports after the Cuban officer had returned to the armored cruiser New York, and anchored at Daiquiri. On the 20th of June a reconnoissance was made east and west of Santiago Bay, and the commanding general went ashore at Asseredero, about eighteen miles west of Santiago. This point was in the

Troop E, Tenth Cavalry.

hands of the Cubans, and the landing was made for the purpose of a conference with General Garcia, the Cuban leader.

"On June 21st plans for landing were made and transmitted to the various commanders. On the morning of the 22d the navy bombarded all the villages along the coast in the vicinity of Daiquiri, and under the cover of this fire an unopposed landing was made by our troops at Daiquiri.

"At 5:25 P.M. June 22d a lieutenant ascended a steep hill at Daiquiri and planted our flag on the top of a blockhouse. As Old Glory was being hoisted to the top of the flagpole every boat in the bay whistled with all their might; the bands played 'The Star Spangled Banner,' and thousands of cheers went up from the brave Americans. Indeed, it was a sight never to be forgotten.

"As the water in the bay was not deep enough for ships to come alongside of the wharf it was necessary to make the landing in small boats belonging to the transports and the navy. The navy furnished the steam launches to tow these boats back and forth between the shore and the transports. The work was slow and very difficult, as the surf was rough and the breakers very dangerous. Two men were drowned while effecting a landing. Their bodies were found next morning and buried. These were the first of our expedition to be placed under Spanish soil. Several horses died on the voyage.

"As soon as our troops landed they formed and marched inland, taking position along the banks of the Daiquiri River, and extending to a distance of about three miles from the village of that name. A number of Cubans who had been landed the night previous at a point east of Daiquiri marched westward and entered

Daiquiri from the land side about the same time that our first troops landed.

"Our landing was slow. No horses were landed the first day, and less than one division of soldiers succeeded in getting ashore. On June 23d the landing of troops continued and the advance pushed on to Siboney, a coast village about nine miles distant from Daiquiri. Horses and mules were landed by swimming and guiding and towing them by the use of small boats. We used our boats, as all of the steam launches were engaged in carrying the soldiers ashore. It was hard work to land the horses and mules; the surf being rough, we had to land them through breakers. Several of the boats were thrown up against the rocks and rendered useless. In the afternoon of the 22d we began to land troops at Siboney where the beach was smoother than at Daiquiri. There was at first no wharf at Siboney, but later a very small one was built by the engineers from timber found in a saw mill nearby. At Daiquiri we found that the Spaniards had burned a car and a roundhouse and set fire to the wharf; but we reached shore before any damage was done the wharf.

"Perhaps a battalion of Spaniards would have been captured at Siboney if a single staff officer could have had a horse to carry the order, but the Spaniards retreated toward Santiago.

"Early in the morning of the 24th we reached a point, Las Guasimas, about four miles west of Siboney where a skirmish had occurred the day before between Cubans and Spaniards in which one Cuban was killed and eight wounded. Here we met a portion of the enemy posted behind stone walls on a very high and steep hill, and facing a point in the road which it was necessary for our troops to pass in marching from a sunken road into an open space. The march from Daiquiri to this point was made in such great haste that our men threw away several thousand blankets and clothing of almost every kind—blouses, trousers and underwear. The sun was so very hot that the men found it impossible to carry such a large roll.

"Here occurred what has since been called the battle of Las Guasimas. The First and Tenth (colored) regiments of regular cavalry (dismounted) deployed and charged up the hill in front. The First Volunteer Cavalry deployed upon the other ridge road from Siboney, which forks at this point with a valley road and charged in flank on the left, driving the enemy from their position, but not until we had sustained a severe loss in both killed and wounded.

"Our forces pushed on and at nightfall occupied a line a mile or more in advance of the position occupied by the enemy in the morning. The conduct of the troops, both white and colored, regular and volunteer, was most gallant and soldierly, and General Young's dispositions, plans and executions were skillful, dashing and successful. Generals Young and Wheeler, and all the other officers, displayed great bravery by walking the skirmish line encouraging the men to keep under cover and take deliberate aim. The fire from the enemy was terrific.

"The disembarking of stores continued a fateful task. We met no resistance in disembarking troops or stores. On June 25th our advance occupied the high ridge of Savilla, in full view of Santiago, about five or six miles distant from it. General Lawton's division (the Second) was in advance; General Wheeler's dismounted cavalry some distance behind General Lawton's and General Kent's first division coming up in rear of General Wheeler's division. We camped on the battlefield. Our detachment packed pieces and camped

TROOP F, TENTH CAVALRY.

twenty-five yards from Corporal White's grave. On the morning of the 26th we marched as far as Savilla-El Pozo on the Santiago road. Our advance continued, the outpost having reached points within three or four miles from the city of Santiago. The light batteries as they came up passed through General Kent's division and went into camp near General Wheeler's division, about the center of the entire army as it stood. The mounted squadron of the Second Cavalry occupied a position near the light batteries. On this date, also, transports containing reinforcements began to arrive (the transports that were considerably out in Santiago Bay).

"The 26th was a trying day. Two-thirds of our packing outfit having been left in the boat, we had to pack ammunition on our gun carriages. We had to travel over a rough and rocky road. I carried a box of Hotchkiss shells for a long distance over a rough road, and was sick several days from being strained, but did not go on the sick report. The sun was very hot. We reached Savilla-El Pozo at 11:30 A.M. and camped on the road leading to Santiago. On our arrival we found a large force of insurgents in camp in a mango grove.

"On June 27th a Spanish spy was captured about two and a half miles from our camp near El Caney by a Cuban. This spy was up in a mango tree on a high knoll drawing a map of our camp and pickets. He was taken before the commander of the Cuban division. Four Cuban officers and two sentinels took him to General Wheeler's headquarters, only 250 yards away. On being examined several important papers were found under the sweatband of his hat. This spy was recognized by several Cuban officers as a deserter from the Spanish lines who entered the lines of the Cubans.

Troop G, Tenth Cavalry.

Soon after he surrendered to the Spanish, giving them much information. He was then taken before General Young. Two Cuban officers, mounted, and two sentinels, dismounted, took the spy and went up the road towards General Shafter's camp. Our gun detachment was in camp at the entrance and to the left of a large gate; as the Cuban officers passed us I brought the men to attention and saluted, they returned with a machete salute. Our spy went the way of all spies in war time.

"June 27th to 30th we camped and bivouacked in front of Santiago and near the San Juan River. On the 29th General Shafter came ashore with his staff, moved out to the front, and there established his headquarters beside General Lawton's. General Ludlow had assumed command of his brigade and reconnoitered the commanding ground on the left of the road well beyond El Pozo.

"June 30th the command mustered at 7:30 A.M. General Lawton commanding the Second division accompanied by his brigade commander, and June 30, 1898, the regiment camped at El Pozo instead of El Caney and made a thorough reconnoissance around and about the village of El Caney, which lies some three miles northeast of Santiago. There was afterwards a gathering of general officers on the afternoon of this date at General Shafter's headquarters. Orders were issued for an attack to take place July 1st on El Caney, with a view of making a turning movement, swinging well to our right and passing through the village of El Caney, striking the left flank of the enemy, perhaps ultimately reaching to the northern side of Santiago In order that the troops should be in position to begin this movement early in the morning, we were moved out of camp late in the afternoon of the 30th. Each man was given three days' rations—eighteen hard-tacks and nine slices of raw bacon. We marched the early part of the night, bivouacking near the road ready to take up our position in the battle line at earliest dawn. It is worthy of note that the moon favored us during all the latter part of June and the early part of July, enabling us to use many hours of the night that would not have been possible in darkness.

"The Second Brigade was composed of the First and Tenth Regular Cavalry, the First Volunteer Cavalry (Rough Riders) and the little battery, consisting of one officer, First Lieutenant Hughes, and twenty-eight men of the Tenth Cavalry; twelve mules and four Hotchkiss guns. At early dawn of July 1st the troops of General Lawton's division started into the position previously designated for them to occupy. The one battery of artillery was assigned to duty with this division. For the day, they occupied a position overlooking the village of El Caney, 2,400 yards distant. General Chaffee's brigade took up a position east of the village, ready to carry the town as soon as it should be bombarded by the artillery. General Ludlow's brigade took up a position to the west of the village in order to cut off the retreat of the Spaniards when they should be driven out and attempt to retreat to the city of Santiago.

"The artillery (Capron's Battery) opened fire with shrapnel at what appeared to be a column of cavalry moving along the road from El Caney toward Santiago, firing a few shots at the blockhouses, then a few at the hedges where the enemy's infantry seemed to be located, and then firing a few shots at the village. All this time a continuous fire of musketry, partly firing at will and partly by volleys, was kept up in all parts of the lines. These lines were drawn closer toward the enemy's works and the brigade in reserve was brought up on the line. General Bates' Independent Brigade reached the position in the afternoon and also went into the line, all closing in toward the village.

"Between 1 and 2 o'clock the division commander directed the battery of artillery to concentrate its fire upon the stone fort or blockhouse, situated on the highest point in the village, on the northern side. This fort was built of brick, with walls about a foot thick, about 35 x 45 feet. The practice of the artillery against it was very effective, knocking great holes in the fort. The infantry of Generals Chaffee, Bates and Miles' brigade then made an assault upon the work and carried it. There were a number of small blockhouses on the other side of the village, from which a strong fire was kept up for some time after the stone fort had fallen. Word was sent to the commander of the artillery to bring his battery down so as to take these blockhouses, but by the time the battery arrived the fire had ceased. But there was another blockhouse still occupied by the Spaniards, and at this the battery fired four shots, resulting in the loss of a number of Spaniards. Orders reached the division commander in the meantime to withdraw his forces as soon as possible and come in touch with the cavalry division on his left. The troops were not moved into the village, but were ordered to bivouac near the main road leading into the city of Santiago."

Troop H, Tenth Cavalry.

TROOP I, TENTH CAVALRY.

CHAPTER VI.

CONTINUATION OF SERGEANT BIVINS' NARRATIVE.

General Garcia—General Joseph Wheeler—Progress of the Tenth United States Cavalry—Captain Grimes—The Part Played by the Balloon—Spanish Become Confused—The Great Charge Up San Juan Hill—The Tenth Win Unfading Glory.

We continue to quote from Sergeant Bivins' account:
"June 30th while lying under a mango tree drawing a map of our camp (our camp was seventy-five yards below General Young's headquarters; we camped with either brigade, or division headquarters), I received orders from detachment commander to march our detachment to regimental headquarters for muster. This was about 8 A.M. The order was obeyed. Our detachment was mustered under a big mango tree. About 11 A.M. I received orders to get our detachment in readiness to move. Each man of our brigade was given three days' rations. General Garcia's command of about 5,000 insurgents began to pass as early as 7:30 A.M. They were still passing at 1:30 P.M. In this command I saw soldiers of all sizes and complexions, some carrying guns, some machetes, some ammunition, some large sacks of rations (such a load as one of our pack mules could scarcely carry), some large sacks of mangoes and with several so sick that it was difficult for them to walk. At 2 P.M. General Wheeler's division, First Cavalry brigade, composed of Third, Sixth and Ninth Cavalry, General Sumner commanding; the Second Cavalry brigade, consisting of the First, Tenth and First Volunteer Cavalry (Rough Riders), General Young commanding, took up the march for El

Pozo. El Pozo is the name of a ruined plantation about three miles from Santiago. General Lawton's division, as I have stated, turned off to the north in advance of us (General Wheeler's division).

"A general movement of all the troops was begun. The road trail and its condition were wretched. The dense thicket confined men and teams to a single trail. Our battery had to stop 143 times in the three miles' march. There were several fords across the Rio Seco and other small streams, which, with the mudholes, caused long delays for the artillery and prohibited a rapid advance of our troops. Night overtook us before we had gone half the distance. The utmost confusion prevailed; bodies of troops in their eagerness to go forward cut others in two repeatedly. It was midnight before the march of three miles was accomplished. (Several did not find their command until next morning, although the moon shone brightly). After we reached camp the boys made coffee in their tin cups, ate their two hard-tacks and a slice of bacon, after which we were told that we would advance on Santiago early in the morning. The boys were cheerful and whistled 'The Star Spangled Banner' and sang 'A Hot Time in Cuba To-morrow.' We then had a few hours of sleep.

"July 1st we were up long before dawn, made coffee, ate our usual breakfast and by dawn were ready for the perilous duty. Soon after sunrise El Caney, the Ducurot house and other buildings where General Lawton's division was operating, were plainly visible about three miles toward the northeast. Soon after dawn we began to hear cannonading and musketry firing in the vicinity of El Caney, which told us that General Lawton's division had attacked the enemy. Our little battery was packed twenty feet from a large sugar house. The troops of the cavalry division and the insurgents were

TROOP K, TENTH CAVALRY.

scattered about without order and with no thought of their protection from the enemy's fire.

"Grimes' Battery was ordered into position on El Pozo Hill at 6:43 A.M. He opened fire on blockhouses out from the city. After we had fired several shots the enemy replied with shrapnel fire at correct range and with accurately adjusted fuse. When the battery opened fire I was so anxious to get the range that I went upon the hill (one hundred yards away). Just as I reached the battery Captain Grimes gave the command: 'With shrapnel at 2,800 yards, load!' Several general officers were at the battery in action. At that moment I heard a deep roar near the city, like distant thunder. In a few seconds a shell came over the battery just a few feet above it and went 100 yards beyond and burst among our men, killing two and wounding several. An officer was near me, mounted; the shell passed so near him that his horse shied and the saddle turned, throwing him to the ground. I went to his assistance, then ran down the hill to my battery. Just as I reached it a shell burst about ten feet directly over me, wounding Private Watson, Troop F, Tenth Cavalry, and a piece of it struck one of our ammunition boxes, exposing the shells. It was lucky that it did not explode, as there were 175 shells in the pile. I reported to our battery commander: 'Sir,' I asked, 'do you wish to bring the battery into action?' He directed that the mules should be taken to shelter and ammunition placed out of range of the Spanish guns.

"The third shell landed on Grimes' Battery, killing one officer, two gunners, and wounding several. The firing was kept up for some time. At 8:30 A.M. the cavalry division begun to march toward Santiago. The dynamite gun in front, with our little hotchkiss battery (colored) following close behind. General Wheeler's division was in rear of the battery. General Kent's division followed and moved across a stream. A balloon was hoisted in our advance. As we reached the balloon the officer in it asked: 'Is there a general officer present?' and dropped a message directing a mounted messenger to carry it to General Wheeler as quickly as possible. Then he said: 'Tell General Wheeler to prepare for an attack; the Spaniards have formed a battle line three hundred yards in front of us.' The next moment shot and shell began to rain at the balloon and the advancing columns. Lieutenant Hughes' battery with the dynamite gun was hurried to the front and placed in position seventy-five yards beyond the San Juan River (we forded the river). The dynamite gun took position a short distance to our right. We planted our guns near the spot where the Spaniards had formed their battle line. They had retreated only a short distance and concealed themselves in the tall sage brush, but kept up a steady fire.

As we reached the stream I found Lieutenant Ord (afterward killed in this battle) making a reconnoisance from a large tree on the banks of the stream. Mauser bullets were flying through this tree clipping off twigs all around him. He gave valuable information as to the position of the enemy, and the condition of the ground over which we had to pass. He remained up this tree until repeatedly ordered down. After crossing the stream the command was given orders to go to the front and in less than five minutes we were in position training our guns on the blockhouses on San Juan Hill. A delay of one hour and a half was caused by waiting for all troops to get into position then the whole force advanced. The charge was made and carried the enemy's first line of intrenchments. The Tenth Cavalry charged up the steep hill and captured the blockhouse and San Juan Hill.

"Our battery kept up the fire on the blockhouse and intrenchments on San Juan Hill until the blockhouse to the right was taken by the Rough Riders and the Tenth Cavalry. When we opened up with artillery (our little battery firing black powder instead of smokeless) we instantly drew all the fire in the vicinity. Ten minutes after we had opened fire two of our gunners were wounded. Sergeant Taylor, Troop E, and Sanders, Troop B, Tenth Cavalry. They landed several shots among the enemy before they fell victims to the Spanish mauser bullet.

"While sighting my gun to fire the eighth shot, a bullet passed through the thick iron plated hub of the gun carriage wheel and struck me near the left temple. It stunned me for about two minutes. I recovered, resighted my gun, pulled the lanyard, then watched with my glasses the result of the shot. It dropped in the Spanish trenches. Great confusion occurred. I could see Spanish officers with raised pistols or drawn swords at each end of the trenches. Some were using their swords on the men to keep them from retreating. I fired several shots—loading and firing the gun myself. Every time the gun was fired it would jump back from five to eight feet. I would load, place it in position, sight it, pull the lanyard, then watch the result of my shot.

"The dressing station (hospital) was under the bank at the ford sixty yards in our rear. When our gunners were carried to the station by our cannoneers they (the cannoneers) were detained to help dress the wounded (as they began to come in so fast), and some were overcome by heat. Our detachment commander received orders to take position on the right near the first blockhouse already taken by the Tenth Cavalry. At this time having had four gunners wounded, and several having fainted, Major Hayes, United States Volunteers, made a suggestion to our commander to take some of his guns and plenty of ammunition—one hundred shells. Major Hayes then accompanied us. We countermarched five hundred yards, crossed the stream and passed down a road. I found several hundred Cubans intrenched along a fence in an open field about one thousand yards in the rear of Generals Wheeler and Kent's division. I have wondered why they were there and when and how they reached that point. Probably they were under orders. After traveling several hundred yards we came to another open field going down this road leading along a wire fence; we were within one thousand yards of San Juan Hill. We halted; Major Hayes and Lieutenant Hughes were mounted and in the lead; our detachment was walking, having one mule drawing a gun and two boxes of ammunition. They selected a good position. Major Hayes cut the wire fence with my wire cutters. I cleared the bushes so that I could get a clear view of the blockhouse on San Juan Hill. Our commander, Lieutenant Hughes, Tenth Cavalry, said: 'Sergeant Bivins, I want you to put a shell into that blockhouse. The elevation is about eight hundred yards.' I replied: 'Sir, it will require an elevation of one thousand yards to reach that house.' 'All right, take that elevation then.' 'Very good, sir.' I loaded my gun and sighted it. At that moment we could hear yelling and saw men walking around the house, and colors flying. I said: 'Sir, I believe our men have that blockhouse. If they are our men and I fire this shot it will do great damage.' Major Hayes said: 'Hughes, I will ride down the road near enough to find out who has that house.' He rode as Sheridan did when going from Winchester. He soon met several of the Tenth Cavalry men wounded and coming to the rear. They told him that our men had taken the blockhouse and had possession of San Juan Hill. I was ordered to unload my gun. We moved down the road, crossed a small stream, turned to the right and took position on a ridge between the two blockhouses. We passed several dead and wounded. I passed my troop commander, First Lieutenant William H. Smith and First Lieutenant William E. Shipp, Tenth Cavalry lying dead, but did not know them. We were then ordered to take position on San Juan Hill.

"We reached that point about 1:30 P.M., and then opened fire on the blockhouse and trenches in the basin in which Santiago lies at six hundred yards range. About fifty sharpshooters were stationed in this house, which had portholes all around it and even holes cut through the roof large enough to sight a gun. Our shots were very effective, knocking great holes in the house, rendering it untenable and killing a large number of men. During our shelling some would attempt to run out of the blockhouse only to be mowed down by Lieutenant Parker's (of the Rough Riders) gatling guns and mausers. We captured several prisoners and about two thousand mauser and brass explosive cartridges. The mauser cartridges were used by Lieutenant Parker in his two mauser guns, against the enemy. Many a Spaniard bit the dust pierced with his own cartridges. At 5:15 we withdrew from the field, having used nearly all of our ammunition in firing from the hill. In the afternoon of the 1st our commander would fire three shots, Corporal Jones, C Troop, would fire three, then I would fire three alternately. It was a hot day and we had no water. Some of us had canteens but they had been pierced by bullets. All of this time we were under a terrific fire. We camped at the dressing station on San Juan River where we first went into action. Just

TROOP L, TENTH CAVALRY.

before dark Major Wint, Tenth Cavalry, was brought in wounded. At the close of the first day's battle our men were occupying the crest all along San Juan Hill, six hundred yards from the enemy's intrenchment, and one and a half-miles from the city of Santiago. Our casualties in regiment were: Officers killed, 2; officers wounded, 9; enlisted men killed, unknown; enlisted men wounded, unknown.

"As soon as our troop took San Juan Hill they began to dig intrenchments. The work was pushed day and night. All night our men were digging as they were under constant fire during the day.

"July 2d we were up early and ate whatever we could pick up. At dawn the battle began. Our commander received orders to move his detachment near division headquarters. We loaded our ammunition and moved and established our camp ninety yards from General Wheeler's headquarters. On this morning three batteries of the artillery went into action near Fort San Juan. Firing black powder instead of smokeless they of course instantly drew all the fire in the vicinity, and being unable to work the guns we were obliged to withdraw. As I came up I saw one of the gunners digging out a shot that a Spanish gunner had landed in the muzzle of his gun.

"During the day there were a great many casualties resulting not entirely from aimed fire, but from bullets clearing the crest of our intrenchments and going far beyond, striking men as they were coming up into position, or as they were going back and forth bringing water and caring for the wounded. Many casualties also resulted from the fire of sharpshooters stationed in trees so thick with foliage that they could not be seen. Just as we were about to break camp a doctor was shot dead within twenty feet of me, while in the act of mounting his horse to go upon the firing line. Notwithstanding the deadly fire of the sharpshooters men were to remain within our lines and continue firing. How very inhuman was it for the enemy to fire upon our Red Cross—shooting doctors and members of the hospital corps while dressing a wound or carrying a wounded man to the rear! This seems incredible. I know of one wounded man being carried to the hospital by three men; when near the hospital one was shot dead, then the second man fell, while the third man dragged his wounded comrade into the bushes and waited until a squad of men came along and assisted in carrying the wounded man to the desired place.

"On reaching our new camp a report came to the brigade commander that the sharpshooters were stationed in the trees shooting whenever they saw one or two men together. It was generally thought that the casualties were caused by bullets that had scaled the crests of the intrenchments. I took a look through the woods with my glasses and thought that I had spied a sharpshooter in a tree covered with leaves. I said 'Give me two men and I will clean the woods of all of those cowards who fired on our Red Cross.' General Sumner and some members of his staff heard me. He said: 'Sergeant, where is that sharpshooter?' I tried to show the brute to him. I said: 'General, if I am given two men I will clean the woods of all the sharpshooters.' He replied that the object I was trying to show him was a buzzard and remarked that 'he was probably there but had flown off.' Then he rode off. I said to the other boys: 'Well, boys, what I was trying to show the general might be a buzzard. You will see before the sun goes down that some man will be shot opposite that tree.' By 2 P.M. two men of the Seventy-first Volunteers had been killed and several wounded. I said: 'Boys, buzzards don't shoot.' A detail was sent out from the Ninth Cavalry and before night six sharpshooters were killed out of one tree and four were killed in the vicinity of the hospital.

"About 9 P.M., everything being quiet, the boys were lying around on the ground when the sentinel said in a very loud voice: 'Halt, who comes there?' Then the crack of a gun was heard and several shots followed. We then knew that the Spaniards were making a night attack. A general fire all along the line of pickets began. General Wheeler ordered reinforcements to be brought up, which were only one hundred yards in the rear, under the crest of the hill. Then the crack of thousands of guns was heard. Lieutenant Parker opened up with his machine guns (four gatling guns and two mauser guns). The fire was kept up about one hour. The Spaniards were repulsed with a great loss, so reported.

"On the 3d a Spaniard, a deserter from the Spanish lines, came into our lines and said that on the night before they were given rum and were told that they must capture San Juan Hill that night. They charged up near our lines but the fire was so terrific they retreated in disorder and their loss was very heavy. It was the first time that they had ventured out of their intrenchments. Our loss was very small. General Hawkins was wounded.

"About 2:30 P.M. I received orders from my detachment commander to take four pack mules and one man and go back to El Caney and bring up our rations, packs, etc., which were left on the 1st; also to bring up one of our hotchkiss guns which had been carried nearly a mile down the stream from where we left it on the 1st at San Juan River, where we first put our guns into action.

"Major Hayes went to help locate the gun. We found it. I never knew who carried the gun and box of shells there. Major Hayes went straight to it. It had been wheeled down the stream, I suppose, with a view of placing it on the left on San Juan Hill, but the river bank was so steep they probably gave up the idea. After Major Hayes showed us the gun we escorted him back, then went on to El Caney, loaded on rations, etc.; but night overtook us and we could not get the gun. I reported the facts to the commander, who gave me orders to go for the gun next morning. At 3 A.M. of the 3d, with two other men, we started for the gun. We reached it about the dawn of the day and lowered it over the embankment and pulled it through the water, which was waist deep. Starting back we came upon three men lying dead near the river bank. They were killed July 1st. On reaching camp I reported the matter and steps were taken to bury them. The firing began all along the line. Bullets were whizzing around us and very frequently we would hear the crack of a mauser in the trees near us.

"Soon after 9 A.M. we began to hear a great cannonading in front of Morro Castle, which soon told us that the Spanish fleet had left the harbor and that we were about to witness the greatest naval fight in the history of man. The very earth seemed to tremble while the battle was raging. Firing on either side of the land forces nearly ceased.

"Every one was eager to hear the result of the naval battle. Negotiations for surrender began at 1 P.M. General Shafter sent a flag of truce to General Linares, commander of the Spanish forces, asking for his unconditional surrender which was refused. At 2 P.M. Major Hayes brought the good news that the Spanish fleet was destroyed by our navy without the loss of a single ship to us. What joy! But we could not cheer. Monday, July 4th, there was no fighting. A telegram of congratulation was received from General Miles. It also contained the information that he would reach us with strong reinforcements within five days.

"July 5th a flag came over from the Spanish lines at 9 A.M. At 9:30 A.M. troops began to take position behind intrenchments for battle. By this time we had thrown up intrenchments all along the line. We had advanced our line to within three hundred and fifty yards of the enemy's trenches. Our little battery was ordered to camp near the Tenth Cavalry headquarters.

"July 6th we planted our guns on the right of our brigade. The dynamite gun and a battery of mortars were on our right. It was the hottest day that I had felt while in Cuba, but our detachment worked all day with the pickax and shovel and had to carry material to build bomb proof several hundred yards. Several men fell under the tropical sun overcome by the heat.

"July 7th was a great day. The exchange of prisoners took place. Lieutenant Hobson, the hero of the Merrimac, and his brave men were exchanged. As he passed our lines the bands played several pieces. Lieutenant Hobson and his men shook hands with all near them. A storm of cheers went up from thousands. Lieutenant Hobson said that he observed our movement from where he was on the 1st of July when we took San Juan Hill. He said that he remarked that none but Americans could do that.

"We worked all night. Colonel Baldwin having received several thousand sacks they were filled with earth and breastworks were made of them. The Spaniards were not idle. Every morning one could see quite readily that a large amount of work had been done by them. They even went so far as to cover their trenches with earth like our bomb proofs to protect them from our shrapnel fire. The city of Santiago by this time was completely invested on the eastern and northern sides.

"July 8th the work of planting the mortars was about completed, and we were ready to do some great work, notwithstanding we had been toiling day and night, and had to go a mile for water and get wood wherever we could. Our food was hardtack, bacon, roasted beef and a few tomatoes (we had to buy the most we got). Our men began to get sick. Several were dragged out of the river. They were either wounded in battle and died or were drowned. The doctors gave orders that all drinking water should be boiled. This order was not strictly carried out. It was so hot that the men in many cases paid no attention to it. I found two springs near a mango and cocoanut grove and reported it. It was fixed up and a guard from the Ninth Cavalry was stationed to guard these springs day and night. All of our drinking water came from them. I have been there when more than a hundred men would be in line waiting for their turn.

"July 9th several deserters from the Spanish lines came over to our lines and reported that food was very scarce in the city. The white flag was still flying over the Spanish trenches.

"Sunday, July 10th, the white flags were taken down and everything was ready for action. At 4:40 P.M. the battle began.

Our hotchkiss gun, though small, did effective work. The bombardment of the lines and city was made by our artillery and lasted until dark. There was but very little small-arm firing on either side. Our casualties were small. A heavy rain began to fall in the afternoon.

"July 11th notwithstanding the heavy rain firing was resumed early in the morning, but with very little effect on account of the rain. By noon the firing ceased and the white flag was displayed again.

"July 12th General Miles arrived at headquarters in the afternoon. A conference was held with the Spanish commander on the 13th. After being present at the capitulation on the 14th, General Miles returned to his ship in the port of Siboney. The articles of surrender were signed under a mango tree between the lines.

"On July 15th we moved all along our line out of the mud and water that we had been in since July 1st. Our mattress was the ground and our cover the sky. Every night a heavy dew would fall, such as has never been seen in any part of the United States. The sun was extremely hot. We had to kneel or lie down in the trenches to avoid its rays. It was no uncommon thing to see a man taken out of the trenches overcome by the heat. Our men began to show their exposure, but not half so much as our white comrades did. July 16th was a quiet day. We received a few papers dated June 29th and 30th, and three reached us dated July 4th and 5th.

"July 17th a telegram of congratulation reached us. At 11:45 we were assembled and heard the reading of it. Then we were drawn up in line to witness the surrender. At 12 M. the Spanish column began to march toward us. Our band played several pieces.

"On July 18th the whole cavalry division moved to Camp Hamilton, about four miles northeast of the city. The day was very hot. Several of the men (mostly white) had to fall out of line, overcome by the heat.

"At one time nearly all the packers and teamsters were sick, and soldiers had to be taken off the firing lines and out of the trenches to do their duty. Most of the packers were of the Tenth Cavalry.

"On July 26th, as I rode over the battlefield, I could plainly see in many places the earth drenched in human blood. On my return to camp I was taken sick with the fever and had camp dysentery. I was carried to the hospital on a litter and for twelve days lay at the point of death. The doctors gave me up to die. For six days I did not eat anything. Our hospital was situated on the brow of a hill, our only covering was a fly stretched above us. There were fourteen of us under this one fly. We had to lie with our heads uphill and dig holes in the ground with our heels to keep from slipping down on our comrades. It rained daily and as our tent fly did not shed water very well and both ends of course being open, we kept wet day and night. We had to lie on the wet ground. Some of us had only a shelter tent half for bedding, some had shelter tent half and slicker, and some had one blanket. For myself, I had a slicker and one blanket. A colored surgeon, Dr. A. M. Brown, United States Volunteers, was assigned to our regiment, but before his arrival, our chaplain, William T. Anderson, who is also an M.D. by profession, had arrived and had given relief to many of the sick men of our regiment. He had a large case of medicine with him, and I owe my life to his treatment. He administered to us until he was stricken down himself. Words cannot tell the change of affairs in our regiment after Surgeon Brown's arrival. He moved the hospital to where General Wheeler's headquarters were, put in bunks for all of the sick and members of the corps. It seemed as though he was just in time to save us. We received our meals from our respective organizations, but, indeed, it was so rough that the sick could not eat it. Under Surgeon Brown's supervision our sick list soon began to decrease.

"I returned to duty August 10th and was placed in

charge of Troop G of our regiment. Ever since August 1st different regiments of our division would embark to return to the United States. We began to think that we would be left to do patrol duty, and were very much discouraged. It rained every day, two-thirds of our men were without blankets, and a thousand other little things that I could speak of disheartened us; but at 9:30 A.M., August 11th, a telegram came ordering our regiment to prepare to return to the United States. We broke camp the next day at 7:30 in the morning and began our march for the railroad station, a distance of one mile and a half. Here we boarded the Spanish battle cars and arrived at Santiago at 11 A.M. These cars were lined on the inside with steel plates of one-half inch thickness and extended to the height of a man's breast with a two-inch space on both sides of the car as portholes, large enough to admit a rifle. I had read of battle cars, but this was my first time to see the real cars. Arriving at Santiago we took shelter under a large shed to protect us from the rain, yet it blew in and gave several of us a severe wetting. We embarked on the transport at 4 o'clock in the afternoon, but did not leave the dock until 2 P.M. next day. During our embarkation Trumpeter Lewis, of Troop F, fell overboard, a distance of about fifty feet. His brave comrades rescued him. He was almost dead when rescued, but under the skillful treatment of Surgeon Brown, he was talking in less than one hour.

As we sailed out of the harbor we passed within a few feet of the Merrimac, made famous by Lieutenant Hobson's daring deed. We had done our duty as United States soldiers and were now sailing for our home. Although leaving a few of our comrades behind us to await the great resurrection morning, we were indeed glad to get away from the direful distress that we were forced to witness each day."

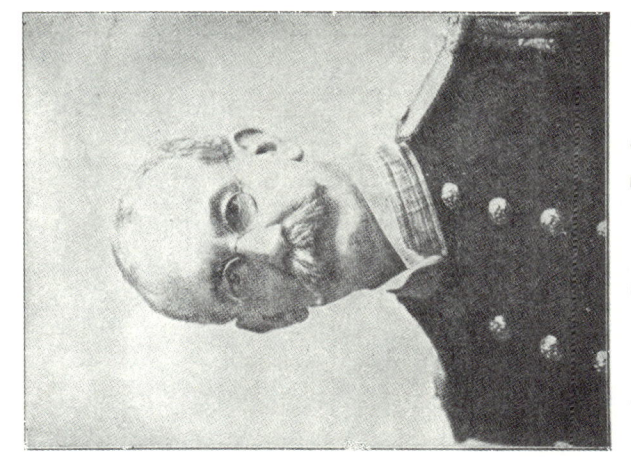
Captain Charles D. Sigsbee.

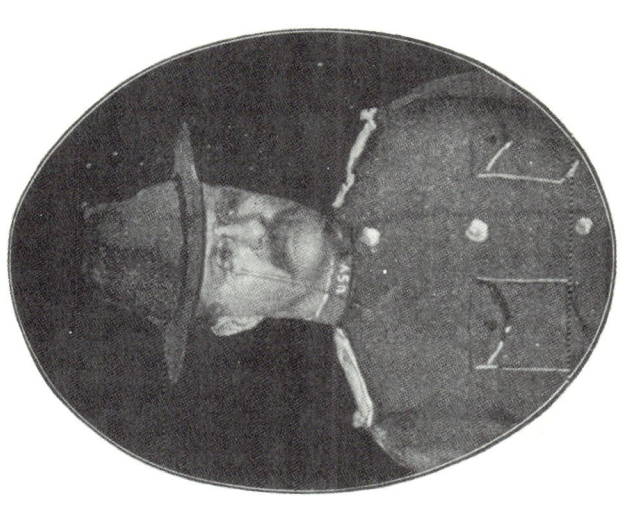
Lieut.-Col. Theodore Roosevelt.

Lieutenant Richmond P. Hobson.

TROOP M, TENTH CAVALRY.

CHAPTER VII.

THE NINTH UNITED STATES CAVALRY.

The Part Taken by the Ninth Regiment of Cavalry—A Famous Regiment of Great Fighters—Road Building in Times of War—Echoes from San Juan Hill—Troop C Initiates the Assault on San Juan Hill.

It was about April 10, 1898, when orders from the War Department came to Fort Robinson, Nebraska, ordering the Ninth Cavalry to make preparation and proceed with the least delay to Chickamauga Park, Georgia, and there to await orders to go to Cuba.

Six troops stationed at Fort Robinson, Nebraska, left the post April 20, 1898, and arrived at Chickamauga Park, Georgia, April 23d. The journey was a very pleasant one. They were treated and greeted with great demonstration and patriotism by the people all through the West.

On April 28, 1898, orders were issued from the War Department to proceed immediately to Port Tampa, Florida. They broke camp on that day and on the 29th, at 7:30 A.M. they marched to Chattanooga, Tennessee, arriving at 10:30 A.M. At 6 30 P.M , they left Chattanooga on the Southern Railroad, and on May 2, 1898, arrived at Port Tampa, Florida. The entire regiment was together the first time in ten years. On or about May 12, 1898, orders from the War Department announced that the Ninth Cavalry with others of the Fifth Army Corps, under General Joe Wheeler, should get in readiness to embark for Cuba at a "moment's notice." Chaplain George W. Prioleau, being confined to his bed with a slight attack of malaria, the following order was issued:

"Headquarters Ninth United States Cavalry,
"PORT TAMPA, Fla., May 13, 1898.
"Special Order, No. 55.
"1. Upon the expected departure of this regiment for Cuba, Chaplain George W. Prioleau, Ninth Cavalry, will remain at Port Tampa, in charge of property stored there in warehouse. . . .
"By order of LIEUT. COL. HAMILTON.
"W. S. WOOD,
"First Lieutenant Ninth Cavalry, Adjutant."

While preparations were being made to yield to the seemingly inevitable, the following order was issued:

"Headquarters Ninth United States Cavalry.
"PORT TAMPA, Fla., "May 14, 1898.
"General Orders, No. 14.
"2. Under authority granted by Par. 4, G. O. 29, A. G. O., 1898, Chaplain George W. Prioleau, Ninth Cavalry, will proceed with least practicable delay to Tuskegee, Alabama, and thence to Orangeburg, South Carolina, and vicinity on special recruiting duty for the Ninth Cavalry. Chaplain Prioleau is appointed acting quartermaster of his rendezvous. The travel enjoined is necessary for the public service.
"By order of LIEUT.-COL. HAMILTON,
"W. S. WOOD.
"First Lieutenant, Ninth Cavalry, Adjutant."

Three officers and six enlisted men were detailed for this work; the Ninth Cavalry had, at the beginning of the strife, ten troops of sixty men each, making a total of six hundred men and officers.

By the order of the War Department, each regiment should be increased to the strength of twelve hundred

MAJOR CHARLES YOUNG.
First Lieut., 9th Cav. (Reg), now Maj. Volunteers.

men. This necessitated a detail of officers to enlist for the regular army. The recruiting officers for the Ninth cavalry detailed May 14, 1898, were Captain Joseph

Garrard, Troop A, with Sergeant Joseph M. Moore and Corporal George Washington of the same troop. Chaplain George W. Prioleau, with Sergeant C. H. Cooper, Troop C, and Corporal William H. Withers, Troop E. First Lieutenant Frank S. Armstrong, Troop A, with Corporal Eugene Caldwell, Troop A, and Private John D. Miller, Troop D. They were out until August 4, 1898, when they were relieved by Adjutant-General Corbin, and ordered to report to that portion of the regiment then in Florida, under command of Captain Guilfoyle. The troops of Ninth Cavalry were: A, commanded by First Lieutenant J. E. Ryan; B, commanded by Captain Finley; C, commanded by Captain C. W. Taylor; D, commanded by Captain McBlain; E, commanded by Captain C. A. Stedman; G, commanded by Captain Philip P. Powell; H, commanded by First Lieutenant McNamee; K, commanded by Captain M. B. Hughes, with Majors Forbush and Dimmick. Under command of Lieutenant-Colonel Hamilton, these troops embarked from Port Tampa Bay, Florida, June 8, 1898, on board the transport Miami, for the Island of Cuba.

Five troops of Ninth Cavalry were disembarked at Daiquiri, Cuba, June 23, 1898. The sea became so rough that it was deemed unsafe to disembark the remainder that day; the transport was ordered to proceed to Siboney, eight miles nearer Santiago, where the other three troops were disembarked at 10:30 that night. This was made possible by the Spaniards having been driven out of there by the troops from Daiquiri, assisted by the war vessels.

Bivouac was made that night directly in rear of the Rough Riders.

Early on the morning of June 24, 1898, General Young's cavalry brigade, composed of the First and

Tenth Regulars, and the First Volunteer Cavalry (the Rough Riders), pushed out to drive the Spaniards from

CHAPLAIN GEORGE W. PRIOLEAU.
Ninth U. S. Cavalry.

a position they had taken up between there and Santiago, and this brought on the fight of Las Guasimas.

About 8 A.M. a hatless and breathless courier rode

into Siboney with the intelligence that General Young had struck the enemy, was having a hard time of it, and needed help. Without waiting for orders, and within ten minutes of the time the courier arrived, Captain E. D. Dimmick, Ninth Cavalry, with Troops C, Captain Taylor commanding, D, Captain McBlain and H, First Lieutenant McNamee, was on his way to the support of the troops engaged at Las Guasimas. Their hard march failed to get them there in time to participate in this, the first fight of the war; but they tried, and their coming was hailed with joy by the tired troopers who had driven the Spaniards from their chosen and strong position.

These three troops were at once put on outpost to protect the front of the army, and remained there until relieved by General Chaffee's infantry brigade when they returned to their bivouac.

June 25th and 26, 1898, Troops A, B, E, G and K, worked hard in unloading transports and building roads for artillery. At 3 A.M. June 26th, Lieutenant-Colonel Hamilton with First Lieutenant W. S. Wood, Troop E, under Captain Stedman and Sergeant-Major John W. Anderson, joined Colonel Sumner and marched eighteen miles southeast with Troops C, D and H, Major Dimmick's squadron, and forming a cavalry brigade with other bodies of cavalry then within about five miles of Santiago. They laid in this camp until the evening of the 30th of June, sending out scouts and patrols, watching the enemy, while Troops A, B, G, and K, were still building roads.

The march began at 5:30 on the evening of June 30th. They bivouacked at 1 o'clock that night in rear of El Pozo. Early in the morning of July 1st the cavalry division marched to the line of battle. It was first intended to let the Cubans form the first line with the cavalry division second, but circumstances soon compelled a change so as to give first place to the cavalry division. The Ninth Cavalry had the advance, and Troop H moved forward as advance guard, giving Troop D the head of the column. The character of the country was such that it was impossible to keep up organization formation, and being in advance the Ninth Cavalry got into such impenetrable thickets that the rest of the first cavalry brigade, the Third and Sixth Regulars, kept on the road and crossed Bloody Ford ahead of the Ninth. It was just after making this crossing that lines were formed; the Third and Sixth in double lines in front and the Ninth in double lines, the first being Troops E and C, and the second D and H in rear of the Sixth Cavalry. Orders caused us to extend our lines to the right so that the Ninth Cavalry line formed left to right; at this time the Rough Riders were being passed by our rear to the right, and it was this movement that first drew the enemy's fire, which was heavy, and from which direction they did not know, so that the men were made to hug the earth pretty closely.

First Lieutenant W. S. Wood, Sergeant Walls and Private Turner of Troop D, were wounded almost at the first fire of the enemy. Captains Taylor and McBlain, in order to get their men out of this fire, pushed their troops forward to a road that was in front of them and got some shelter from the timber skirting it. After remaining in this position for some time until the men got restless under the heavy fire that they were subjected to, C Troop got out into the open; seeing which, Captain McBlain called to Captain Dimmick, "C Troop is in the open and should be supported," and got orders: "Go in," which he did with his Troop D. This was the initiation of the assault on San Juan Hill.

San Juan Hill was not intrenched, but it was a

good natural position, surrounded by a substantial house. In the assault C and D Troops were joined by others, among them being many Rough Riders. Troop D and a part of C got to the right of the building, and after remaining on this hill for awhile, during which time Lieutenant-Colonel Hamilton, Ninth Cavalry, was killed, and Captain Taylor and others wounded, the line was pushed forward to the intrenched crest; Troops C and D and some of the Tenth Cavalry and some of the Rough Riders, under Captain McBlain, occupying the extreme right until the evening of July 2d, when an adjustment of the lines brought the Ninth from the extreme right to the center, when Troops C and D reached the Spanish crest. The men did not average five cartridges to the man at this time, so heavy and continuous had been the firing.

Troop B with the balance of the first squadron were ordered to report to General Hospital. Here they were assigned to the duty of looking after the sick and the Spanish prisoners and issuing rations to 20,000 starving people. Here they remained at El Caney until the morning of the 9th, when they were relieved by Troop D, Second Cavalry. They joined the first and second squadrons, Ninth Cavalry, commanded by General Wheeler, on the firing line. They arrived on the firing line about 4 P.M. of July 9th. Here they were assigned to duty digging trenches, preparatory to the bombardment of Santiago, which took place on July 10 and 11, 1898. Troop B was ordered to the front trenches about 3 P.M. of July 10, 1898, and almost immediately commenced firing on a body of Spanish troopers, who responded most vigorously. First Sergeant Charles Jefferson, Troop B, Ninth Cavalry, was wounded in the right hand shortly after firing began, while in the act of loading his carbine. He went to the hospital, had his wound dressed and returned to his troop in the midst of heavy firing from the Spanish trenches, with a painful wound, and suffering with a high fever. For this act Sergeant Jefferson was recommended for a certificate of merit by his troop and squadron commanders. Private Thomas Sinclair, Troop B, Ninth Cavalry, was wounded in the left shoulder, at the same time as Sergeant Jefferson. Sergeant George Lyman, color bearer, had several narrow escapes. At one time his gun barrel was hit, bullets passed through his clothes, he was stunned and was about to be left for dead. Corporal Irvine, one of the color guards, was struck twice by a piece of shell.

After the cessation of hostilities and the surrender of the Spaniards the Ninth Cavalry and the whole cavalry brigade, moved from San Juan Hill to near El Caney and established Camp Hamilton. Here they remained until August 13, 1898; they struck camp, moved to Santiago, where they boarded the Rio-Grande and sailed for Montauk Point, New York, arriving on August 23, 1898. After remaining in detention camp five days they joined the Ninth Cavalry detachment, which consisted of Troops I and F, and six hundred recruits. Here they remained recuperating their strength and health, for they were badly used up from exposure and the fever of the island, until September 27, 1898, when they broke camp and departed for their new station, Fort Grant, Arizona.

Their departure was all that soldiers could desire. They were heartily cheered by their comrades in battle as they marched through Camp Wikoff. At New York they were met by the Red Cross Society and provided with supper. While crossing the Hudson to Brooklyn the Ninth Cavalry band played patriotic airs and were saluted by steam tugs and steamers, and by hundreds of New York and Brooklyn's patriotic citizens. On arriving at Brooklyn the Red Cross Society again provided them with refreshments. They then started on their westward journey at 11:30 P.M. on September 27, 1898, via the Baltimore and Ohio Railroad, arriving at Wilcox, Arizona, on October 4, 1898, at 8 A.M. They camped that day and night at Wilcox, and at 8 A.M. they mounted their horses, and for twenty-eight miles over a hot and dusty prairie marched to Fort Grant, arriving at 2:30 P.M. All along the line from New York to Wilcox, they were greeted with cheers and appreciation from the American people.

For the statements and dates of their engagements in Cuba, we are indebted to Captain McBlain, Troop D; First Sergeant Charles Jefferson, Troop B; Color Sergeant George Lyman, Troop A; and George W. Prioleau, Chaplain Ninth Cavalry.

The promotions for meritorious service were as follows, viz.:

Sergeant-Major John H. Anderson, Sergeant Elisha Jackson, Troop H; Saddler Sergeant John W. Brown, Troop A.

First Sergeant John C. Proctor, Troop I; First Sergeant William Washington, Troop F, to second lieutenants of volunteers, and Sergeant Joseph M. Moore, Troop A, to first lieutenant of volunteers.

The detachment of Ninth Cavalry, consisting of Troops F and I and recruits, left Port Tampa, Florida, under command of Captain Joseph Garrard, August 6, 1898, for Montauk Point, New York, and arrived August 11, 1898. Honorary mention is here made of Second Lieutenant Lanning Parsons, and Sergeants W. H. Brown and William Washington, who received recruits at Fort McPherson, Georgia, and trained them for the service.

CAPTAIN ALLEN ALLENSWORTH.
Chaplain 24th Regiment U. S. Infantry.

CHAPTER VIII.

THE TWENTY-FOURTH INFANTRY.

The Story of the Twenty-fourth Infantry—What Her Men Accomplished on the Battlefields in Cuba—Great Victories Won —General Kent's Appeal to 71st N. Y. Volunteers—His Joy at Sight of His Colored Boys—"Liscum, Turn to Your Right, Ford the Stream and Fight Everything Before You"—Their Worst Night in Cuba—Nursing Yellow Fever Patients Without a Murmur—Last Regiment to Leave Cuba.

THE Twenty-fourth Infantry, like other regiments of the American Army, was destined to share the horrors of actual duty in the hostile field of action; and accordingly, on April 19, 1898, was ordered to proceed to New Orleans without delay. Pursuant to these instructions, on the 20th day of the same month, under command of Colonel J. Ford Kent—that brave and noble soldier who distinguished himself so admirably by his cool, deliberate generalship in the battle of San Juan— formed in line and after receiving a soul-stirring and patriotic address from that hero, Chaplain Allen Allensworth, which ended with the memorable appeal to the men of that command in these words: "Acquit yourselves and fight like men"—began the march which was to impress the world with the Negro's ability as a soldier and a man.

It is needless to attempt a description of patriotism displayed by the liberty loving people of this country along our line of travel until reaching the South, where cool receptions told the tale of race prejudice and every other element inimical to Negro welfare, even though these brave men were rushing to the front in the very face of grim death to defend the flag and preserve the country's honor and dignity.

Having received countermanding orders at Pueblo, Colorado, the regiment did not go to New Orleans, but pursuant to instructions, proceeded without delay to Chickamauga Park, Georgia, where many regiments were being mobilized, preparatory to going to Cuba. The Twenty-fourth upon arriving at the above-named place on Sunday, the 25th day of April, immediately pitched camp and on the morrow began practice in the field maneuvers—as did all the regiment at this place.

It was here that they suffered very much from the excessive heat to which they had not been exposed for many years, having been kept almost constantly at frontier posts in the northwest since their organization.

Matters had now assumed a very grave aspect since rumors were afloat that the Spanish government had sent a formidable fleet east. As to its whereabouts no one was able to say; but fears were entertained of having our seacoast cities bombarded and attacked by Spanish forces, and it was deemed necessary by the War Department to rush our land forces to the front as well as to give new instructions to our navy. It now seemed that the colored soldiers would be rushed first into every danger, when on Saturday, April 30, 1898, the Twenty-fourth Infantry received orders to proceed to Tampa, Florida, without delay. Arriving at Tampa May 2d, camp was made on Tampa Heights, and immediate preparations began for thorough drill in field tactics.

It was exceedingly hot at this place and many were prostrated while drilling four and five hours each day, generally in heavy marching order, as they were unaccustomed to the climate, water and other surroundings.

Many became quite ill and so great was the decimation of the ranks at one time that it was recommended by the surgeon in charge that all troops should be moved from this place as soon as possible.

Colonel J. Ford Kent was promoted to brigadier-general while at Tampa, on the 15th of May, and placed in command of the Third Brigade, First Division, being succeeded in the colonelcy of the Twenty-fourth by Lieutenant-Colonel E. H. Liscum. This soldier and fighter, as he proved himself to be, in the battle of San Juan, was loved by the brave boys of his command, and he made every possible arrangement conducive to their welfare. This regiment, destined to become conspicuous in the San Juan Hill charge, like that of the famous Tenth Cavalry, in the Rough Rider massacre, and the gallant Twenty-fifth Infantry before El Caney, was not to be left in idleness, but, according to orders, on the 8th of June boarded the train and proceeded to Port Tampa, arriving and embarking the same day for Cuba.

An amusing incident connected with the embarkation might well be mentioned here. The steamship City of Washington had been assigned to this regiment, but being larger and of greater draft than her sister transports, was unable to come up in the harbor and was anchored about eighteen miles down the bay. On arriving at Port Tampa the regiment embarked aboard the steamer Margaret and was taken down the bay to the transport, which transferred the men and returned to the port. It was about 1:30 A.M. when the boys, fatigued by the constant movement of property and burdensome accouterments, were sleeping as comfortably as the accommodations of the ship would allow, that the same steamer returned with orders to proceed to shore at once, as there were three Spanish vessels within a few hours' run of us. This command of course was promptly obeyed. Boarding the steamer they returned to the harbor and rested quietly until morning, when their transport steaming inland again received the boys who had so readily abandoned her the night before. After remaining in the bay until the 15th of June the whole squadron left for Cuba, convoyed by several men-of-war. They presented a fine sight as they swung out upon the emerald gulf in three long columns of fifteen vessels each, and the never-ceasing signal lights flashing their brilliant rays from left to right, bearing imperative orders to be cautious, and asking if any danger had been discovered ahead.

On the morrow, on arriving off Key West, the booming of the Indiana's thirteen-inch monsters, as she joined the brilliant command, added new vigor to the men who were now *en route* to a land unknown, to fight in the cause of Christianity, freedom and honor. Early in the morning of June 20th the fleet appeared off Santiago Bay, and after a conference with Admiral Sampson, the troops prepared to land. The Twenty-fourth Infantry, with one battalion of the Twenty-first Infantry, aboard the City of Washington, were the last regiments to land. They were kept coasting around in front of Morro Castle until June 25th, when they received landing orders. The object of keeping this regiment in front of Morro Castle cannot be explained unless it was to draw the Spanish fire from the castle and surrounding forts, in order to locate their whereabouts. This was demonstrated when, on the morning of the 22d, while the second and a portion of the first division was landing at Daiquiri and Siboney; the vessel, with about six hundred colored troops aboard, was ordered to close in on Morro Castle, which it did, immediately attracting its attention, and drawing their fire. Luckily none of the shells fired at her struck the ship, but this was apparently due to bad marksmanship, since shells fell beyond her, showing plainly that she was wholly within range.

Landing on the morning of June 24th, the regiment immediately marched about one mile below Siboney, and made camp on the same ground previously occupied by the second division, which had now moved to the front, about five miles, toward Santiago. The Twenty-fourth was now a member of the third brigade, of the first division, and being held in reserve was the last of the brigade to move to the front. On the morning of the 27th of June, this regiment, headed by the Ninth and Thirteenth Infantries—the two advance members of the third brigade—marched out of Cocoanut Hollow (so called by the men on account of its numerous cocoanut trees) and moved five miles to the front, making camp at Las Guasimas, the hill on which the fighting and gallant Tenth Cavalry saved the Rough Riders from being massacred. The regiment remained here until the 30th of the same month almost rationless, due to lack of transportation to bring up supplies. Detachments of men had gone back to Siboney, where abundant supplies and provisions were being wasted and stolen by Cubans, to bring provisions a distance of five miles to the hungry troops. The writer was one of a detachment and well remembers how surprised the tired men were who had packed whole boxes of hard-tack over almost impassable trails, when, on returning to the camp they had left in the morning full of lively, busy, and anxious men, to find it entirely deserted, and not a tent to mark the site of their former abode. But presently a messenger came in great haste with orders from the regimental commander to bring up the detachments at once.

Already fatigued by the burdensome march with the

provisions from Siboney the men could hardly realize how they could accomplish the journey mapped out for them; but with the true spirit of loyalty and patriotism they set out over a road almost impassable by human feet. On they went, plowing through mud and mire that sometimes would rise above their knees; sometimes fording streams up to their waists, again tearing their way through thorny underbrush, until about 12:30 at night, when completely exhausted they lay down and made camp on the damp, miry soil that had been occupied by a thousand horses the night before. The memory of this night's work cannot be expressed in the few words now at my command, and it was only surpassed in hardship by our famous march from Santiago to Siboney, on the night of July 15th, of which you will learn later. Joining the regiment at this place, orders were issued to the men to "lie down—do not pitch tents, but get all the rest you can." This of course was suggestive of something unusual, and was not fully understood until July 1st, about 4:30 A.M., when the booming of a gun from Sampson's fleet told the boys on shore that it was time they were "up and a-doing." Immediately upon this signal Capron's mighty deluge of shell and shrapnel; Grimes' never ceasing flame and the sharp and stinging whiz of the wel-ldirected bullet of the fighting Tenth and stubborn Twenty-fifth, in company with a few other regiments, told Toral at El Caney that on that day they "would abide at his house." A signal was all that was necessary. Colonel Emerson H. Liscum, commanding the Twenty-fourth Infantry, stepped to his orderly musician, and quietly commanded him to blow "general call."

This trumpeter was William Brent, of Company H.

The command formed without discord, and, being in reserve, followed the Ninth and Thirteenth Infantries in the march to the front as had been ordered.

While hurrying to the front as fast as the roads and trails would permit, the constant roar of musketry of the second division, of which the Twenty-fifth was a member, then contending every inch of ground before El Caney, animated the black boys soon to become heroes, and becoming weary of the apparent reluctance of the white regiments that led them, complained to their commander and begged to be allowed to pass and take the lead. Colonel E. H. Liscum, no less a hero, no less brave than the demons he commanded, weary himself of the apparent reluctance of his leading commander, seized the opportunity at the first wide road where a passing might be effected, told the lieutenant-colonel of the Ninth Infantry, that his men were becoming aroused and desired to go to the front. The Thirteenth Infantry needed no further invitation but immediately stepped to the left of the road and allowed us to take the lead, while they accosted us with such epithets as, "There go the fighters"—"There go the men that will make Spain tremble." They know this is true, and not one dare deny it.

Having passed the Ninth and Thirteenth there remained nothing to impede our progress but the thorny underbrush and numerous streams peculiar to Cuban roads. Coming now within full range of the Spanish fire, our regiment was met by an orderly with orders to pull off all luggage and retain nothing but gun, belt and two hundred rounds of ammunition to each man, to send out scouts to bring in information as to the enemy's whereabouts. This was at the Sugar House near El Pozo and Capron's battery (on our left and rear) was firing directly over our heads. The writer was the first scout named from his company, and on advancing well into the dense shrubbery was surprised to see every twig, to the size of a man's finger, pierced by mauser

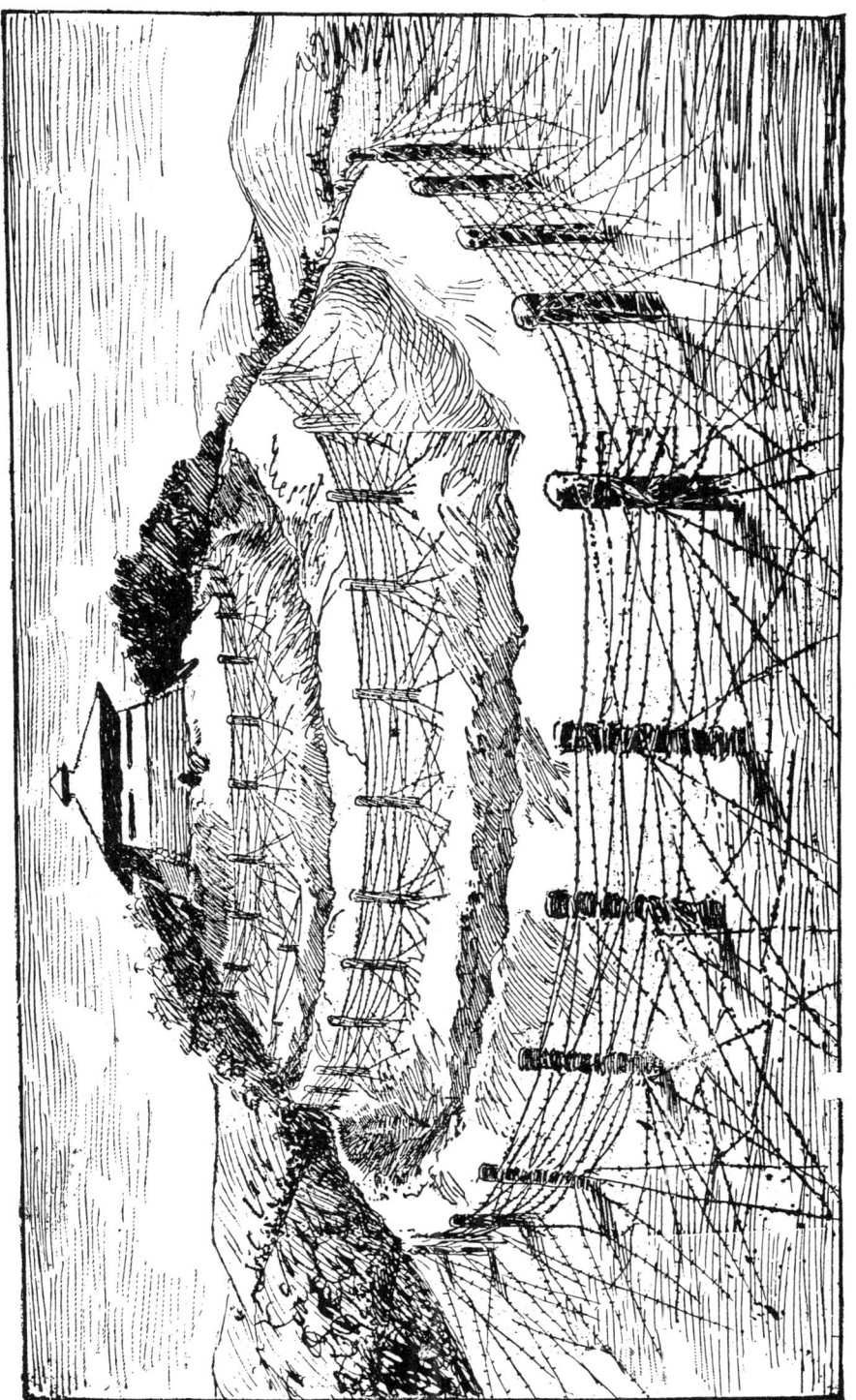

Typical Blockhouse in Cuba with Barbed Wire Fortification.

bullets or broken by shell or shrapnel. Before the scouts were far enough to discover the enemy's line of intrenchments recall was sounded and they came in. As soon as the command could be formed again, Colonel Liscum stepped to the head of his column and commanded "Forward! March!" Moving up at double time we soon came to the fork of the road where General J. Ford Kent was standing, disgusted, with tears running down his cheeks, begging, admonishing, persuading and entreating the Seventy-first New York Volunteers (white), "for the love of country, liberty, honor and dignity; in the name of freedom, in the name of God; for the sake of their dear mothers and fathers to stand up like men and fight, and go to the front." But all in vain, they fled like sheep from the presence of wolves.

On seeing Colonel Liscum and the boys whom he had formerly commanded, and whom he so well knew, he seemed almost wild with joy. At his first sight of the colored boys who were then double-timing and almost breathless, he ran out, grasped Liscum's hand, exclaiming in his deep voice: "Liscum, turn to your left, pass over all troops you see there (the Seventy-first New York were rushing to the rear and laying down under cover), turn to your right, ford the stream and fight everything before you." These were his exact words --I heard them distinctly. Liscum smiled and with perfect composure replied. "General, my boys will not disgrace the flag."

Turning to the left along the San Juan road, running parallel with the river of the same name, those dark heroes, maddened by terrible and trying fire to which they were being subjected, rushed over the prostrated bodies of the bewildered and stampeded Seventy-first, and halted where their commander decided to cross,

Turning to his command, after a moment's deliberation, he gave his last command, before the battle, which was: "Deploy as skirmishers, forward, march!" In the river they rushed like madmen. They swam the stream which took them up to their necks, tearing through the wire fences which were perplexingly and intricately interwoven among the dense shrubbery. Emerging from these stubborn impediments they rushed wildly across the open field, attracting the attention of the entire Spanish line, and drawing their concentrated fire, which would have completely demoralized and defeated any body of men of less determination and bravery than the dark heroes with whom they were now contending. Having given the command to advance two hundred yards and lie down under cover, on arriving at this point Colonel Liscum changed his mind. He saw that to stop was death and destruction to his men; to go ahead was little less dangerous, but he chose the latter and ordered a charge. The flood of flame that now fell upon these men is almost beyond description. From early morn had the Sixteenth Infantry striven against hope to charge this impregnable summit, but in vain. They had bravely attempted repeatedly to charge this point, but were as often repulsed. Their ranks had been fearfully depleted and there seemed no hope of success against such a formidable foe, but when the colored boys of the Twenty-fourth Infantry showed their brilliant faces upon this bloody field matters assumed a different aspect.

Colonel Liscum, standing on tiptoe, viciously waved his sword toward the "Hill," and never did men obey their leader with more determination. Turning to his orderly he commanded him to sound "to the charge" and William Brent, with all the courage of a patriot and a soldier, obeyed. While thus directing the movements of his troops Colonel Liscum fell, pierced by a bullet in his left shoulder, but his men did not falter a moment. Captain Ducat and his second lieutenant, John A. Gurney, fell within fifty yards of each other, but Sergeant William H. Ellis took command of the company; two minutes later he also fell badly wounded, but the boys did not want for a commander; Sergeant Lewis W. McNabb, stepping to the head of his company, led them on up the hill and to success.

After capturing the hill, General Kent, seeing the noble work they had done, sent his congratulations to them and ordered that they be not required to fire another gun that day. So great had been the loss of this regiment that when the roll was called, after darkness had put an end to the fighting, companies originally numbering one hundred men reported only seventeen, twenty, and twenty-three present.

Early the next morning, long before sunrise, the enemy, irritated by their dreadful defeat of the night before, opened volley after volley upon our men, who now occupied the most important position along the whole line; but too late—the men had worked all night with improvised implements, using, in many cases, their muskets for shovels and their bayonets for spades, and had thus fortified themselves against the enemy's fire. All day long with nothing to eat or drink did these heroes lay in those narrow trenches, beneath the parching rays of a tropical sun. Every stitch of their clothes wringing wet from fording the river and from the dense dew for which Cuba is noted; lying on the bare ground with not a stitch to protect them or keep them warm; kept constantly on duty, while other regiments lurked about at the foot of the hill, and went to the rear where they could get abundant provisions—these men were yet cheerful through it all.

For fourteen long days did they endure almost unbearable hardships until almost demoralized by sickness, fatigue and hunger, when, to the joy of every man the surrender was announced. Relieved greatly by this peaceful announcement they hoped soon for better fare; to be sent somewhere that they might rest and recover, but this was not to be. At 4 P.M. of the 14th of July, the day on which the surrender was announced, volunteers were called for to nurse the sick inmates of the rapidly increasing yellow fever hospital already established at Siboney. When eight regiments had been consulted and refused, the colored troops were called upon, and without a murmur they gladly accepted, marching from Santiago to Siboney, a distance of about fifteen miles, through almost complete darkness, passing through places so dense and dark that they were compelled to clasp hands in order to find their way. This was the worst night experienced while in Cuba.

Arriving at Siboney about 4 A.M. of July 16th they lay down with clothes soaked in perspiration on the ground that was daily drenched by rains. The next day nurses were called for, and almost all volunteered. However, only eighty-four were chosen, but within two weeks eighty more were called upon to fill the places made vacant by sickness and death—for only four of the first relay remained for duty.

Their fare was better here, but the awful scourge of the yellow fever soon thinned their ranks to a minimum. One month and ten days they remained at Siboney, nursing the sick, burying the dead, building tents, burning and disinfecting buildings, and performing every other duty of camp life.

On the 24th of August, after all other regiments had been ordered home and had departed, excepting several regiments of immunes, the Twenty-fourth received orders to pack up and prepare to leave for home.

On the 26th day of August they started for Montauk Point, Long Island, arriving there on the 2d day of September and remaining at that place to recuperate until September 25th, when they were ordered to their old station at Fort Douglas, Utah

LIEUT. A. J. SMITH,
8th U. S. Volunteer Infantry. Late Sergeant 25th Infantry. Promoted for bravery at El Caney.

LIEUT. WILLIAM McBRYAR.
Eighth U. S. Volunteer Infantry. Late Quartermaster-Sergeant 25th U. S. Infantry.

CHAPTER IX.

THE TWENTY-FIFTH INFANTRY.

A Private Letter Reproduced—How the Battles were Won—Troop Commander Lieutenant W. H. Smith Killed—Lieutenant Robertson Wounded—Troop Commanded by Sergeant Saint Foster—Sergeant Foster Promoted—Chaplain T. G. Steward of the 25th Infantry gives Account of the Negro Soldier—General Reports are Quoted.

IF the entire story of the campaign in Cuba is ever told in all its details, it will be told by individuals who actually took part in it. The tragic accounts of the battles fought can be given best by those who heard the whiz of the bullets, the boom of the cannons, the fierce yells of the brave boys as they rushed up the hills and through the wild undergrowth. In the reminiscences of officers and privates much valuable information is gleaned.

"We came in sight of Morro Castle, June 21st, at 1:30 P.M. I saw the most beautiful scenery of my life. To see our ships in line of battle guarding the harbor of Santiago, in which Admiral Cervera's fleet had been bottled up for several days, was indeed a wonderful spectacle. A sight once seen never to be forgotten.

"We effected a safe landing June 22d, at Daiquiri, about twenty-five miles southeast of Santiago. Here an active campaigning began. Our march on the island was over very rough roads, causing much fatigue. Our first battle took place at Las Guasimas, June 24th.

The Rough Riders, one squadron of the First Cavalry, and one squadron of the Tenth Cavalry, drove more than six thousand Spaniards from their fortifications. The contest lasted about two hours. The only artillery used was our hotchkiss battery, of which I am gunner of Section No. 1. The fight was indeed a hot one; but twenty-one shots from our battery and the charging of the Tenth Cavalry up the crest of the steep hill and at short range pouring several volleys of steel into the enemy, caused them to fall back and retreat in confusion, leaving one hundred of their dead on the field. Our casualties were small. My regiment lost one killed and eight wounded. June 30th we camped at El Caney, two and a half miles from Santiago. Each man was given three days' rations, consisting of eighteen hardtack and nine slices of bacon, and was told that in the morning we would advance on Santiago. We were several thousand strong. General Garcia commanded two thousand insurgents. The boys were very cheerful and sang 'A Hot Time in Cuba To-morrow.' We arose early July 1st, made coffee in our tin cups and ate our two hard-tacks and bacon. At 5 A.M. we were ready for the task before us. Captain Capron's Battery E, First Artillery, was ordered to be planted on the crest of El Caney, overlooking the city and the guns turned on the enemy's blockhouses. At 6:20 A.M. the battery opened fire; twenty-one shots were fired before the Spaniards answered. Our little battery was one hundred yards in the basin and in the rear of the battery in action. The first shot from the Spanish battery fell about twenty feet from our battery and exploded, killing one Cuban soldier, and wounding nine. The second shell exploded ten feet above and directly over me, wounding one gunner of our battery, Pat Watson, Troop F, Tenth Cavalry. A piece of shell struck one of our ammunition boxes, exploding the shells, but luckily it didn't explode our shells. For half an hour or more, a continual rain of shells came from the Spanish battery. Their aim was very accurate and they soon began to drop shells on Captain Capron's battery; an hour later they withdrew, after several were killed and wounded. Our little battery was ordered to advance on Santiago.

"We followed close in rear of the dynamite gun. Down a narrow and rough road full of undergrowth we went. A balloon was hoisted in advance, guided by several hundred feet of rope, and about twenty-five men. Two officers were in the balloon, and located the enemy. As we passed under the balloon one of the officers said: 'Tell General Wheeler to prepare for an attack. The Spaniards have formed a battle line three hundred yards in front of us.' The next moment, shot and shell began to fly at the balloon and our advancing columns. The dynamite gun and our little battery moved forward and across the San Juan River seventy-five yards beyond- unlimbered and planted our battery on the spot where the Spanish line was first formed. They had retreated a short distance and concealed themselves in the tall sage brush and bushes, pouring in a deadly fire upon us. The dynamite gun took position seventy-five yards to our right.

"By the aid of my glasses I saw so much game I did not know where to direct my first shot. In front of me, was a squadron of cavalry; one hundred yards to the right of the cavalry, were several Spanish trenches; on the left of the cavalry Spaniards were as thick as sand crabs along the seashore. Through the thick undergrowth, I sighted my gun on the blockhouses. As No. 1 pulled the lanyard, I watched with my glasses the result of the shot. It hit its mark. Several Spaniards took refuge in the trenches. I directed my second shot at the trenches. As they were packed like sardines, the shell exploded about ten feet in front of them. Knowing that I had the range, I gave it to the other gunners. My elevation was 1,000 yards or 148 degrees. There were two shots fired from my gun before the others got in position. A shot was fired from the dynamite gun and the shell got jammed so the gun was carried to the rear, having fired only one shot.

"During the day all four of our guns were playing on the enemy; but we were receiving a heavy musketry and artillery fire from the Spaniards. The battery fire was terrific and our black powder gave them a good mark. The screeching and bursting of shrapnel, the whiz of the mauser bullets were seen and heard all around us. Two gunners were wounded: Sergeant Taylor, Troop E, and Sanders of Troop B, Tenth Cavalry; but not until they had displayed great bravery did they fall victims to the Spanish mauser. Several of our regiments deployed in line of battle on our right and left. The gallant Rough Riders on the left, the Tenth Cavalry in the center and the First Cavalry on the right made assault after assault on the enemy's strong intrenched position, cutting their way through several barb-wire fences. Our battery ceased firing, for fear that we might drop a shell among our own men. I then became an eyewitness of the desperate work. By the aid of glasses I observed that my troop was advancing too fast. It was far in advance of the other trooops and was receiving a crossfire from two blockhouses and the trenches. They were cut down as if a mowing machine had been run through the platoons. At this point, our troop commander, First Lieutenant William H. Smith, fell dead, a mauser bullet having passed through his head. And Second Lieutenant Robertson, wounded, leaving the troop without an officer. The first sergeant, Saint Foster, took command of the troop, led it onward, and with a yell the Rough Riders and the Tenth Cavalry carried the works by storm and planted their colors upon San Juan Hill.

"For this gallant work, Sergeant Foster was ordered back to the United States to be appointed commissioned officer. The Spaniards retreated into the basin in which Santiago lies. We received orders to take position on San Juan; we reached that point at 1:25 P.M. and planted part of our battery upon the brow of her hill. We opened fire on the blockhouses and trenches. At 5:15 we withdrew from the field as our ammunition ran short.

"The gallant Rough Riders, the Tenth Cavalry, and other regiments have baptized San Juan with their life's blood, fighting for our country's honor and the bleeding 'Pearl of the Antilles.' As we withdrew our forces from the field I passed over the trenches and examined the blockhouse on which we had first opened fire. As I gazed upon the dead my heart sank. A Spanish major was lying dead near a tree, half his head having been carried away by a shell. The trenches were full of dead Spaniards. Oh! what a terrible sight. God grant I may never behold such a piteous spectacle again. I can never forget what I saw on San Juan Hill July 1st. From 8:30 A.M. until the close of the battle for the day the only artillery used (except one shot fired from one of the dynamite guns) was our hotchkiss gun battery commanded by Lieutenant Hughes. The battle was resumed at 4:30 lasting all day, and at 9 P.M. the enemy made a night attack, which lasted two hours. On the morning of the 3d, the battle began to rage at an early hour, lasting until 11:30 A.M. At 1 P.M. a flag of truce met between the two lines. General Shafter demanded the surrender of General Toral and his forces, but the surrender was not effected until July the 17th at noon. I am glad that I am an ex-student of Hampton, where I received my first military training. I was with my gun and under fire from 8:30 A.M. until 5:15 P.M. and when my gun got too hot, I used my carbine and made Spaniards bite the dust as easy as it was for me in '94 to carry off the two department gold medals and the first army gold medal. Time cuts off further remarks, hence I will close. HORACE W. BIVINS."

Chaplain T. G. Steward, of the Twenty-fifth Infantry, furnishes the following account of the Negro's work in the army of invasion. It is interesting to note that he does not attempt to give too much credit to a few; but would like to have the honors equally divided.

"All the army made history during the short Cuban war; but the colored regulars in three days practically revolutionized the sentiment of the country in regard to the colored soldier, and as a result more than one hundred Afro-Americans are bearing commissions in the United States Army.

"The entire colored contingent—the Ninth and Tenth Cavalry and the Twenty-fourth and Twenty-fifth Infantry—did well. It has been said by one who knows: 'Not a colored soldier disgraced himself on Cuban soil.' Indeed, the converse of this is practically true. Every colored soldier honored himself.

"Without desiring to take away one leaf or sprig from the laurels won by the other colored regiments, and with a full recognition of the valor of the entire army, I invite attention to the following official story of the action of the Twenty-fifth United States Infantry in the Cuban campaign.

"I may summarize in advance by saying that the Twenty-fifth was the first regiment to leave its home station, the first to go into camp, was a part of the first

CAPTAIN T. G. STEWARD.
Chaplain 25th Regiment U. S. Infantry.

UNDER FIRE. 141

expedition to Cuba, and the second to land, and had the honor of digging the intrenchments nearest to the enemy's line. In physique and discipline it was so nearly perfect that only one man from its ranks died on Cuban soil from climatic disease, and only two from diseases of any sort. The men are mostly large, many of them being six-footers, and weighing, when in good condition, two hundred pounds and over, and the standard of intelligence among them and the language used are about up to what obtains in the army generally. In marksmanship, drill and general military knowledge and skill they have attained a high degree of efficiency, and as a whole are of excellent character and temper.

"The present regimental commander is Lieutenant-Colonel A. S. Daggett, a highly accomplished officer, who rose to the rank of colonel in the Civil War and was brevetted brigadier-general for gallant and meritorious services in the battle of the Wilderness. He came to the command of the regiment in Tampa but a few weeks before it embarked on the transports for Cuban shores.

"The story that I am now to present is woven almost entirely from the official reports and orders of Colonel Daggett, who commanded the regiment most successfully through the fierce fight before Santiago. Any one who saw the regiment as it passed the camp of the Second Massachusetts on its way to its own camp would have witnessed an open and cordial tribute to its valor. As these worn and dusty—and dusky—veterans swung by the cultivated well-bred amateur warriors of Massachusetts the young heroes gave them such cheers and applause, as soldiers seldom give. 'They have a good feeling for us,' said a sergeant of the Twenty-fifth to me. 'They think you are soldiers,' I remarked. 'They know we are soldiers,' he replied.

"The Twenty-fifth, with all the other colored regiments, is known as a band of fighters.

"The history of the campaign of the Twenty-fifth is succinctly and graphically told in the following general orders published near Santiago August 11, 1898:

"'Gathered from three different stations, many of you strangers to each other, you assembled as a regiment for the first time in more than twenty-eight years on May 7, 1898, at Tampa, Florida. There you endeavored to solidify and prepare yourselves, as far as the oppressive weather would permit, for the work that appeared to be before you. But who could have foretold the severity of that work? You endured the severe hardships of a long sea voyage, which no one who has not experienced it can appreciate.

"'You then disembarked amid dangerous surroundings, and on landing were for the first time on hostile ground. You marched under a tropical sun, carrying blanket roll, three days' rations and one hundred rounds of ammunition, through rain and mud, part of the time at night, sleeping on the wet ground without shelter, living part of the time on scant rations, even of bacon, hard bread and coffee, until, on July 1st, you arrived at El Caney. Here you took the battle formation and advanced to the stone fort more like veteran troops than troops who had never been under fire.

"'You again marched day and night, halting only to dig four lines of intrenchments, the last being the nearest point to the enemy reached by any organization, when, still holding your rifles, within these intrenchments, notice was received that Santiago and the Spanish army had surrendered.

"'But commendable as the record may be, the brightest hours of your lives were on the afternoon of July 1st. Formed in battle array, you advanced to the stone fort against volleys therefrom, and rifle pits in front, and against a galling fire from blockhouses, the church tower and the village on your left. You continued to advance skillfully and bravely, directed by the officers in immediate command, halting and delivering such a cool and well-directed fire that the enemy was compelled to wave the white flag in token of surrender.

" 'Seldom have troops been called upon to face a severer fire and never have they acquitted themselves better.

" 'The regimental reserve was called upon to try its nerve by lying quiet under a galling fire without returning it, where men were killed and wounded. This is a test of nerve which the firing line cannot realize, and requires the highest quality of bravery and endurance. You may well return to the United States proud of your accomplishments, and if any ask what you have done, point him to El Caney.'

"The history of that part of the battle performed by the Twenty-fifth is further detailed by the regimental commander in his official reports to his superiors. These reports and the orders just quoted from constitute the whole official literature on the subject, and hence the present story may be regarded as both authentic and exhaustive.

"According to Colonel Daggett's report, the regiment occupied the right of a short reconstructed line, with the Fourth Infantry on its left. To the right of the Twenty-fifth somewhere were about fifty Cubans, but the testimony is that they did not help in the fight.

"The firing line of the Twenty-fifth consisted of two companies—H and G. Company D was then ordered to deploy as flankers on the right. This battalion was commanded by Captain W. S. Scott, and advanced in line with the Fourth Infantry, all being under fire, until within about five hundred yards of the fort. Here the line found cover, halted and delivered an effective fire.

At this point the Fourth Infantry was blocked by natural obstacles, and could make no further advance, but continued to pour a telling fire into the fort.

"Colonel Daggett ordered an advance, which was quickly made by the Twenty-fifth, but in doing so it broke away from the Fourth, which was halted on its left, and thus separated itself from the brigade and exposed its left to a severe oblique, or nearly crossfire from the village and blockhouses which were on the left and a little in front of El Caney. Company C was then ordered to reinforce the left of the line, and Lieutenant Kinson's company was called from the reserve to replace Company C in the line of support, thus making five companies in action.

"The battalion in this formation continued to advance from cover to cover until it reached a point within fifty yards of the fort. Here these companies opened so cool, steady and sure a fire that a Spaniard could not show himself but he was immediately hit, and fifteen or twenty minutes before any other troops came up the enemy put out the white flag.

"The space, however, between the front of the Twenty-fifth and the fort was so swept by the crossfire from the church and blockhouses on the left that it was impossible for one of our officers to cross to receive the surrender of the fort or for a Spanish officer to bring the flag to our lines.

"At the end of about twenty minutes one company of the Twelfth Infantry, which had gotten round to a point where they were thoroughly screened from the fire of both the fort and the village, under protection of the fire of the Twenty-fifth, entered the fort and received the surrender which the bullets of the Twenty-fifth had brought about. Two of our men—Butler of H company and J. H. Jones of I company—entered the fort at the same time with the men of the Twelfth, and while an officer of that regiment received the white flag of surrender, these two men seized the Spanish standard. They were immediately ordered to give it up by an officer of the Twelfth, and obeyed, but before doing so they each tore a piece from the flag. One of these pieces I have seen and examined, and the man who has it I have known for years, and I do not hesitate to accept his story. The fact, indeed, is so well attested that it is embodied in official reports.

"The conduct of the regiment and the skill and courage of the commanding officer, as well as of the company officers, were such as to elicit highest praise. From the regiment four sergeants have been promoted to commissions, and Lieutenant-Colonel Daggett has received most flattering mention, the whole action of the regiment being regarded as especially brilliant."

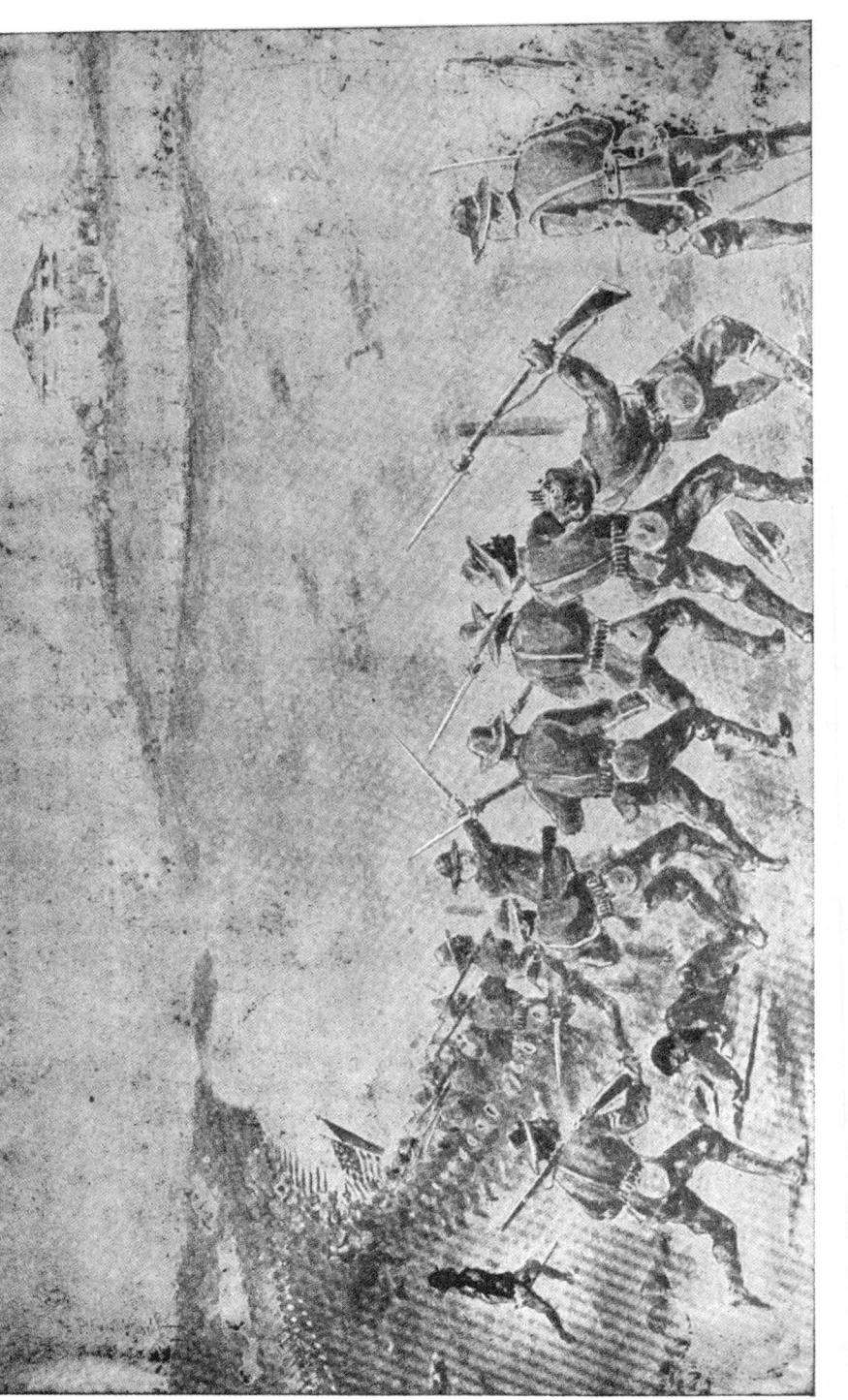

Twenty-fifth Infantry Deploying to Right in Assault on El Caney—Co. D, Extreme Right.

CHAPTER X.

THE NINTH AND TENTH CAVALRY.

What Colonel Theodore Roosevelt, Governor of New York, has to Say of the Ninth and Tenth Cavalry—Major-General Nelson A. Miles—General Field Orders—General Wheeler's Testimony—Major-General Shafter—Lieutenant-Colonel T. A. Baldwin—Captain Woodward Announces the Retirement of Sergeant George Berry, Who Spent Thirty years in the Service.

COLONEL THEODORE ROOSEVELT said in a private letter to John E. Bruce, Esq., of Albany, New York:

"DEAR SIR: The Ninth and Tenth Cavalry Regiments fought one on either side of mine at Santiago, and I wish no better men beside me in battle than these colored troops showed themselves to be. Later on, when I come to write of the campaign, I shall have much to say about them."

We also quote the following letter from Major-General Nelson A. Miles:

"Headquarters of the Army,
"WASHINGTON, D. C., November 21, 1898.
"CHAPLAIN W. T. ANDERSON,
"Tenth United States Cavalry, Huntsville, Ala.
"MY DEAR SIR: Replying to yours of the 11th instant, I inclose copy of General Field Orders No. 1, in which you will find a paragraph marked that will indicate my opinion of the colored soldier in unmistakable language. Very truly yours,
"NELSON A. MILES.
"Major-General Commanding."

The following are the Field Orders above referred to:

"Headquarters of the Army,
"SIBONEY, Cuba, July 16, 1898.
"General Field Orders, No 1.

"The gratifying success of the American arms at Santiago de Cuba and some features of a professional character, both important and instructive, are hereby announced to the army.

"The declaration of war found our country with a small army scattered over a vast territory. The troops composing this army were speedily mobilized at Tampa, Florida. Before it was possible to properly equip a volunteer force, strong appeals for aid came from the navy, which had inclosed in the harbor of Santiago de Cuba an important part of the Spanish fleet. At that time the only efficient fighting force available was the United States army; and in order to organize a command of sufficient strength, the cavalry had to be sent dismounted to Santiago de Cuba with the infantry and artillery. The expedition thus formed was placed under command of Major-General Shafter. Notwithstanding the limited time to equip and organize an expedition of this character, there was never displayed a nobler spirit of patriotism and fortitude on the part of officers and men, going forth to maintain the honor of their country. After encountering the vicissitudes of an ocean voyage, they were obliged to disembark on a foreign shore, and immediately engage in an aggressive campaign. Under drenching storms, intense and prostrating heat, within a fever-afflicted district, with little comfort or rest, either by day or night, they pursued their purpose of finding and conquering the enemy. Many of them trained in the severe experience of the great war and in frequent campaigns on the Western plains, officers and men alike exhibited great skill, fortitude and tenacity, with results that have added a new chapter of glory to their country's history. Even when their own generals in several cases were temporarily disabled, the troops fought on with the same heroic spirit until success was finally achieved. In many instances the officers placed themselves in front of their commands, and under their direct and skillful leadership, the trained troops of a brave army were driven from the thickets and jungles of an almost inaccessible country. In the open field the troops stormed intrenched infantry, and carried and captured fortified works with an unsurpassed daring and disregard of death. By gaining commanding ground, they made the harbor of Santiago untenable for the Spanish fleet, and practically drove it out to a speedy destruction by the American navy. While enduring the hardships and privations of such a campaign, the troops generously shared their scanty food with the five thousand Cuban patriots in arms and the suffering people who had fled from the besieged city. With the twenty-four regiments and four batteries, the flower of the United States army, were also three volunteer regiments. These, though unskilled in warfare, yet, inspired with the same spirit, contributed to the victory, suffered hardships and made sacrifices with the rest. Where all did so well, it is impossible by special mention to do justice to those who bore conspicuous part.

"But of certain unusual features mention cannot be omitted namely, the cavalry dismounted fighting and storming works as infantry; and a regiment of colored troops, who having shared equally in the heroism as well as the sacrifices, is now voluntarily engaged in nursing yellow fever patients and burying the dead.

"The gallantry, patriotism and sacrifices of the American army, as illustrated in this brief campaign, will be fully appreciated by a grateful country, and the heroic deeds of those who have fought and fallen in the cause of freedom will ever be cherished in sacred memory, and be an inspiration to the living.

"By command of Major-General Miles:
"J. C. GILMORE.
"Brigadier-General U. S. V."

We append the general orders of Major-General Joseph Wheeler, who commanded the cavalry division with such conspicuous ability and gallantry:

"Headquarters Cavalry Division,
"CAMP WIKOFF, L. I., September 20, 1898.
"To the Officers and Soldiers, of the Cavalry Division, Army of Santiago:

"The duties for which the troops comprising the cavalry division were brought together have been accomplished.

"On June 14th we sailed from Tampa, Florida, to encounter in the sickly season the diseases of the tropical Island of Cuba, and to face and attack the historic legions of Spain in positions chosen by them and which for years they had been strengthening by every art and contrivance known to the skillful military engineers of Europe.

"On the 23d one squadron each of the First and Tenth Regular Cavalry and two squadrons of the First Volunteer Cavalry, in all nine hundred and sixty-four officers and men landed on Cuban soil. These troops marched on foot fourteen miles, and, early on the morning of the 24th, attacked and defeated double their number of regular Spanish soldiers under the command of Lieutenant-General Linares. Eagerly and cheerfully you pushed onward, and on July 1st, the First, Third, Sixth, Ninth and Tenth Regular Cavalry and the First Volunteer Cavalry, forded San Juan River and gallantly swept over San Juan Hill, driving the enemy from its crest. Without a moment's halt you formed, aligning the division upon the First Infantry division under General Kent, and, together with these troops, you bravely charged and carried the formidable intrenchments of Fort San Juan. The entire force which fought and won this great victory was less than seven thousand men.

"The astonished enemy though still protected by the strong works to which he had made his retreat, was so stunned by your determined valor that his only thought was to devise the quickest means of saving himself from further battle. The great Spanish fleet hastily sought escape from the harbor and was destroyed by our matchless navy.

"After seizing the fortifications of San Juan ridge, you, in the darkness of night, strongly intrenched the position your valor had won.

"Reinforced by Bates' Brigade on your left and Lawton's Division on your right, you continued the combat until the Spanish army of Santiago Province succumbed to the superb prowess and courage of American arms. Peace promptly followed, and you return to receive the plaudits of seventy millions of people.

"The valor displayed by you was not without sacrifice. Eighteen per cent., or nearly one in five, of the cavalry division fell on the field either killed or wounded. We mourn the loss of these heroic dead, and a grateful country will always revere their memory.

"Whatever may be my fate, wherever my steps may lead, my heart will always burn with increasing admiration for your courage in action, your fortitude under privation and your constant devotion to duty in its highest sense, whether in battle, in bivouac or upon the march.

(Signed) "JOSEPH WHEELER,
"Major-General U. S. V., Commanding."

Here follow the General Orders of Major-General Shafter in command of the expedition:

"Headquarters United States Troops in Cuba,
"SANTIAGO DE CUBA, July 19, 1898.
"General Orders No. 26.

"The successful accomplishment of the campaign against Santiago, resulting in its downfall and the surrender of the Spanish forces, the capture of large amounts of military stores, together with the destruction of the entire Spanish fleet in the harbor, which upon the investment of the city, was forced to leave, is one of which this army can well be proud.

"This has been accomplished through the heroic deeds of the army, and to its officers and men the major-general commanding offers his sincere thanks for their endurance of hardships heretofore unknown in the American army. The work you have accomplished may well appeal to the pride of your countrymen and has been rivaled upon but few occasions in the world's history and excelled by none. Landing upon an unknown coast, you faced dangers in disembarking and overcame obstacles that even now, in looking back, seem insurmountable. Seizing, with the assistance of the navy, the towns of Daiquiri and Siboney, you pushed boldly forth, gallantly driving back the enemy's outpost in the engagement of Las Guasimas and completed the concentration of the army near Sevilla, within sight of the Spanish stronghold at Santiago de Cuba.

"The outlook from Sevilla was one that might well have appalled the stoutest heart; behind you ran a narrow road, made well-nigh impassable by rains, while to the front you looked out upon high foothills, covered with a dense tropical growth, which could only be traversed by bridle paths, terminating within range of the enemy's guns. Nothing daunted, you responded eagerly to the order to close upon the foe and attacking at Caney and San Juan, drove him from work to work, until he took refuge within his last and strongest intrenchments immediately surrounding the city.

"Despite the fierce glare of a southern sun and rains that fell in torrents, you valiantly withstood his attempts to drive you from the position your valor had won. Holding in your vise-like grip the army opposed to you, after seventeen days of battle and siege, you were rewarded by the surrender of nearly twenty-four thousand prisoners—twelve thousand being those in your immediate front, the others scattered in the various towns of eastern Cuba; freeing completely the eastern part of the island from Spanish troops. This was not done without great sacrifices. The death of two hundred and thirty gallant soldiers, and the wounding of twelve hundred and eighty-four others, shows but too plainly the fierce contest in which you were engaged. The few reported missing are undoubtedly among the dead as no prisoners were lost.

"For those who have fallen in battle with you, the commanding general sorrows, and with you will ever cherish their memory. Their devotion to duty sets a high example of courage and patriotism to our fellow-countrymen.

"All who have participated in the campaign, battle and siege of Santiago de Cuba will recall with pride the grand deeds accomplished, and will hold one another dear for having shared great sufferings, hardships and triumphs together. All may well feel proud to inscribe on their banner the name of 'Santiago de Cuba.'

"By command of Major-General Shafter:
(Signed) "E. J. McClernand,
"Assistant Adjutant-General."

We close this chapter with the report of Lieutenant-Colonel T. A. Baldwin, through the acting adjutant-general of the Tenth United States Cavalry:

"Headquarters Tenth United States Cavalry,
"Camp Hamilton, Cuba, July 23, 1898.
"Adjutant-General, Second Brigade, Cavalry Division,
Fifth Army Corps.

"Sir: I have the honor to submit the following report of the part taken by the Tenth Cavalry in the battle of July 1, 2 and 3, 1898, before Santiago de Cuba.

"On the morning of July 1st the regiment, consisting of Troops A, B, C, D, E, F, G and I, field and staff, occupied a position on the left of the Second Cavalry Brigade, the line extending nearly north and south on a ridge some three or four miles from Santiago.

"At about 6:30 A.M. a battery of artillery, posted a short distance from our right, opened fire upon the works of Santiago, the regiment being exposed to much of the return fire of the enemy's batteries. After the artillery firing had ceased, the regiment moved to the right, passed the Sugar Mill, and proceeded in rear of the brigade down the road bending toward Santiago. The movement was delayed as we approached the San Juan River, and the regiment came within the range of fire about one-half mile from the crossing. Upon reaching the river, I found that the Seventy-first New York Volunteers was at the crossing and that the regiment preceding mine had moved to the right. The Tenth Cavalry was here subjected to a converging artillery and infantry fire from the three blockhouses and intrenchments in front and the works further to the left and nearer to Santiago. This fire was probably drawn by a balloon which preceded the regiment to a point near the ford where it was held. I was directed to take a position to the right behind the river bank for protection. While moving to this position, and while there the regiment suffered considerable loss. After an interval of twenty or thirty minutes, I was directed to form line of battle in a partially open field facing toward the blockhouse and strong intrenchments to the north occupied by the enemy. Much difficulty was found on account of the dense undergrowth crossed in several directions by wire fences. As a part of the cavalry division under General Sumner, the regiment was formed in two lines; the first squadron under Major S. T. Norvell, consisting of Troops A, B, E and I, leading. The second line under Major T. J. Wint, consisting of Troops C, F and G. Troop D, having crossed further down the river, attached itself to a command of infantry, and moved with that command on the two blockhouses. The regiment advanced in this formation under a heavy converging fire from the enemy's position, proceeding but a short distance when the two lines were reunited into one. The advance was rapidly continued in an irregular line toward the blockhouses and intrenchments to the right front. During this advance the lines passed some troops of the First Cavalry which I think had previously been formed on our right. Several losses occurred before reaching the top of the hill, First Lieutenant William H. Smith being killed as he arrived on its crest. The enemy having retreated toward the northwest, toward the second and third blockhouses, new lines were formed and a rapid advance was made upon the new positions.

"The regiment assisted in capturing these works from the enemy, and with the exception of Troop C and I, who in the meantime had joined the First Volunteer Cavalry, then took up a position north of the second blockhouse, remaining there during the night. With some changes in the positions of troops, they held this line on the 2d and 3d, under a very heavy and continuous fire from the enemy's intrenchments in front, and the regiment now occupied a part of the most advanced intrenched positions. Some troops lost their

Map Showing Relative Positions of Ninth and Tenth Cavalry and Rough Riders.

relative positions in line during the first day of the battle, but attached themselves to others and continued to move forward. During the entire engagement the regiment acted with extraordinary coolness and bravery. It held its position at the ford and moved forward unflinchingly after deploying through the dense brush under the heavy fire from the enemy's works.

"The officers and men in general, throughout, exhibited great bravery, obeying orders with unflinching alacrity while attacking with small arms an enemy strongly posted in intrenchments and blockhouse and supported with artillery. Words cannot express my gratification at such conduct and I would request that such service receive some special recognition. It is difficult to distinguish between officers and men, all of whom are so deserving, but of the officers whose conduct on the field came under my direct personal observation, I would especially mention Major S. T. Norvell and Major T. J. Wint, squadron commanders. First Lieutenant John J. Pershing, quartermaster, and First Lieutenant M. H. Barnum, adjutant, for their untiring energy, faithfulness and gallantry during this engagement, and would recommend the officers named for brevet commissions.

"I desire to recommend the following medical officers, attached to the Tenth Cavalry: Captain and Assistant Surgeon M. M. Brewer, First Lieutenant and Assistant Surgeon L. A. Fuller, for their untiring zeal and fearless energy in their attendance, under fire, of wounded officers and men of my own and other commands during the entire day of July 1st and succeeding days of the engagement.

"I would invite attention to the following list of men especially recommended in the inclosed reports forwarded herewith.

"Troop A, Corporal John Anderson and Private R. A. Parker.

"Troop C, First Sergeant Adam Houston.

"Troop E, First Sergeant Peter McCown, Q. M. Sergeant William Payne, Sergeants Benjamin Fasit, Ozrow Gaither and Corporal Thomas H. Herbert.

"Troop I, Private Elsie Jones, previously recommended. Very respectfully,
(Signed) "T. A. BALDWIN,
"Lieutenant-Colonel Tenth Cavalry, Commanding.
" A true copy:
"Second Lieutenant, Tenth Cavalry. Acting Regimental Adjutant."

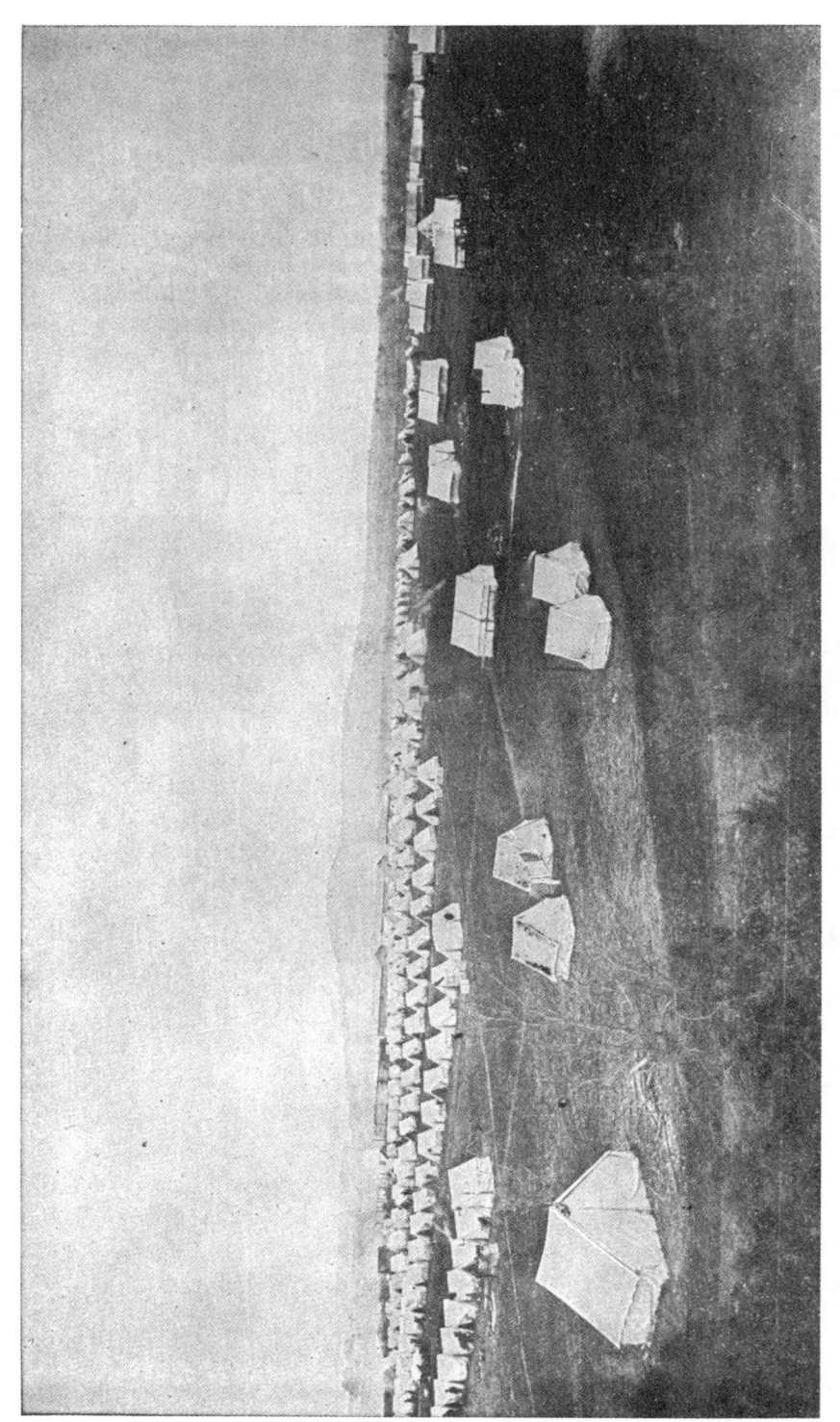

CAMP OF TENTH U. S. CAVALRY NEAR HUNTSVILLE, ALABAMA.

CHAPTER XI.

THE CONDUCT OF THE NEGRO TROOPS.

The Powerful Press—Spontaneous Outburst of Splendid Commendation of the Negro's Right to Share in the Glory Won by American Arms—Report of Captain John Bigelow, Jr., of Troop D, Tenth Cavalry—Evidences of Negro Heroism—Death of Lieutenant J. G. Ord, Sixth Infantry, Avenged by Corporal Walker, Tenth Cavalry, who Narrates Particulars.

FROM the New York *Mail and Express:* "All honor to the black troopers of the gallant Tenth. No more striking example of bravery and coolness has been shown since the destruction of the Maine than by the colored veterans of the Tenth Cavalry during the attack upon San Juan. By the side of the intrepid Rough Riders they followed their leader up the terrible hill from whose crest the desperate Spaniards poured down a deadly fire of shell and musketry. They never faltered. The rents in their ranks were filled as soon as made. Firing as they marched, their aim was splendid, their coolness was superb, and their courage aroused the admiration of their comrades. Their advance was greeted with wild cheers from the white regiments, and with answering shouts they pressed onward over the trenches they had taken close in pursuit of the retreating enemy. The war has not shown greater heroism. The men whose own freedom was baptized with blood have proved themselves capable of giving up their lives that others may be free."

From the Springfield *Republican:* "At San Juan Hill three companies of the Twenty-fourth Infantry (colored) lost every one of their officers before the fighting was over. Four of the regimental captains were knocked over by Spanish bullets within a minute of each other, and the lieutenant-colonel was severely wounded. Company F in a short time had only its captain left, and no other commissioned officer. It is said that the Twenty-fourth bore the brunt of the battles around Santiago, the Spaniards directing their main attack upon them on the theory that the Negroes would not stand the punishment. Yet whole companies remained steady without a single officer. As a final display of their remarkable discipline and nerve, this regiment of Negroes under the hottest fire of the day, 'charged front forward on its tenth company,' which is called a maneuver not altogether easy on a peaceful parade ground at home. The value of the Negro as a soldier can hardly be doubted after that day's work. While we are distributing cards of merit to generals and commodores, let us‧ not forget the colored soldiers of the Twenty-fourth Infantry."

From the Washington *Post:* "If it had not been for the Negro cavalry, the Rough Riders would have been exterminated. I am not a Negro lover. My father fought with Mosby's Rangers and I was born in the South, but the Negroes saved that fight, and the day will come when General Shafter will give them credit for their bravery."

From the New York *Sun:* "Meanwhile the Ninth Cavalry (colored) advanced steadily. At 3 o'clock in the afternoon the First and Tenth Cavalry came up, as did also the Rough Riders. Captain Taylor took the Ninth out and flanked the enemy on the left between our troops and the river. The jungle was up to their shoulders. All the troops advanced into this. The enemy had recovered meanwhile, and was sending a heavy fire into our ranks. Men were dropping everywhere. Some one set up the old-fashioned rebel yell, and the others took it up as one man. The soldiers leaped forward, charging and shooting across the field of manigua to the river. The steep banks were muddy, but our men dashed and slid down them, yelling like mad. Across the stream they went, and up the other side, the Spaniards pouring shot into them at a lively rate. They could no more stop the advance, however, than they could have stopped an avalanche.

"The blockhouse, a hundred yards away, continued its fire and contested every inch of the advance. The yelling and enthusiastic Americans charged on the blockhouse, driving the enemy before them. The enthusiasm of the Ninth Cavalry was at its highest pitch, and so it was with the other troops. Only annihiliation could drive them back; the Spaniards could not."

Though we had read columns upon columns of news from the scene of the battles around Santiago, our interest in the achievements of our men had not really reached its highest point, until an opportunity was presented to hear the story directly from the lips of some of the heroes themselves. Lately there have been landed at Fortress Monroe several shiploads of sick and wounded soldiers from Cuba, and they have been besieged by solicitations to give accounts of the battles. Their stories in the main agree with the best newspaper accounts, but many personal reminiscences are given which have not found their way into the papers. Four of the men, at the earnest solicitation of one of the pastors of the town, and with permission of the post surgeon, consented to give a public account of their part in the fray. They were members of the Ninth and Tenth Cavalry, and the Twenty-fourth Infantry. One of them, from the Twenty-fourth, was wounded in the hand, and carries around as a memento the bullet from a mauser rifle which struck him; another was wounded in the arm; a member of the Ninth had been incapacitated for duty by the deadly malaria contracted in that terrible siege in the trenches; the worst wounded of the four, a member of the Tenth, had two ribs broken before San Juan by a bursting Spanish shell. They are all of ordinary intelligence and told their stories in a modest, unassuming, but remarkably graphic way.

They told of the difficulties of landing from the transports, how they had to literally crawl on their hands and knees through the briars, thorns, and underbrush for five miles, and how their hands and knees and bodies were torn, bleeding, and blistered at the end of the journey. They described the rugged, rough condition of the country, how at times they had to wade through water up to their necks, and at the next instant to climb up some rocky eminence. Pathetically they told of how they suffered for food and water, and finally of that awful baptism of fire they received before San Juan, and the terrible trials in the trenches.

Said one of them, after describing the landing and the trying march to the front: "The Rough Riders had gone off in great glee, bantering us, and good-naturedly boasting of how they were going to lick the Spaniards without any trouble; and telling us to just wait there until they returned, that they would bring back to us some Spanish heads as trophies. Soon we heard firing in the distance, and our captain remarked that somebody ahead was doing good work. The fusillades kept up with so much persistence and vigor that our officers, without orders, decided to move forward and reconnoiter.

"When we got where we could see what was going on, we found that the Rough Riders had marched down a narrow valley; the Spaniards had men posted at the entrance, and as soon as the Rough Riders had gone in, had closed up behind them, and were thus firing on them from both front and rear. When the Spaniards received a volley from our men (the Tenth), who fired without command, they feared we were going to flank them, and rushed out of ambush in front of the Rough Riders, throwing up their hands and shouting 'Don't shoot, we are Cubans!' The Rough Riders thus let them escape, and gave them a chance to take a better position ahead. During this time all the men were in tall grass and could see even their own men, and I fear the Rough Riders in the rear shot many of their own men in front, mistaking them for Spanish soldiers. By this time the Tenth had taken in the situation, and adopting the method used in fighting Indians, were able to turn the tide of the battle, and repulsed the Spaniards. I don't think it an exaggeration to say that for the timely aid of the Tenth Cavalry, the Rough Riders would have been exterminated; this is the opinion freely and openly expressed by the men of that regiment themselves."

"Were you in the fight of July 1st?" he was asked. "Yes, that is where I received my wounds. We were under fire in that fight forty-eight hours or more, without food and with but little water. We had been cut off from our pack train, as the Spanish sharpshooters shot our mules as soon as they came anywhere near the lines, and it was impossible to move supplies. Very soon after the firing began our colonel was killed, and most of our other officers were killed or wounded, so that the greater part of that desperate battle was fought by the Ninth and Tenth Cavalry without officers; or at least, if there were any officers around, we neither saw them nor heard their commands. The last command we heard our captain give was: 'Boys, when you hear me whistle lie down flat on the ground.' Whether he ever whistled or not, I don't know. The next move we made was when, with a terrific yell, we charged up to the Spanish trenches and were bayoneting and clubbing them in their faces. Some of the men in one of the colored regiments say the last command they heard was, 'To the rear!' but this command they entirely disregarded, and charged to the front until the day was won, and the Spanish—those who were not left dead in the trenches—fled back to the city. At San Juan, it was I who had the pleasure of helping to take some of those blockhouses you have heard so much talk about, and I had the privilege of hauling down the Spanish flag, and planting the Stars and Stripes in its place. The sides of the blockhouse gave absolutely no place for a foothold or anything to catch hold of with the hands. So one member of the Seventy-first New York placed his old Springfield rifle on the ground, and by placing my foot on the hammer, I climbed upon it and was pushed up on the stock to the roof of the house. After I had hauled down the Spanish flag, and was just about to plant the Stars and Stripes, a bullet came whizzing in my direction, cutting a hole through my hat and burning my head slightly; that's what I call a close shave.

"In the charge before San Juan my twin brother, who was fighting at my side, was wounded and I could stop only long enough to drag him off the firing line. I returned to the fight, and in a few moments a shell burst directly in our midst, and a portion of it broke two of my ribs. Our men didn't care at all about the small shot, but they feared the shells from the large Spanish guns, and there was often a lively struggle among us as to the proprietorship of a particular tree to which several of us would flee at once for refuge.

"We were greatly worried by the sharpshooters. In going toward the front, I noticed at one point that several of our men and officers were shot, and no one seemed to be able to locate the shooter. I concluded that I had better not go around that way, so I turned in another direction, and as I went near an old tree I noticed that the dirt had been washed from around its roots, and happening to look under it, I spied a Spanish sharpshooter, the one who had been picking our men off. I slipped up behind him, whacked him in the neck, and broke it; our men were no longer molested in that locality."

Another told of how he picked off a sharpshooter who was hidden in a tall cocoanut tree. "They had been getting our officers in great shape, and we couldn't for the life of us locate the man or men who were doing it. Finally, bang! came a bullet which struck one of my comrades near me. I decided it was now about time to look after that Spaniard; so I kept a sharp lookout, and all at once saw part of a head peeping from behind a bunch of cocoanuts, drew a bead on it, and instantly a Spaniard tumbled out of that tree. As a memento of the occasion, I hold in my hand a watch with an iron case and a brass chain, which I took from this man who had played such havoc among our men."

Another of the speakers, after giving other reminiscences, said:

"A foreign officer standing near our position, when we started out to make that charge, was heard to say: 'Men, for Heaven's sake don't go up that hill; it is impossible for human beings to take that position, and you can't stand the fire.' Notwithstanding this, with a terrific yell, we rushed up to the enemy's works, and you know the result. Men who were near said that when this officer saw us make the charge, he turned his back on us and wept."

"Camp A. G. Forse,
"HUNTSVILLE, Ala., December 1, 1898.
"The Adjutant-General United States Army, Washington, D. C.
"Through Military Channels.
"SIR: I have the honor to submit the following report of the part taken by Troop D, Tenth Cavalry, in the engagement before Santiago de Cuba, so far as it is known to me.

"On the 30th of June the troop marched with the second squadron of the Tenth Cavalry, Major Wint's, from Sevilla, and encamped a few hundred yards beyond El Pozo on an eminence overlooking the basin of the San Juan River, or creek. My troop served as support to Lieutenant Smith's, which was on picket about one hundred yards to its front. In the morning it was placed on picket, relieving Lieutenant Smith's troop. Soon after my sentinels were posted I was ordered to withdraw my troop and prepare to march. Having done so, I took my place with my troop in the column, and after waiting from half an hour to an hour for the column to move, marched past El Pozo and the Division Hospital in the direction of San Juan. The military balloon passed over our regiment from rear to front while we were at a halt. At a halt made soon afterward I was ordered to have my men strip themselves of everything but arms and ammunition. The rolls, haversacks, and canteens of my men were taken off and laid on the ground near the road, and two men detailed to remain with them as a guard.

"About this time our balloon commenced coming down near the head of our regiment. When about one hundred feet from the ground it was fired at by the enemy's artillery. About the same time we received a volley of infantry fire coming down the road over our heads, too high to strike any one. The troop ahead of mine started to the rear, but was soon checked. I understand that the impulse to break to the rear was imparted to it by the Seventy-first New York. My men were lying down in the road facing to the left by order of the squadron commander, Major Wint. The enemy's fire, delivered in volleys, kept raking the road and riddling the dense foliage about us. I thought that the enemy had the range of our position, or at least the direction of this road, and that the situation demanded that the troops be moved off the road either to the right or left; or formed so as to face in the direction from which the fire was coming. I looked around for the squadron commander to get his permission to move my troop off the road, or make a change of front with it to the right. He was not anywhere in sight. I had seen him some time before going toward the right of our line or head of our column. After waiting some time for him to return, I acted on my own responsibility by bringing my troop around at right angle to the road; its right resting on the road, its left lying in the wood. In this position I was free from the troop on my right, in case it should again break to the rear. I was under the impression that we were much nearer the enemy than afterward proved to be the case, and expected the regiment to deploy across the road at any minute.

"From my studying of tactics and the drill regulations, together with my limited experience in field exercises, I knew that in dismounted fighting, especially in a densely wooded country, the time comes when the direction of operations is necessarily left to the company commanders, and I judged that this time had come or could not be far off. I did not know but that the squadron commander was disabled, and I was determined that my men should not be decimated without doing any execution, through fear of responsibility or lack of initiative on my part. I felt that I would be erring on the right side to anticipate slightly the proper time for independent action on the part of company commanders. After waiting a minute or two in my new position, the enemy's fire not abating, and no superior officer appearing, I faced my troop to the left, and pushed into the wood far enough to clear the road by about ten or twenty yards with the rear of my column, when I came upon a line of infantry skirmishers apparently without officers. I had my troop face to the right or in the general direction in which the road ran, and prepared to advance.

"In anticipation of the difficulty of penetrating the dense undergrowth, I took immediate charge of one platoon, and gave my lieutenant, Second Lieutenant J. F. Kennington, Tenth Cavalry, charge of the other with instructions to keep his platoon in touch with mine. I then proceeded to advance in a direction generally parallel to the road which I had just left. I expected that by the time I arrived abreast of the head of my regiment I would find it deployed or deploying. Under the enemy's unaimed fire we pushed through the dense wood and undergrowth, waded a creek about knee deep and a short distance beyond it came upon a line of troops lying in a road; but it was not our regiment. Here I received word from my lieutenant that he, with his platoon, was some distance to my right. He inquired whether he should join me. As there was a heavy fire coming down the road, and I did not wish him to expose his men unnecessarily, I answered in the negative. The bearer of the message to and from me was Sergeant George Dyals, of my troop, who was afterward wounded so that he lost the sight of one eye. He has since been discharged for physical disability.

"The wood terminated in a thin belt just beyond this road. After lying a few minutes in the road I proceeded with my platoon through this belt of wood and came upon open ground overgrown with tall grass reaching nearly to the waist. Here the enemy's fire seemed to come principally from our left. I accordingly faced my men to the left, and filed off in that direction. As a number of bullets dropped near us, Sergeant James Elliot of my troop came to me, and pointing to a tree on our right, said that he saw something stirring in it; that it looked like a Spaniard, and that he would like my permission to fire at it. I looked at the tree, but it was so dense that I could not see into it. I had been cautioned by troops whom I had passed against firing as there were troops of ours in front. Remarking that it might be a Cuban or one of our own men, I refused the permission.

"Soon afterward, while we were lying down, Private George Stovall, of my troop, was shot through the heart and killed; the same shot wounded Private Wade Bledsoe in the thigh. About one hundred yards farther on we came upon a squad of infantrymen sitting under some trees on the edge of the aforementioned belt of wood, around an officer who was lying on his back bleeding from the face, and who died while we were there. I believe that this officer and Privates Stovall and Bledsoe were shot by the sharpshooter whom Sergeant Elliot wanted to fire at.

"The infantrymen stated that our men were falling back and the Spaniards advancing. We could not see any enemy. On our left was a stream which I took to be the one which we had crossed. From the other side of it came the sound of voices and loud reports of firing. We could not tell whether they were Spanish or American, but I thought it was best to take our chances on their being American. We accordingly waded the stream and pushing into the wood on the opposite bank, found ourselves among the men of General Hawkins' brigade. They were lying in a road on the edge of the wood. Beyond them stretched a plain about six hundred yards wide, overgrown with tall grass like that through which we had just passed. At the further edge of the plain was a hill about one hundred and fifty feet high, now known to our troops as San Juan Hill, or a part of it. On the top of this hill was a blockhouse, and a structure that looked like a shed. Here and there a puff of light smoke indicated that the position was manned by infantry, who were firing at us. About one hundred yards in front of the line which I joined was a thin line of infantry firing at the enemy on the hill. It seemed to be falling back on the main line. There was no firing in the latter. My men and myself laid down in this road with the infantry.

"Everybody whom I could then see was lying down except one officer of infantry who was walking up and down the road in the rear of the line exposed to a fire which raked the road. From conversation with officers of the Sixteenth Infantry I understand that this was Captain George H. Palmer of that regiment. I asked him whether it was not about time to advance to the support of the line out in the plain which seemed to me to be falling back. He replied that he supposed it would be pretty soon, and kept on walking as before.

"Sergeant Elliot of my troop asked permission to go up to the fence and do some firing. I replied: 'Go ahead, sergeant, if you think that you can do any good.' He accordingly stood up by the fence and fired seven shots, when having attracted the enemy's fire, he fell back, and laid down.

"Immediately in front of us beyond the road ran a barbed wire fence. There were no wire nippers in my troop. With a view to an advance through this fence, I dug with my hands at one of the fence posts, but soon concluded that I could not accomplish anything in that way. I then stood up, and pulled and pushed at the post, but made no appreciable impression on it. So I lay down again and continued looking out on the plain for signs of an advance. After awhile I observed near the edge of the open plain on our left a swarm of men breaking forward from the road. I went up to the top of the wire fence by stepping from wire to wire near a post, and jumped off the top, calling to my men as I struck the ground to come on. Corporal John Walker of my troop got a bayonet, and cut the wire. My men and a number of infantrymen went through the opening thus made. I struck out as fast as the tall grass would permit me toward the common objective of the mass of men which I now saw surging forward on my right and left toward San Juan Hill. The men kept up a steady double time and commenced firing of their own accord over one another's heads and the heads of the officers who were well out in front of the men. I tried to stop the firing as I thought it would seriously retard the advance and other officers near me tried to stop it. But a constant stream of bullets went over our heads, the men halting in an erect position to fire. The men covered, I should say, about fifty yards from front to rear. They formed a swarm rather than a line. When they were not firing they seemed to be all cheering and yelling. Our firing, though wild, was not altogether ineffective and retarded the advance less than I had thought it would. I could see the side of the hill dotted with little clouds of dust thrown up by our bullets. We evidently peppered it pretty hotly from top to bottom, and I have learned since then that many dead and wounded Spaniards were found in the trenches on the top of the hills. These casualties, however, were caused in part, perhaps mostly, by the fire of our small advance line prior to the assault. This line was composed, I understand, mostly of classified marksmen and sharpshooters.

"As we approached the foot of the hill our artillery commenced firing over our heads at the enemy on top of it. This caused a slowing up of the general advance. When I was about halfway up the hill I was disabled by three bullet wounds received simultaneously. I had already received one but did not know it. What took place subsequent to my disablement, in the direction of the enemy, is known to me only through the statements of my men and others, substantiated by the depositions inclosed herewith. My platoon went to the top of the hill with the infantry, and was soon afterward conducted by Lieutenant J. J. Pershing, R. O. M. Tenth Cavalry to the line of the Tenth Cavalry, a short distance to the right.

"The following men of the platoon especially distinguished themselves: Sergeant James Elliot, Corporal John Walker, and Private (now corporal) Lucius Smith. Sergeant Elliot and Private Smith, were, during the ascent of the hill, constantly among the bolder few who voluntarily made themselves ground scouts, drawing the attention of the enemy from the main line upon themselves. Corporal Walker was with the handful of fearless spirits who accompanied Lieutenant J. G. Ord of the Sixth United States Infantry, forming with that splendid young soldier, the point of General Hawkins' gallant brigade, the head and front of the assault, and it was Corporal Walker who avenged the death of Lieutenant Ord. I recommend Sergeant James Elliot and Corporal Lucius Smith for certificates of merit, and Corporal John Walker for a medal of honor.

"First Sergeant William H. Givens was with the

platoon which I commanded. Whenever I observed him he was at his post exercising a steadying or encouraging influence upon the men and conducting himself like the thorough soldier which I have long known him to be. I understand to my great satisfaction that he has been rewarded by an appointment to a lieutenancy in an immune regiment.

"I think it due to the other men of my troop to say that with one exception they proved themselves ready to follow me wherever I would lead them. Their conduct made me prouder than ever of being an officer in the American army and of wearing the insignia of the Tenth United States Cavalry.

"The movements of the platoon commanded by Lieutenant Kennington have, I believe, been reported to you by that officer.

"I took into action, including Lieutenant Kennington's platoon, but not including the two men left to guard the packs, two officers and forty-eight men. My losses were as follows:

"Killed, Private George Stovall; wounded, Captain John Bigelow, Jr., Sergeant George Dyals, Sergeant Willis Hatcher, Private J. H. Campbell, Private Henry Fearn, Private Fred Shockley, Private Harry Shurgis, Private James F. Taylor; missing, Private James Clay.

"The accompanying map is intended to show roughly the courses taken by my troop after it left the regiment and the general direction of the attack made by the regiment.   Very respectfully,
  (Signed) "JOHN BIGELOW, JR.,
"Captain Tenth Cavalry, Commanding Troop D."

As throwing light on the death of Lieutenant Ord and as revealing his avenger, we invite attention to the subjoined affidavit by Corporal John Walker, of Troop D, Tenth United States Cavalry:

State of Alabama, }
County of Madison. } ss.

"PERSONALLY appeared before me the undersigned, John Walker, corporal, Troop D, Tenth Cavalry, who being duly sworn according to law, deposes and says, that on July 1, 1898, he was engaged in the assault on San Juan Hill at a point where there was a blockhouse, a shed, and a line of intrenchments; that just before the foremost assailants reached the foot of the hill our artillery commenced firing over the assailants at the enemy on the top of the hill; that when the deponent was about halfway up the hill, the only persons near him except an officer who was disabled, were Lieutenant Ord of the Sixth United States Infantry, and Private (now corporal) Lucius Smith, Troop D, Tenth Cavalry; that the main line was about fifty yards in rear of this party with a light scattering of men between it and this party; that the said Lieutenant Ord, evidently observing that our artillery fire had caused a slowing up in the main line, called out in a loud tone, looking toward the main line and waving his hat: 'Come on, men, we've got them on the go,' having repeatedly before urged the men on with voice and gesture: that the deponent reached the intrenchments about fifty yards in advance of the main line; that the only persons near him at the time were the said Lieutenant Ord, a private of the Sixth United States Infantry and a private of the Sixteenth United States Infantry; that about twenty yards to his left and about on a line with him was the said Lucius Smith; that about twenty-five yards in the rear of the deponent was a scattering of other soldiers, foremost among whom was Sergeant James Elliot, Troop D, Tenth Cavalry; that the deponent found two Spaniards alive and a number dead and wounded in the intrenchments; that the two former threw up their hands and surrendered; that the deponent took from one of them a pearl-handled pistol, and gave it to the said Lieutenant Ord; that the Lieutenant said: 'Let us go to the blockhouse, and capture these men in it;' that having gone about four yards in the direction of the blockhouse, the lieutenant stopped behind a tree and leaning to one side, looked in the direction of the retreating enemy: that as he did so he was shot with a pistol directly under the chin by a Spaniard on the other side of the tree; that as he fell at the cor-

poral's feet he said: 'If we had the rest of the Tenth Cavalry here, we could capture this whole command;' that the lieutenant died about five minutes afterward, or about ten minutes after he was shot; that the man who shot him ran off: that the deponent fired at him twice, and saw him fall: that he and the aforementioned private of the Sixteenth United States Infantry examined the man who had shot Lieutenant Ord immediately after the corporal had fired at him, and found that he was shot through the body twice, both shots going through the small of the back. That he was apparently dead: and that he, the deponent, is firmly convinced that the man in question was killed by him the deponent. Further deponent sayeth not.
  (Signed)   "JOHN WALKER,
                 "Corporal Troop D, Tenth Cavalry.

"Sworn to and subscribed, before me at Camp A. G. Forse, Huntsville, Alabama, this — day of December, 1898.   S. D. FREEMAN,
         "First Lieutenant, Tenth Cavalry,
      "Judge-Advocate, General Court Martial."

CHAPTER XII.

TENTH CAVALRY OFFICERS' REPORT.

Daring Expedition of Lieutenant Carter P. Johnson, Carrying Supplies to General Maximo Gomez's Army—Words of Praise from President William McKinley—Commissioned and Non-Commissioned Officers Make Reports—Statements Made for this Work Only—Strong Arguments Offered for the Negro Troops—Captains and Lieutenants Pleased with Results. The Close of Hostilities—Blanco's Cunning Letter—General Maximo Gomez Replies.

"During the Spanish-American war, Troop M, Tenth Cavalry, left Port Tampa on the steamer Florida, June 20th, under the command of First Lieutenant Carter P. Johnson, of Troop H, Tenth United States Cavalry, with supplies for General Gomez's army. Besides ammunition, rations, and rifles there were five companies of Cuban soldiers on board under the command of General Nunez, who was accompanied by his staff. These Cubans called themselves American citizens. Our expedition consisted of three vessels—two transports and one gunboat. We were out thirteen days before we sighted land. The sea was perfectly smooth and the tropical heat very intense. We had to give special attention to our horses; for they were situated near the boiler room where the heat was so very great that it was almost unbearable. Our horses got along very well. Our losses were very small considering the condition of the weather.

"Our first combat with the Spanish was on the 30th of June, when we tried to effect a landing in the southeast corner of Santa Clara Province. We were told by the Cuban general on board of our transport that General Maximo Gomez would meet us at this point.

"On the 25th of July, the Cubans on board of our transports attempted to land, but were met by a volley of mauser bullets from the Spanish forces. At this point we had to fight, and General M. Gomez, who saw the effort we put forth, said that he had never witnessed greater bravery than was exhibited by our men. Troop M gained a reputation that each member should well be proud of. The commander-in-chief of the Cuban army, General Gonzellas, said of the troop when he was approached after the battle in regard to Negro generals: 'If you will be as brave in the future to your country as you have proved yourself to-day it will not be very long before you will have generals in the army of the United States.' Just after we had landed and marched to the place pointed out for our camp, we found dead bodies of Cubans and Spanish soldiers in every direction. We camped in a cocoanut grove. The land was in an awful condition. Buzzards were seen in every direction and if you wanted to locate a Cuban camp all you had to do would be look out for a large number of buzzards.

"In some of the camps, or forts taken by us from the Spanish forces we found an abundance of provision. A great number of cattle and chickens had been penned up for future use. The sights seen in the forts and on the battlefields were awful in their many grim aspects, and Troop M may never witness such sights again. Dead Cubans and Spaniards could be seen lying in an exposed condition, and the buzzards would feast upon them. At the mouth of the Rio de Sasa River we encountered the bitter opposition of the enemy, and thence on until our victory was won.

"SERGEANT JAMES B. JELKAS,
"Troop M."

The following letter will explain itself:

"Executive Mansion,
"WASHINGTON, December 8, 1898.
"MY DEAR SIR: Your letter of recent date has been received and the contents carefully noted.

"The president greatly regrets that owing to the pressure of important matters upon his time he is unable to make a personal response to many similar requests.

"I take pleasure in sending you, however, the following quotation from the president's speech at Springfield, Illinois, October 15, 1898:

" 'I am glad to be at the home of the martyred president. . . . He liberated a race—a race which he once said ought to be free because there might come a time when these black men could help keep the jewel of liberty in the family of nations. If any vindication of that act or of that prophecy were needed, it was found when these brave black men ascended the hill of San Juan, Cuba, and charged the enemy at El Caney. They vindicated their own title to liberty on that field, and with other brave soldiers gave the priceless gift of liberty to another suffering race.'

"Believing that the above quotation will fully answer your purpose, I am,
"Very truly yours,   J. A. PORTER,
"Secretary to the President.
"REV. WILLIAM T. ANDERSON,
"Chaplain Tenth U. S. Cavalry,
"Huntsville, Ala."

"Troop G, Tenth Cavalry,
"CAMP ALBERT G. FORSE, Ala., Nov. 30, 1898.
"The Adjutant General, Fourth Army Corps.
"SIR: In compliance with the request of Major-General Joseph Wheeler, I have the honor to submit the following report of the action of this troop from the morning of July 1st until 1 P.M. of the same day. The troop was drawn from outpost duty about 6:30 A.M. July 1st, and about 9 A.M. moved from El Pozo down the road toward the Spanish position. While in the road they were passed by a balloon which shortly afterward drew a heavy fire from the Spaniards. A short distance from the point where the road crosses the river we were halted and ordered to lie down, and remained in that place until orders were brought to move to the

right into the bed of the river. This we accomplished with some delay owing to a strong fence of barbed wire through the undergrowth along the river. After reforming in the river bed we moved up stream a few hundred yards and took such shelter as was afforded by the river bank. The fire at this time was very heavy, projectiles from both artillery and small arms falling around and among the troops.

"At about 12:30 P.M. the troop moved up the bed of a small creek that flowed in from our right and by direction of Major Wint came into an open space in sight of, and facing, what I have since heard called the Sugar House ridge. Here the troop was deployed and just as the first advance was ordered I received a wound through the body that prevented my advancing with the troops. When I last saw them they were advancing in good order at the double time toward the two blockhouses in our front. The conduct of the men was good, and I saw no inclination to hesitate or to straggle. I desire to especially mention the conduct of Private William J. Davis, and Trumpeter James Cooper, of this troop, who assisted me from the spot where I fell back to the river under a very sharp fire, and rendered much assistance in trying circumstances both to myself and to Acting Assistant Surgeon Delgado, into whose hospital I was taken, and which was soon to be broken up on account of its becoming too much exposed to the enemy's fire. The conduct of these two men, in my opinion, entitles them to the medal of honor for rescuing the wounded at the risk of their own lives. Referring to the report of Major T. J. Wint, Tenth Cavalry, I have the honor to state that the trumpeter of Troop G, to whom he alludes, is Zachariah Steward, whose conduct I have heard highly spoken of. I regret that I am not able to give a more complete and definite account of this action, but I did not get far enough before being wounded to get a very clear idea of our position with reference to other troops or to the Spanish works.

"Very respectfully,

(Signed) "T. A. ROBERTS,
"Second Lieutenant Tenth Cavalry,
"Commanding Troop G."

"Camp Albert G. Forse, Ala.,
"December 3, 1898.

"I certify on honor that after the fight at Las Guasimas, Cuba, on June 24, 1898, Lieutenant Robert J. Fleming, Tenth Cavalry, spoke to me in very high terms of the conduct of First Sergeant John Buck, of my troop, who on that day had command of the greater part of the troop during the advance on the Spanish fortified position, Lieutenant Fleming stating that he witnessed the fine conduct of Sergeant Buck, who was pushing his men to the front with great coolness, gallantry and intelligence, calling to them by name and telling them what to do, holding his men well in control and in other ways making himself noticeable and conspicuous for his coolness and gallantry under a hot fire.

"Others whose names I cannot now remember spoke to me to the same effect in regard to the gallant conduct of Sergeant Buck. I have written to Lieutenant Fleming for a certificate from himself as to the foregoing, but have not received an answer from him yet. I was on detached service from my troop at the time with some hotchkiss mountain guns and was not therefore an eyewitness of the facts related.

(Signed) "J. W. Watson,
"Captain Tenth Cavalry,
"Commanding Troop B."

"Camp Albert G. Forse,
"Huntsville, Ala., December 4, 1898.

"Personally appeared before me, the undersigned, Judge-Advocate of a General Court Martial Sergeant James W. Ford, Troop B, Tenth Cavalry, who, being duly sworn according to law, deposes and says 'I was present on duty with the attacking line of Troop B, Tenth Cavalry in the battle of Las Guasimas, Cuba, on June 24, 1898, when it attacked the Spanish fortified position. Private Arthur G. Wheeler, Troop B, Tenth Cavalry, while advancing on the enemy by crawling through the jungle was hit by a bullet which passed through the fleshy part of the calf of his right leg. Although the wound got to be very painful and I told him he had better go back to the hospital at the rear, he still

persisted in going on and continued in the advance toward the Spanish position until the enemy fled.
 (Signed) "JAMES W. FORD,
 "Sergeant Troop B, Tenth Cavalry.

"Sworn to and subscribed before me this 4th day of December, 1898.
 (Signed) "S. D. FREEMAN,
 "Judge-Advocate, General Court-Martial."

"Camp Albert G. Forse,
 "HUNTSVILLE, Ala., December 4, 1898.
"Personally appeared before me, the undersigned, Judge-Advocate of a General Court-Martial, Sergeant William Bell, Troop B, Tenth Cavalry, who being duly sworn according to law, deposes and says:

" 'I was present with the attacking line of Troop B, Tenth Cavalry, at the battle of Las Guasimas, Cuba, on June 24, 1898, and saw Private Arthur G. Wheeler, same troop, keeping up with the advance for several hundred yards and until near the Spanish fortified position, when the Spanish retreated; and this under a hot fire and notwithstanding the fact that Private Wheeler had received two wounds in his right leg—one in the thigh and one in the calf.'
 (Signed) "WILLIAM BELL,
 "Sergeant Troop B, Tenth Cavalry.

"Sworn to and subscribed before me this 4th day of December, 1898.
 (Signed) "S. D. FREEMAN,
 "First Lieutenant, Tenth Cavalry,
 "Judge-Advocate, General Court-Martial."

"Camp Albert G. Forse,
 "HUNTSVILLE, Ala., December 4, 1898.
"Personally appeared before me, the undersigned, Judge-Advocate, General Court-Martial, Sergeant James W. Ford, Troop B, Tenth Cavalry, who being duly sworn according to law deposes and says:

" 'I was present with the attacking line of Troop B, Tenth Cavalry when it advanced on the Spanish fortified position at the battle of Las Guasimas, Cuba, on

June 24, 1898. I noticed Private William M. Bunn, Troop B, Tenth Cavalry, during the advance, whose conduct was conspicuous for coolness and gallantry, shown by the deliberate manner in which he kept firing at a Spaniard up in a tree, although the bullets were falling thick around us at the time. After one of Private Bunn's shots I saw the Spaniard fall out of the tree and I feel sure that Private Bunn killed him.'
(Signed) "JAMES W. FORD,
"Sergeant Troop B, Tenth Cavalry.

"Sworn to and subscribed before me, this 4th day of December, 1898.
(Signed) "S. D. FREEMAN,
"First Lieutenant, Tenth Cavalry,
"Judge-Advocate, General Court-Martial."

"Camp Albert G. Forse,
"HUNTSVILLE, Ala., December 4, 1898.
"Personally appeared before me, the undersigned, Judge-Advocate, General Court-Martial, Private Marion W. Murphy, Troop B, Tenth Cavalry; who being duly sworn deposes and says:
" 'I was present with the attacking line of Troop B, Tenth Cavalry when it advanced on the Spanish fortified position at the battle of La Guasimas, Cuba, on June 24, 1898. I noticed Private William M. Bunn, Troop B, Tenth Cavalry, during the advance, whose, conduct was conspicuous for coolness and gallantry in the cool and deliberate manner in which he kept firing at a Spaniard up in a tree, although the bullets were falling thick around us at the time. After one of Private Bunn's shots I saw the Spaniard fall out of the tree and I feel sure that Private Bunn killed him.'
(Signed) "MARION W. MURPHY,
"Private Troop B, Tenth Cavalry.

"Sworn to and subscribed before me, this 4th day of December, 1898.
(Signed) "S. W. FREEMAN,
"First Lieutenant Tenth Cavalry,
"Judge-Advocate, General Court-Martial."

"Camp Albert G. Forse, HUNTSVILLE, Ala.

"Troop I belonged to the first squadron of the Tenth Cavalry, commanded by Major Norvall, Tenth Cavalry.

"The troop landed at Daiquiri the afternoon of the 22d of June, and camped that night at that place, remaining there until 5 P.M. of the afternoon of the 23d. The troop then marched out about two miles and joined the other three troops of the squadron. After a short rest the troop (with the squadron) proceeded on the road to Siboney.

"We camped along the road in a downpour of rain, at about 10 P.M. We broke camp in the morning about 3:30 and proceeded to Siboney, arriving there about 7 A.M. There we took the road to the right and proceeded on the road to Santiago. At about 8:10 A.M. we reached Las Guasimas where the Spaniards opened fire on us. The First Cavalry went into action first, followed by Troop A of the Tenth Cavalry, which connected the First and Tenth Regular Cavalry with the First Volunteer Cavalry.

"Troops B and I of the Tenth Cavalry were ordered to support the four troops of the First Cavalry in front.

"The troop advanced out into the open, directly in rear of that regiment and while crossing the open space, not more than twenty yards wide, three of the men were wounded.

"The troop then advanced, turned to the right of the road until well into the woods, when it turned to the front and advanced up the hill.

"Our position was then to the right of the right troop of the First Cavalry and slightly in rear. This position was maintained during the entire ascent.

"We were constantly under fire while crossing the open spaces, but after commencing the ascent of the steep part of the hill, we were concealed by the very thick growth of underbrush. These were so thick in places that we found it necessary to cut a path with knives. Notwithstanding the fact that no one knew the number of the enemy or the strength of his position, every man pressed forward eagerly and was among the first to enter the Spanish works at the top of the hill, a detachment of Troop K of the First Cavalry being only a few yards ahead.

"The troop advanced beyond the Spanish position until it reached the extreme edge of the ridge, where it was halted. The troop commander was here ordered by Colonel Wood, of the First Volunteer Cavalry, to throw out outposts, which was done. The hill was captured about 10:30. We remained on guard until about 3 P.M. when we were relieved and marched back to camp. The wounded were Privates Mayheny, Redd, and Wesley Jones. The entire troop behaved with great gallantry and all equally distinguished themselves. The troop commander especially noticed the gallantry and coolness under fire of the following men·

"Farrier Sherman Harris, Wagoner John Boland, Private Elsie Jones. The men were named in the report as deserving of special mention.

"We remained in camp until the morning of the 26th of June, when the entire regiment moved out on the road to Santiago. We marched about three miles and went into camp alongside the road. We remained here until the afternoon of the 29th, when we marched to El Pozo and took position in the rear of Battery A, Second Artillery, where we remained all night. At about 7:55 A.M. the battery opened on the Spanish position at San Juan. The troop remained here until about 9:30 A.M. when we retraced our steps until we reached the road to San Juan. Marched about a mile, and while halted, a volley from the Spaniards wounded two men, Privates Berkley and Wesley Jones.

"The packs carried by the men were here taken off and left near the road under guard. The troop was then marched to the fight, until we reached the creek, when we again turned to the right and marched down the creek bed in the water about thirty yards. Here we halted and lay down on the bank for probably twenty minutes.

"During this time we were in almost direct line of fire of the enemy, who were firing at the balloon over our heads. Luckily nobody was hit, although shrapnel were exploding all around us. The troop was then marched forward through a wire fence and deployed in open order in rear of A and B troops, of the first squadron. We advanced about twenty yards at a time, always under a heavy fire, until we reached the San Juan River. Troops A and B after crossing marched to their left front. Troop I marched to the right front until it reached the road, down which it marched until opposite Kettle Hill.

"We then crossed through wire fences and passed over to the hill, and we remained here about ten minutes, exchanging volleys with the enemy. We then advanced on the run toward the enemy's works, passed the pond to the right and reached the top of the hill at a trench, midway between the two blockhouses. In this charge, as far as observed, were men of the First and Tenth Regular Cavalry and the First Volunteer Cavalry. The Spaniards abandoned their position when we had arrived within three hundred yards of them. The troop commander at this time was the senior officer at this part of the hill and had under his command men of the three above-mentioned regiments. We remained here for about twenty minutes exchanging volleys with the enemy in the trenches immediately in front of the city.

"Troop I then moved forward up the plateau in the direction of the city until we reached the extreme forward crest. We remained here for about three-quarters of an hour, being joined by Troop C under command of Lieutenant Anderson and other men of the Tenth and men from the First Regular and First Volunteer Cavalry. This position was about eight hundred yards from the Spaniards and had very little cover. We here exchanged volleys with the enemy, and several men were wounded. This position was the most advanced of any part of the army that day. Word was brought forward that a line was being formed in the rear. We retired until we reached the line, where intrenchments were afterward dug and we formed on the left of Colonel Roosevelt's command, with Troop C, under Lieutenant Anderson.

"During the night of the 1st dug intrenchments on our part of the line. Ten men of the troop occupied them next day until 3 P.M. The remainder lying down a short distance in rear. At that time the men in trenches were relieved by ten others and the remainder of the troop joined Colonel Roosevelt's command at the bottom of the hill. During the next attack on July 2d Troop I was ordered to form the reserve of the First Volunteer Cavalry and formed on the crest of the hill in rear of that regiment's position. The troop remained with the First Volunteer Cavalry until the afternoon of the 3d of July, when we were ordered to join the regiment, which we did, reporting at 3:30 P.M. The troop then took its share of digging and guarding trenches until the surrender.

"The wounded in this engagement were: First Sergeant Millbrown, Sergeant Gunter, Private Berkely, Private Hardy, Private W. Jones, Private Bennett, Private Riddell, Private Chinn.

"None were killed. The troop commander claims for Troop I especial credit for two things: First being among the first body of men to reach the blockhouse on the right and the trench midway between the two blockhouses Second, reaching and maintaining under heavy fire the most advanced position gained by our army on the 1st of July.

"The entire troop behaved with great gallantry, and when such is the case, it is hard to pick out any particular man as deserving a special mention. First Sergeant Millbrown, Sergeant Dunton, Corporal Reed, Corporal Smith, Trumpeter Oden, Wagoner Boland, Farrier Harris and Privates Hardy, Piersaul, Humphreys and Elsie Jones, were especially noticed by the troop commander for their conspicuous gallantry and coolness. The troop commander takes pleasure in certifying to the coolness and gallant conduct of Second Lieutenant A. M. Miller, Jr., Tenth Cavalry, who was with the troop in both engagements. This officer was especially distinguished for his coolness and gallant conduct. There were many brave men who fought in the battles around Santiago and much honor was gained, but none were braver, or gained more honor than Second Lieutenant A. M. Miller, Jr., of the Tenth Cavalry.

(Signed) "First Lieutenant ROBERT J. FLEMING,
"Tenth Cavalry Commanding,
"Second Lieutenant A. M. MILLER, JR."

"Camp Albert G. Forse,
"HUNTSVILLE, Ala., December 5, 1898.
"Adjutant, Tenth Cavalry,

"SIR: In compliance with indorsements of the 17th of November, in letter of 14th of November from adjutant-general's office to commanding officer Tenth Cavalry, I have the honor to submit the following recommendations:

"For conspicuous gallantry and daring in advancing two hundred yards beyond where the main attacking line stopped in the assault on San Juan Hill, Cuba, July 1, 1898, and assisting to hold this advanced position without cover and in the face of greatly superior numbers in fortified positions an hour or more until reinforcements had been ordered up:

"I recommend for medals of honor the following officers and non-commissioned officers (see certificate 'A'): First Lieutenant P. E. Traub, First Cavalry; First Lieutenant E. D. Anderson, Tenth Cavalry; Second Lieutenant, A. M. Miller, Tenth Cavalry; Sergeants Bailey, Ford, Holliday and Bell, Troop B, Tenth Cavalry.

"For the conspicuous gallantry and cool self-possession with which he advanced his men under a hot fire to the attack of the Spanish fortified position at the battle of Las Guasimas, Cuba, June 24, 1898, he being at the time in command of a greater part of his troop, I recommend for a medal of honor, First Sergeant John Buck, Troop B, Tenth Cavalry (see certificates 'B' and 'C').

"For courage and pluck in continuing to advance under a hot fire on the Spanish fortified position at the battle of Las Guasimas, Cuba, June 24, 1898, after being shot through the thigh and calf of his right leg, I recommend for a medal of honor Private Arthur G. Wheeler, Troop B, Tenth Cavalry (see affidavits Nos. 1 and 2). The foregoing recommendations are made in accordance with my interpretation of General Orders No. 135, A. G. O., of September 3, 1898. After reading those orders over carefully, for bravery, coolness and steady marksmanship under a hot fire while advancing on the Spanish fortified position at the battle of Las

Guasimas, Cuba, June 24, 1898, I recommend for a certificate of merit Private William M. Bunn, Troop B, Tenth Cavalry, (see affidavits Nos. 3 and 4.)
"Very respectfully,
(Signed) "J. W WATSON,
"Com. Troop B, Tenth Cavalry."

"PHILADELPHIA, November 28, 1898.
"The Adjutant, Tenth Cavalry, Huntsville, Ala.

"In compliance with your request of the 22d inst. I have the honor to submit the following report of the action of Second Squadron, Tenth Cavalry, Troops C, D, F and G, on July 1, 1898, at San Juan Hill:

"The second squadron following the first, marched to near crossing of the creek at foot of hill, where, after a short halt packs were deposited and the marching continued to crossing and then up creek about seventy-five yards, where the troops were placed under the best shelter to be found, but which was not sufficient to prevent quite a heavy loss from the enemy's fire, which opened immediately after the packs were deposited and which was quite heavy during the march, and for half an hour after taking a new position.

"Upon halting, I found one of my troops (Troop D) absent, and reported its absence to the regimental commander, who sent his staff officer and others to find it, but without success. At about 2 P.M. the second squadron was formed in support of first squadron and advanced in the direction of Sugar House ridge, between the two blockhouses, keeping a distance of twenty-five yards in rear of first squadron.

"After advancing a short distance, we came in view of troops to our right front at Sugar House, and on the left front troops were advancing on blockhouse. From this point a strip of thick woods continued to San Juan Hill with open ground to the right in the direction of Sugar House, with a slight ridge running from the house to near the woods.

"Finding vacant ground at the lower part of the ridge, near woods, the second squadron, three troops, took position there, connecting with other troops on its right and opened fire on the earthwork, located between the blockhouses, and on the blockhouse to the left of it, against which troops were advancing. For a time the enemy's fire was very heavy on our position, but our fire soon had effect; as the enemy's fire slackened, the squadron advanced without check to the crest of the San Juan Hill. Two of my troops, C and F, went to the right of a body of water in our front and Troop G passed through the left end of it, with myself. The troop commander, Lieutenant Smith, with Lieutenant Shipp, were killed at the last position. Troops C and F arrived on the hill to the right of the road and Troop G to the left of it at earthworks. I sent for C and F troops to join me on the left of the road, as there were no other troops at that point at that time, but before the order was complied with, other troops of the regiment came up and my two troops were ordered to remain to the right of the road.

"Captain Beck with his troop joined on my left and Captain Ayres with his troop joined about twenty minutes later from the direction of the woods to our left and rear. A few men of Troop D also came in line.

"He reported his arrival to Colonel Wood and was placed on line to left of road; later I was ordered by regimental commander to take charge of troops on that part of line and open fire, which continued about ten minutes, when firing ceased and line was withdrawn behind the crest of the hill, at which time I was wounded, about 5:45 P M., and taken to the rear. During the action up to this time the officers and men of the troops with me behaved in a manner to entitle them to the highest praise. Officers were cool and quick to carry out orders, and the men prompt and fearless in obeying. Captain Jones, Lieutenants Smith, Anderson Roberts and Whitehead came specially under my notice and conducted themselves in a most satisfactory manner. Lieutenant Pershing, R. O. M., was with second squadron when posted on Sugar House Hill, and during its advance on San Juan Hill he conducted himself in a most gallant and efficient manner.

"I would like to mention several enlisted men of Troop G for their coolness and daring, but am not sufficiently acquainted with them to state their names positively, and without reference to records. Among the number were the first sergeant, a trumpeter I believe White by name, two men who came to my assistance in dragging Lieutenant Smith from under fire, after he was hit and two men who dragged me from under fire after being wounded. The first sergeant was very active and efficient in commanding the troop after the death of Lieutenant Smith, and the trumpeter kept with me and was prompt in sounding calls as ordered. By inquiry, no doubt, all these men can be identified and proper credit given them.

"I remain, Very respectfully,
(Signed) "THEO. J. WINT,
"Major Tenth Cavalry."

The sergeant referred to by Major Wint is Sant Foster, since promoted to Second Lieutenant of the Tenth United States Volunteer Infantry for gallantry.

The trumpeter referred to is Zachariah Steward.

The men referred to who dragged Lieutenant W. H. Smith from under fire after he was killed was Corporal Charles E. Parker (only one man).

The two men who dragged Major Wint from under fire when he was wounded were Corporal Charles E. Parker and Corporal James M. Watkins.

All of the above named persons are of Troop G, Tenth Cavalry.

"During the campaign in Cuba, I remember well the morning of July 1, 1898. The Tenth Cavalry, under the command of Lieutenant-Colonel Baldwin, left El Pozo and marched toward the enemy in a narrow roadway.

"I carried the 'guidon' and was at the head of the column. Soon the command 'Halt, take off packs, forward, march!' was given. We had not gone very far before the command 'Halt!' was given again and at this point volley after volley came whizzing through the bushes. This was my first experience of warfare;

however, I stood as firm as a wall built of stone. Then the command was given to move by the right flank; we did so and crossed the San Juan River.

"Then we came in contact with the barbed wire fence. First Sergeant, Troop C, Tenth Cavalry, Adam Houston called for the noncommissioned officers. Sergeant Thomas Griffin, of the same troop, was the first one to rush forward and perform the noble duty of cutting the barbed wire and while doing this several men were killed and wounded. Our gallant major, Theodore J. Wint, gave the command: 'By the right flank, march!' This, I think, covered the left flank of our enemy. He then gave command, 'By the left flank march!' 'Halt!' 'Lie down!' He was then ready to make a charge. Major Wint got in the center of Troop C and gave the command, 'Rise, forward march, guide center!' and I was the guide during this time.

"The charge was made with brilliant success. I was without food or water and in the heat of the fight was lost from my troop and reported to the regimental adjutant July 1st. I found my troop on July 2d and was made acting first sergeant until July 27, 1898. I was on sick report one day during the campaign.

"WILLIAM ANCRUM,
"Sergeant Troop C, Tenth Cavalry."

"Camp Albert G. Forse,
"HUNTSVILLE, Ala., December, 1898.

"I certify on honor that while I was advancing in command of my troop before the Spanish fortified position at the battle of Las Guasimas, Cuba, on June 24, 1898, I witnessed the fine conduct of First Sergeant John Buck, Troop B, Tenth Cavalry, who was in command of the greater part of that troop, and who was pushing his men to the front with great coolness, gallantry and judgment, calling to them by name and telling them what to do, holding his men well in hand and in other ways making himself noticeable and conspicuous for his coolness and gallantry under a hot fire which was coming on this part of the attacking line.

(Signed) "R. J. FLEMING,
"First Lieutenant, Tenth Cavalry."

"There was much doubt as to whether this position could be held, and the Thirteenth Infantry was ordered up in support, but for an hour or more it was held by this small force without any backward movement whatever on their part.

"At this time there were no trenches here or any other cover whatever.

"This position was slightly in advance of the position which was afterward occupied on July 2d by the First Volunteer Cavalry on the left and the Tenth Cavalry on the right, and held *with trenches.*

"I certify on honor that the foregoing statement is correct and that I was present and an eyewitness of all related.

(Signed) "J. W. WATSON,
"Captain Tenth United States Cavalry,
"Commanding Troop B."

"CAMP ALBERT G. FORSE, Ala.
"December 3, 1898.

"In the assault on San Juan Hill in the battle of Santiago de Cuba, on July 1, 1898, the main attacking line stopped on the crest of this San Juan Hill after driving the Spaniards out of their intrenchments, which were at the crest of this hill.

"But there were some who did not stop at this crest but continued the advance for one hundred and fifty or two hundred yards to the front and toward the enemy. There were about fifty of these in all, of whom about ten were officers. The position occupied by this force in its further advance was about one hundred and fifty or two hundred yards nearly northwest from the right San Juan blockhouse. In this position they were exposed to the fire from a large Spanish trench seven hundred yards to their left front, from another Spanish trench five hundred yards to their right front, and from a small Spanish trench two hundred and fifty or three hundred yards directly in front of them.

"The position with reference to other parts of our advance line to the right and left of it was a salient jutting cape-like out into the Spanish lines.

"The officers here whom I knew at the time of advancing to and taking this position were: Colonel Roosevelt, Captain Charles Morton, Third Cavalry; Captains J. G. Gailbraith, First Cavalry; John F. McBlain, Ninth Cavalry; First Lieutenants P. E. Traub, First Cavalry; E. D. Anderson, Tenth Cavalry; Second Lieutenant A. M. Miller, Tenth Cavalry. All of these officers were performing their parts with the utmost coolness and gallantry. This advanced line was made up of small detachments from various troops and regiments. Among the men of my own troop present, Sergeants Bailey, Ford, Holliday and Bell, attracted my attention by their coolness and gallantry, all of them firing into the Spanish trench to the left front without any attempt to take advantage of cover although a galling fire which killed some of the line and wounded others, was coming from the trench on the right front.

"The position occupied by this small line of about fifty men in all was so exposed that it seems likely that if the enemy had opened fire on them from all three of their trenches referred to the force must have been annihilated unless they had retreated under the hill fifty yards or so to their rear. But the Spaniards with the exception of their right front trench, reserved their fire, apparently in expectation of a further assault."

Just before the beginning of our war with Spain Ramon Blanco, appreciating his certain downfall in case the American army should invade the Island of Cuba and open hostilities, wrote the following cunning letter to General Maximo Gomez, commander of the Cuban forces:

"General Maximo Gomez, Commander-in-Chief of the
    Revolutionary Forces·
  "SIR: It cannot be concealed from you that the Cuban problem has radically changed. We Spaniards and Cubans find ourselves facing a foreign people of different race, of a naturally absorbent tendency, and with intentions not only to deprive Spain of her flag over the

Cuban soil, but also to exterminate the Cuban people, due to its having Spanish blood.

"The supreme moment has, therefore, arrived in which we should forget our past misunderstandings, and in which, united by the interests of our own defense, we, Spaniards and Cubans, must repel the invader.

"General, due to these reasons, I propose to make alliance of both armies in the City of Santa Clara. The Cubans will receive the arms of the Spanish army, and with the cry of 'Viva España!' and 'Viva Cuba!' we shall repel the invader and free from a foreign yoke the descendants of the same people.

"Your obedient servant,
"RAMON BLANCO."

To this General Gomez replied as follows:

"SIR: I wonder how you dare to write me again about terms of peace when you know that Cubans and Spaniards can never be at peace on the soil of Cuba. You represent on this continent an old and discredited monarchy. We are fighting for an American principle, the same as that of Bolivar and Washington.

"You say we belong to the same race and invite me to fight against a foreign invader, but you are mistaken again, for there are no differences of race and blood. I only believe in *one race, mankind*, and for me there are but good and bad nations, Spain so far having been a bad one and the United States performing in these movements toward Cuba a duty of humanity and civilization.

"From the wild, tawny Indian to the refined, blonde Englishman, a man for me is worthy of respect according to his honesty and feelings, no matter to what country or race he belongs or what religion he professes.

"So are nations for me, and up to the present I have had only reasons for admiring the United States. I have written to President McKinley and General Miles thanking them for American intervention in Cuba. I don't see the danger of our extermination by the United States, to which you refer in your letter. If it be so, history will judge. For the present I have to repeat

that it is too late for any understanding between my army and yours. Your obedient servant,
"MAXIMO GOMEZ."

From whatever standpoint this sentiment may be viewed it is regarded by the liberal-minded as being the noblest that lives in the human breast. It is this that gives such spirits a place in history and the name of Gomez will live in the memory of generations to come on account of his expressions in this letter.

CHAPTER XIII.

THE CAMPAIGN OF SANTIAGO.

Lieutenant John J. Pershing Gives His View of the Great Campaign—What the Tenth Cavalry and other Negro Troops Accomplished.*

IN the successful conduct of our recent war America has again astonished the world. In four months she has raised and recruited an army of a quarter of a million men, assembled and drilled them in various camps, transported them to distant lands, and, without one single reverse either on land or sea, has victoriously wrested from tyranny and misrule the island possessions of the proudest monarchy of Europe. Conceived and born amid revolution and by tradition the friend of the oppressed, she has stretched out her hand across the ocean to extend to ten millions of human souls the blessings of our own civil and religious liberties.

Fathers and mothers experienced a new sensation and made a new sacrifice when their sons, in response to the call of the president for volunteers, came to them

---

* Lecture delivered by Lieutenant John J. Pershing, of the Tenth Cavalry, at the Hyde Park M. E. Church, Chicago, Illinois, on the occasion of a patriotic thanksgiving service Sunday, November 27, 1898. Lieutenant Pershing was quartermaster of the regiment and was with the headquarters continuously after landing and was acting regimental adjutant after the morning of July 2d, when Lieutenant Barnum, the adjutant, was wounded.

and obtained consent to go to war. They came thrilled by the same patriotism that inspired the heart of the volunteer in '61—the fathers, to extend freedom to a race of slaves at home; their sons, to carry it to a race of worse than slaves abroad.

At the beginning of the war with Spain our government found itself in a deplorably unprepared condition. The admonition of George Washington, 'in peace prepare for war,' had gone unheeded for a third of a century. Congress had turned a deaf ear to the importunities of our military commanders. The staff departments of the army were only large enough to meet the ordinary necessities in times of peace of an army of twenty-five thousand men. They had not transported, even by rail, for over thirty years, a larger command than a regiment. The organization was crude and individual responsibilities were not clearly outlined. These staff departments had then to be increased by the appointment of inexperienced officers, but the unwieldy organization of the staff corps still remained, and yet awaits the action of Congress. In the face of all this, every official, both civil and military, of staff and line, seemingly did his best to overcome these adverse conditions, and though of course mistakes were made, I should hesitate to attribute to any individual other than purest motives of patriotism. The work they undertook was enormous—arms, ammunition, commissaries, medical supplies, tentage, field transportation and all sorts of personal equipment had to be provided at once. Army officers, and all others understanding the difficulties of this great undertaking, under the conditions incident to an aggressive foreign war, can only be filled with wonder and admiration at the boundless resources of the nation. The wonder is it was done at all, the wonder is it was done so well.

That part of the war on land that was to be undertaken immediately was, of course, assigned to the regular army; regiments were assembled and recruited and officers absent on special service reported for duty. The point of embarkation for the first army of invasion was Port Tampa, Florida, and here we find twenty-four regiments of the regular army—in fact, the regular army entire, except the heavy artillery, some light artillery and such few infantry and cavalry regiments as were deemed necessary to garrison the most exposed frontier posts, or were held for other duty. Assembled here, also, were three volunteer regiments—Roosevelt's Rough Riders, the Seventy-first New York and the Second Massachusetts, that had been selected to accompany the expedition to Santiago, or wherever it should be finally decided to send it. There was some delay in the embarkation, due to various causes, one of which was the inexperience of officers in transporting troops by water, and as a result of this inexperience and a lack of proper assignment and dependence upon officers so assigned, property and rations were loaded with but little system. Another cause of delay was the uncertainty as to whether or not the Spanish fleet was really confined in the harbor of Santiago. Certain it is that the transports were held in the harbor at Tampa for several days after they were ready to sail.

On the afternoon of June 14th the fleet steamed out under its naval escort, and a grander and more impressive sight the world has never seen. Fifty transports bearing an American army as splendid in the personnel of the officers and men of its line as ever invaded a foreign country; its officers and men trained in their profession; hardy from their years of frontier service; imbued with an eagerness for conflict born of patriotism and with á confidence in their strength inspired by a righteous cause—this army departed with that firm determination to win, which, in itself, heralded victory. Ship after ship took her place in column amid the cheers of officers and men and the music of regimental bands playing the uplifting strains of national airs, and many eyes dimmed with tears when good-by was waved to dear old America as we started on this voyage which should carry freedom to a down-trodden people and our flag to foreign lands.

Our transports were either combined passenger and freight or ordinary freight vessels hastily fitted up with stationary bunks, made of rough lumber and arranged in tiers, so that troops were really much crowded. In that southern climate the lower decks were very warm, but fortunately the weather was so pleasant that at all times, day or night, men could be permitted to remain on the upper decks.

On such a journey there is issued to enlisted men a travel ration, consisting of cooked corned beef in cans, canned tomatoes, hard bread, sugar and coffee, arrangements being usually made for cooking coffee about twice a day; on this journey fourteen days' rations were issued. The duties on shipboard consist of rollcalls at reveille and retreat, a daily inspection of arms and quarters, guard mounting daily, a general police of the ship and such physical exercise as the commanding officer may deem practicable.

The voyage from Tampa to Santiago was without particular incident, and except for the time occupied with the usual routine duties, officers and men had nothing to do except to lounge about the upper decks and cabins and smoke or sing, enjoying the new and changing scenes of southern waters or discussing the possibilities of the immediate future. There was among the officers a supreme confidence in our ultimate success. I remember also that it was the opinion among officers, and men as well, that one had better die fighting than to fall into Spanish hands a prisoner; and the Spaniards had the same idea of us. We also had rather a contempt for their fighting qualities, but our opinion on both these subjects changed before the campaign was over.

Arriving in the vicinity of Santiago, some time was spent in deciding where to attempt a landing—the selection from a strategical standpoint depending, of course, upon the plan of campaign. Two plans were proposed; one an attack from the west, which it was said would involve, with the assistance of the navy, the capture of the outer defenses of the harbor of Santiago, after which it was thought the city would be easily reduced from the heights to the south and those to the west across the bay. This plan it was said would require the use of heavy artillery at some stages of the advance; but the army was practically without siege artillery. It would have been difficult also to close the avenues of escape to the north and east. The other plan —the one which was adopted—ignored the existence of Morro Castle and the coast defenses, so far as a land attack was concerned, and contemplated an attack on the city from the rear—approaching from the east and north. This decided, a point of debarkation and one least likely to be occupied by the enemy in force was selected at Daiquiri, about thirteen miles east of Santiago.

There were no good maps of Cuba and very little was known of the coast or country, simply because of its occupation, for the last four hundred years, by an unprogressive race of Spaniards. The main source of information as to both the enemy and country was the Cuban insurgents, and the information we obtained was often inaccurate and unreliable—the most valuable information was obtained by reconnoisances conducted by our own officers.

At Daiquiri the navy prepared the way for landing by bombarding the town and outlying blockhouses and driving out the Spanish troops who, before leaving, set fire to the buildings of the town and the machine shops of the mines located there. There were no docks at Daiquiri except a small wooden affair, old and out of repair, the vessels could get no nearer than about three hundred yards from shore and then only in calm weather.

Before landing each officer and soldier was issued three days' field rations of raw bacon, hard-tack and coffee. The regiments selected to make the landing were loaded in the small boats from the naval vessels of the blockading squadron drawn by steam launches—each launch hauling four or five boats. The First Regular Infantry, General Shafter's old regiment, was given the honor of leading, and by wading some distance in the surf, it succeeded in making a landing under protection of the guns of the naval vessels, meeting with practically no opposition from shore.

Nothing was taken ashore with the troops except what they carried on their backs, but the load was so heavy that to fall overboard in deep water meant to drown, though from the entire army but two men were lost. This plan of debarkation was the only one possible and it was tedious and dangerous. Men had often to drop from ten to fifteen feet from the freight porthole to the boat below, which is a very difficult task in a rolling sea; and yet though dangerous it was enjoyed by all as a sport—the many minor mishaps, such as being thrown down by the high waves while wading to shore, bringing forth shouts and peals of laughter from the troops.

UNDER FIRE. 201

On the morning of June 23d, the Tenth Cavalry, colored, my own regiment, together with the First Cavalry and Roosevelt's Rough Riders, three regiments which formed the second brigade of the cavalry division, were sent ashore and moved out northwest passing through Siboney, which later became the place of debarkation, to a point beyond the most advanced outposts toward Santiago. These troops, though belonging to the cavalry, were dismounted and in marching through marsh and bog along the single sunken road, overhung with boughs and vines, clad as they were in heavy clothing, they soon began to feel the wilting effects of a tropical sun; but every man had resolved for the honor of his country to make the best of the situation as a soldier, and whether working, marching or fighting, all behaved as though the success of the campaign depended upon their own individual efforts. It is to this resolution, firmly lodged in the heart of every man, that success was largely due.

During the day information was obtained through insurgents as to the location of a body of Spanish troops in force some three miles beyond Siboney. General Wheeler, the brave old ex-Confederate leader, who commanded our cavalry division, decided to attack this force on the following morning with the three regiments I have mentioned. It is at this battle that the Rough Riders are said to have been ambushed. This is not literally correct, for the battle had been planned the night before and the attack was made practically as planned; but in their commendable eagerness to get forward, the main body of the Rough Riders absorbed the advance guard, except a small portion of the advance, which was allowed by the Spaniards to pass through the lines and return without being fired upon, so that the whole line of Rough Riders came against the enemy before the latter opened fire. There is a trail leading from Siboney along the ridge of hills near the coast which comes into the main road near the position occupied by the Spaniards, while the main road from Siboney inclines to the right and follows up the valley between this coast ridge and the mountain range farther inland. The part of the Spanish line attacked by the Rough Riders was at an angle across this trail, over which the Rough Riders moved, the right flank of this part of the Spanish line trending to the rear.

While the advance of the Rough Riders was in progress the First and Tenth Regiments were moving up the main road to the right, to the attack of the Spanish left, which lay across the main road at almost a right angle. These regular cavalry regiments attacked the Spanish left and drove them from their position in front and occupied it; the Tenth Cavalry having charged up the hill, scarcely firing a shot and being nearest the Rough Riders, opened a disastrous enfilading fire upon the Spanish right, thus relieving the Rough Riders from the volleys that were being poured into them from that part of the Spanish line. This is in brief the story of how the Tenth Cavalry relieved the Rough Riders at Las Guasimas.

During the next week following this battle, the whole army had debarked and brigades and regiments marched to the front along this narrow road, passing and repassing each other, jovially chaffing an old acquaintance here and there, camping in open places on the deserted plantations, among the thorns and cacti at the roadside, long enough to build a shelter of palm leaves and fix a dry place to sleep, only to leave it the next day. In the meantime transports were being unloaded with much difficulty owing to the absence of lighters. Horses and mules were simply thrown overboard by main force and towed ashore, if possible. Many got lose, became bewildered in the breakers, swam back to the transports or out to sea and were drowned. A scant supply of rations was issued daily, and the problem became more difficult as the army advanced and the rainy season came on. Whole companies of our troops were put to work to make the road passable for wagons. Two batteries of artillery came by and were lustily cheered by the soldiers who lined the road to witness the sight—a new one to many in the service. Everything indicated that preparations were being rapidly made for the coming battle; a package for "first aid to wounded" was issued to each officer and man.

On June 29th a part of General Garcia's army of some four thousand Cubans, which had been brought by transports from the west of Santiago, was marched to the front, but they rendered little assistance either in working or fighting and most of them fled at the first explosion of a Spanish shell over El Pozo Hill on July 1st. However, some excuse is theirs; ragged, some half-naked, barefooted, weary from hunger, laden with huge earthen water pots, heavy packs and cooking utensils slung over their backs, armed with every conceivable obsolete pattern of gun—it is no wonder that they dared not face the deadly mauser rifle; we, ourselves, had much less contempt for Spanish arms after we had met them face to face on the battlefield.

On June 30th the general order came to move forward, and every man felt that the final test of skill at arms would soon come. The cavalry division of six regiments, now under temporary command of General Sumner, camped in its tracks at midnight on El Pozo Hill, about three miles due east of Santiago, and awoke next morning to find itself in support of Grimes' battery which was to open fire here on the left, with the idea of diverting the enemy's attention from the main battle which was planned to be fought that day at El Caney.

The morning of July 1st was ideally beautiful; the sky was cloudless and the air soft and balmy; peace seemed to reign supreme; great, quiet palms towered here and there above the low jungle; it was an oriental picture of a peaceful valley; there was a feeling that we had secretly invaded the Holy Land; a hush seemed to pervade all nature as though she held her bated breath in anticipation of the carnage that should that day strew those foreign fields with soldiers slain, and redden with their blood the very waters of the coursing streams.

The command had been aroused before daybreak and the men now stood about in little groups, opposite their places in line, anxiously awaiting the opening gun. From the ridge of the hill we now occupied could be seen, half a mile beyond the river to the northwest, the dark lines of masked intrenchments and the mysterious blockhouses of the hills of San Juan. To the left of the first hill, holding a horse, stood one lone Spanish sentinel; farther to the west were plainly visible the successive tiers of the city's defenses, crowned at the top of the hill by the spires and towers of the apparently lifeless city of Santiago. Around to the northeast in the foothills, on an eminence overlooking all approaches, stood the stone fort and the smaller blockhouses surrounding the outpost El Caney.

As the sun's golden rays tinted the mountain tops and lighted the eastern horizon behind us, the stillness was broken—the suspense was over. Captain Capron's fieldguns had opened fire upon the stone fort at El Caney and the hills resounded with echoes; then followed the rattle of musketry of the attacking infantry; the battery in our front burst forth and the battle was on.

The artillery duel began and in company with foreign military *attachés* and correspondents, we all stood watching the effect of the shots as men witness any friendly athletic contest, eagerly trying to locate their smokeless batteries. A force of insurgents near the old Sugar Mill applauded at the explosion of each firing charge, apparently caring for little except the noise. The smoke hung heavily in front of our guns preventing the accuracy of our aim, but locating us all too plainly for the enemy's gunners. A slug of iron now and then fell among the surrounding bushes or buried itself deep in the ground near us. Finally a projectile from an unseen Spanish gun disabled a hotchkiss piece, wounded two cavalrymen and smashed into the old sugar mill in our rear, whereupon the terrorized insurgents fled and were not seen again near the fighting line until the battle was over. Thus the morning wore along.

A part of the plan it is said was that the cavalry division and Kent's division of infantry should cross the San Juan River, connect with and, if necessary, assist Lawton at El Caney, whose duty it was to carry that outpost early in the day of July 1st; then on the following day, after preparing for further attack by the use of artillery, the whole line was to swing to the left to the attack of the San Juan Hills and the fortified ridge stretching in prolongation to the northwest. The movement of the cavalry division was accordingly begun.

The road from El Pozo Hill leads in a northwesterly direction, follows, tortuous and narrow, along the river through the swampy jungle, then crosses the river and passes toward and between the San Juan Hills and turns nearly west over the ridge into Santiago. The regiment moved slowly along this road under the scorching sun and sweltered; a few men were overcome with heat; already, an occasional bullet nipped a leaf above our heads. Impatient at delay the regiment and brigade finally swung past the waiting infantry and moved farther down the road. The Spaniards had evidently concluded that our plan was to march straight into the city that day, so that they soon began to dispute our progress by opening fire from the San Juan Hills and the trenches about the city upon the war balloon which had preceded us, thus making our immediate deployment necessary. So much has been said about this balloon that it hardly seems necessary to say more; why it was there, no one of the line could tell, as the only information its occupants furnished, so far as we knew, was that the Spaniards were firing upon us —information which at that particular time was entirely superfluous.

When the Tenth Cavalry arrived at the crossing of the San Juan River, the balloon had become lodged in the treetops above and the enemy had just begun to make a target of it—no doubt correctly supposing that our troops were moving along this road and were near at hand. A converging fire from all the works within range opened upon us that was terrible in its effect; the Seventy-first New York, which lay in a sunken road near the ford, became demoralized and well-nigh stampeded; our mounted officers dismounted, the men stripped off at the roadside everything possible, and prepared for business.

We were posted for a time in the bed of the stream to the right, directly under the balloon, and stood in water to our waists awaiting orders to deploy. Re-

UNDER FIRE.

maining there under this galling fire of exploding shrapnel and deadly mauser volleys the minutes seemed like hours. The colonel's son, a lad of nineteen who accompanied his father, was seriously wounded in the side by a piece of shrapnel. General Wheeler and a part of his staff stood mounted a few moments in the middle of the stream. Just as I raised my hat to salute, in passing up the stream to post the leading squadron of my regiment, a piece of bursting shell struck between us and covered us both with water. Pursuant to orders from its commander with myself as guide, the second squadron of the Tenth forced its way through wire fence and almost impenetrable thicket to its position. A surgeon of our brigade, an Americanized Cuban, stood in the water behind the bank in a bend of the river supporting two wounded colored troopers to keep them from drowning. A temporary dressing station was established behind a large tree near by where those first wounded were taken. The regiment was soon deployed as skirmishers in an opening across the river to the right of the road, and our line of skirmishers being partly visible from the enemy's position, their fire was turned upon us and we had to lie down in the grass a few minutes for safety. Two officers of the regiment were wounded here, and there were frequent calls for the surgeon; casualties still occurred and there was a delay in the order to move forward. Whatever may have been the intention as to the part to be played by the cavalry division on that day, the officers present were not long in deciding the part their commands should play, and the advance began.

Each officer or soldier next in rank took charge of the line or group immediately in his front or rear and halting to fire at each good opportunity, taking reasonable advantage of cover, the entire command moved forward as coolly as though the buzzing of bullets was the humming of bees. White regiments, black regiments, regulars and Rough Riders, representing the young manhood of the North and the South, fought shoulder to shoulder, unmindful of race or color, unmindful of whether commanded by an ex-Confederate or not, and mindful only of their common duty as Americans.

Through streams, tall grass, tropical undergrowth, under barbed-wire fences and over wire entanglements, regardless of casualties, up the hill to the right this gallant advance was made. As we appeared on the brow of the hill we found the Spaniards retreating, only to take up a new position farther on, spitefully firing as they retired and stubbornly yielding their ground inch by inch.

Our troopers halted and lay down but momentarily to get a breath, and in the face of continued volleys soon formed for attack on the blockhouses and intrenchments on the second hill. This attack was supported by troops including some of the Tenth who had originally moved to the left toward this second hill and had worked their way in groups, slipping through the tall grass and bushes, crawling when casualties came too often, courageously facing a sleet of bullets, and now hung against the steep southern declivity, ready to spring the few remaining yards into the teeth of the enemy. The fire from the Spanish position had doubled in intensity—the cracking of their rifles was a continuous roar. There was a moment's lull and our line moved forward to the charge across the valley separating the two hills. Once begun it continued dauntless and unchecked in its steady, dogged, persistent advance until, like a mighty resistless torrent, it dashed triumphant over the crest of the hill and firing a parting volley at the vanishing foe, planted the silken standards on the enemy's breastworks, and the Stars and Stripes over the blockhouse on San Juan Hill to stay.

This was a time for rejoicing; it was glorious. For the moment every other thought was forgotten but victory; men shook hands and congratulated each other; some hugged each other like children; rank was waived; their hearts were filled with a new joy. All wondered how they had done it; it was against all modern military theory that men should charge straight at a fortified and intrenched position, unshaken by artillery and defended by modern firearms in the hands of trained troops; and yet here we were. Only American valor could have done it. I remember seeing a second lieutenant of the Sixth Cavalry lying wounded upon the grass at the top of the hill and when I asked him if he was badly hurt, he replied: "I don't know, but we whipped them, any way, didn't we?" A brave man and like his comrades filled with only thoughts of victory.

But among these scenes of rejoicing there were others of sadness. Both American and Spanish troops lay dead and wounded around us; all were cared for alike. I saw a colored trooper stop at a trench filled with Spanish dead and wounded and gently raised the head of a wounded Spanish lieutenant and give to him the last drop of water from his own canteen. Their dead, of whom there were many, had fought bravely and we buried them in the trenches where they gallantly fell.

The losses of the day were heavy—the Tenth Cavalry losing half of its officers and twenty per cent. of its men. We officers of the Tenth Cavalry could have taken our black heroes in our arms. They had again fought their way into our affections, as they here had fought their way into the hearts of the American people. Though we had won, it had cost us dearly; the field was strewn with brave fellows; the dressing stations were crowded with the day's victims. It was sad, indeed, as at night we checked up the losses of that terrible battle—gallant comrades, school-fellows, chums, had there offered up their lives as a heroic sacrifice to humanity. Their cherished names and their heroic deeds are ours to enshrine and ours to bless forever.

An attempt was made that evening to recapture the hill, but our defense was so strong that the attempt was futile, the Spaniards retiring to their first interior line of intrenchments—three hundred to five hundred yards away. The firing on both sides was kept up till dark and ceased only at intervals during the night. Over at El Caney the battle had raged with fury all day, but stubbornly as the Spaniards had held their positions the fierce charges of the gallant Seventh, Twelfth and Twenty-fifth Regiments of infantry were resistless. Soon after San Juan was ours El Caney fell. That night the troops engaged there were hurriedly brought forward to extend and strengthen our own line.

It was rumored that evening that some general officers considered our position untenable. "Our lines were too weak," they said, and it was proposed that the army withdraw to Las Guasimas five miles in rear and there await reinforcements. The movement would have been as unpopular as the advance was popular; the very thought struck a false note—retreat! The line officer and soldier of the regular army did not understand the meaning of the word. No! Not while a man remained. Right here lay Cuba; in holding this position lay the success of the expedition; to yield meant

UNDER FIRE. 211

defeat and failure; they spoke boldly: "We can hold this line against the whole Spanish army." Possibly the temper of the army became known; in any event it was fortunate for the army and the country that these sentiments prevailed and that they were permitted to hold the position they had so nobly won. Weak parts of the line were strengthened by new dispositions of troops; after dark lines of siege intrenchments were laid out; picks and shovels were bought up; companies to dig and others to guard them were designated; the night was spent in digging and men sprang to arms only when interrupted by Spanish volleys or by annoying sharpshooters.

There was but little sleep that night; many men, even of those who had opportunity, forgot to eat, and all thought of water as a luxury; ambulances and even wagons were pressed into service and kept busy until dawn gathering up the wounded; only a few of the dead were buried; pack trains carried ammunition instead of commissaries. By morning the position was strengthened so that our line was fairly well protected; reveille was sounded by Spanish small arms and artillery in chorus, but the signal had been anticipated and all men were in their places on the firing line.

Daylight was barely breaking in the east when both sides began where they had left off the night before and the firing all day was incessant. A few moments after the firing opened some cannoneers permitted a limber from one of the guns of the light battery near us to get away and it went tearing down the hillside to the rear for a quarter of a mile. Our artillery was silenced by the enemy's small arms and compelled to take up a new position; Spanish shrapnel went screeching overhead and bursting beyond; the adjutant of my regiment was stricken by a hidden sharpshooter; the heat soon became intense and there was no shelter. Those men not in the trenches carried water nearly a mile for those who lay there fighting in the broiling sun. A soldier cooked bacon and coffee in the rear of the line while a dozen others were waiting for his frying pan and his quart cup. A cannon ball plunged through the line at the top of the hill and went rolling to the bottom of the valley; bullets spatted against the isolated trees or grazed the newly-made earthworks, covering with dirt the men in the trenches and fairly mowed the grass for many yards in our front. Now and then a man was hit while changing reliefs or carrying water to the fighting line. Thus the day went on and the night and the succeeding day began. Then came the welcome truce; everybody drew a long breath and thanked God; it was possible once more to walk erect; however, the echoes of the last three days were slow to die away and at the breaking of a bough or the rustling of a leaf, there was a temptation to duck.

Officers and soldiers of both armies were glad, and stood in lines facing each other with a curiosity mingled with respect. Meanwhile, we were quietly locating the exact distance of this or that part of the opposing line, and no doubt the Spaniards were doing the same thing. We had taken a position giving us every advantage, and they could plainly see that our lines extended around on the right to Santiago Bay and on the left to the top of the ridge below the city. Our grasp was firm and unyielding; further resistance was useless. Cervera, the naval commander, appreciating this, had accepted the only chance of escape with his fleet and had lost. At noon on July 4th the regiments were formed into line and I had the pleasure of reading to my regiment a telegram from the president, extending the thanks and congratulations of the American people to the army in front of Santiago for its gallantry and success. A message of congratulation and commendation from the commanding general of the army stating that he was soon to arrive with reinforcements was greeted with exultation.

The brave Linares, however, had already realized the hopelessness of his cause, but he would not surrender without permission from his home government. Therefore the city must be bombarded. Pacificos and other noncombatants were ordered out of the city, and were permitted to come within our lines. All day along the hot, dusty road leading from Santiago to El Caney, passed the long, white line; frail, hungry women carried a bundle of clothing, a parcel of food or an infant, while weak and helpless children trailed wearily at the skirts of their wretched mothers. An old man tottered along on his cane and behind him a puny lad helped an aged woman; old and young, women, children and decrepit men of every class—those refined and used to luxury, together with the ragged beggar—crowded each other in this narrow column. It was a pitiful sight; from daylight until dark the miserable procession trooped past. The suffering of the innocent is not the least of the horrors of war.

The days of truce and hostilities alternated; all rollcalls were suspended except the sunset call and retreat, on days of truce. At the evening call we daily ceased our chatting, cooking or working, and groups or lines of officers and men stood with uncovered heads in respectful and reverent attention as the music of the "Star Spangled Banner" and the sight of the flag we had planted on the hill above us lifted us out of ourselves and carried us in thought to home and country; it was the soldier's silent "Ave Maria."

Duty in the trenches was not less arduous because

of the few days of truce; all the available men were required to work at strengthening positions and building bombproof shelters; vigilance never relaxed until the capitulation. The rainy season had set in in earnest and the trenches were at times knee-deep with mud and water. The constant exposure to the heat and rain, together with the fearful strain of battle, began to have its effect upon even the strongest of us. Our sick list gradually grew and the dreaded yellow fever appeared in our ranks; the field hospitals, already overcrowded with wounded, were compelled to accommodate the increasing number of fever patients; medical supplies and food for the sick were lacking, and though many things were furnished by the Red Cross Society, there was yet a shortage.

Officers and men unite in saying that too much praise cannot be given those noble Christian women, Clara Barton and her associates, for their gentle care, their tender solicitude and for their untiring efforts in aiding and comforting our sick and wounded soldiers. They came as ministering angels to the suffering army at Santiago. Army chaplains worked assiduously among the sick in camp and in the hospitals, and the friends of many a soldier who lies buried in that faraway tropical clime have to thank the army chaplain that the last sad religious rites were administered to their beloved here.

The supply departments exhausted every resource to feed the added burden of the insurgent army and the thousands of starving pacificos within our lines. Roads had become well-nigh impassable and swollen streams delayed transportation. The campaign must soon be forced to a conclusion.

Since July 3d, the firing from the Spanish trenches had become irregular, desultory and noneffective. Our artillery gunners now knew the range of every Spanish battery, and our men in the trenches—every one a trained marksman—knew the distance of every Spanish position. We had learned them so accurately that their soldiers could scarcely expose themselves long enough to take aim without being hit. A Spanish captain afterward told me that it was dangerous for them to stick up even a finger for fear of having it shot off; and yet the Spanish commander still held out.

On July 10th, the day set for the ultimatum of bombardment, the white flags of truce were again taken down and the men again climbed into the trenches. At 4 o'clock in the afternoon, at the signal of the first gun from our northern battery, the firing began and the battle raged with the same old fury as of those early July days; shells and bullets whistled violently for a few moments, but the enemy's fire gradually died away and was silenced. They realized their helplessness and the battle was over.

Our reinforcements had begun to arrive and the terms of capitulation dictated by the commanding general were soon agreed upon. On the morning of July 17th the lines of both armies were drawn up to witness the formal surrender. General Toral with an infantry escort rode out from the city to meet General Shafter, who was escorted by a squadron of mounted cavalry. The formalities were courteous though simple. Arms were presented by both commanders, and the Spanish general tendered his sword to our commander.

General Shafter, accompanied by all the general and staff officers, his escort of cavalry and one regiment of infantry, then entered the city.

Shortly before 12 o'clock our troops were again drawn up in line along the six miles of trenches and stood at present arms. An officer ascended to the top of the governor's palace, lowered the Spanish colors and now held the Stars and Stripes, impatient to declare our victory to the world. Suddenly, at exactly 12 o'clock, the enthusiasm burst forth, cannon boomed the national salute, bands played the "Star Spangled Banner," hats were thrown into the air and ten thousand men, as if to burst their throats, joined in one grand American yell. There just beyond the hill, outlined against a clear sky, over the governor's palace in the captured city, though invisible to many of us, floated our own beloved flag. The campaign was over. For us the war was ended.

Although our banners have been planted abroad, and a protocol has been signed conceding to us the victory, we are not yet ready to proclaim to the world the state of peace we hope will soon exist and forever endure. We, as a nation, in the fulfillment of our manifest destiny, have risen in our strength to assert our position among nations, and in our wrath to rebuke a sister nation for her inhumanity. New responsibilities have arisen and we must meet them bravely and without hesitation. Although our prowess by land and sea is conceded abroad, our new condition requires us to stand ready at all times to enforce our demands. It is the duty of every soldier, as well as every citizen who has a true love of country at heart, to stand out against those who stir up strife or who bring us to scorn in the eyes of other nations. That firm support of those in authority necessary to make us strong should not be withheld until our new policy shall be fully determined and we are again at peace with all mankind.

(Signed)   JOHN J. PERSHING,
First Lieutenant, Tenth United States Cavalry,
Major, Chief O. O., U. S. V.

CHAPTER XIV.

GREAT SUFFERING ENDURED.

Predictions Among Enlisted Men as to the Outcome of the War—Sergeants Peter McCown, David T. Brown, and other Non-commissioned Officers give Personal Accounts of Cuban Campaign—Splendid Words from Captain Charles G. Ayres.

FIRST sergeant of Troop E, Peter McCown, had this to say regarding his experience in Cuba:

I enlisted in the Tenth Cavalry at Philadelphia, Pa., December 4, 1885, and was assigned to Troop D. At the breaking out of the Spanish-American war, we were ordered from our post in Montana to Chickamauga Park, where we went into camp April 25th. We were drilled every day in battle exercises. On the 14th of May the regiment left Chickamauga Park for Lakeland, Florida, at which place we arrived on the 16th of May. We remained at Lakeland until the 7th of June when we proceeded to Tampa, Florida. On our arrival in Tampa we immediately boarded transport boat No. 21, and after a week's delay—a week of anxiety to get to Cuba—we were all very happy on the evening of June 14th, when our steamer sailed out of Tampa Bay into the waters of the Gulf of Mexico.

There were all sorts of speculations on the part of the men as to what we would do in Cuba. Some said that it would take about five minutes to knock out the entire Spanish army. Others said that we would not have to fire a single gun. Still I thought we would have to do some fighting. We landed at the town of Daiquiri, June 22d. I had received orders from my troop commander, Captain Charles G. Ayres, to have all the men take three days' rations. My troop had just landed when the first flag was hoisted. Men shouted. The whistles of the steamer blew loud and continuous screeches; everything savored of patriotic zeal and enthusiasm. On the evening of the 23d we marched fourteen miles and camped near Sevilla.

The next morning we were met by General S. B. M. Young. A squadron of the First Cavalry and a squadron of the Tenth Cavalry started on our march toward Santiago. We had not gone more than one mile when we met a number of Cuban soldiers, who told us that the hill in front of us was called Las Guasimas, and that about three thousand Spaniards were intrenched there; which statement we afterward found to be true. We had not gone five hundred yards before the firing commenced from the hill. The First Cavalry deployed to the right and the Tenth Cavalry to the left. This placed the squadron of the Tenth in the center of the Spanish line. Our lines advanced very rapidly to the top of the hill. It was here that we broke the center of the Spanish lines which had been concentrating their fire on the Rough Riders, killing them at long range. Fearing that we might be mistaken we signaled the Rough Riders that we were the United States Tenth Cavalry. All this time the Spaniards kept up a heavy and terrific fire on our lines. But when we crossed the crest of the hill, the Spaniards were retreating toward Santiago.

This was our first battle on the island. In this engagement Corporal William L. White, of Troop E, was killed, Trumpeter Johnson was wounded. All through this fight I saw Generals Wheeler and Young. Troop

E supported the battery that day. The horses were all sent to the rear. When it became necessary to change position, the men would move the pieces themselves. Captain Ayres took charge of the line after Major Bell of the First Cavalry was wounded. He was carried off the firing line by Captain Ayres and three other men.

I feel very proud of the record my regiment made in the battle, notwithstanding the fact I stood at my post and saw my friends fall. It was early on the 1st day of July that I got all the fighting I was looking for. Troop E being on the extreme right of the line I had a splendid opportunity to see everything that took place. Just as we were crossing San Juan River, the Spaniards sent in a volley of musketry that showed no mercy. We opened fire and our gatling and hotchkiss guns were throwing shot after shot into their lines. But that charge on the hill! I hardly know how I reached the top of the hill. I found myself there just behind Captain Ayres, and my troop was lying down firing at one thousand yards.

At 6 o'clock that evening I was approached by Second Lieutenant Parker of the Thirteenth Infantry, who stated that he was in charge of the Gatling Gun Detachment of the Fifth Army Corps, and that four of his men had been killed and quite a number wounded. I reported the facts to Captain Ayres, who immediately ordered me to detail one noncommissioned officer and two privates to work the guns. Sergeants John Graham, Privates William Taylor and John Smith readily volunteered to go. They were each recommended for medals of honor by Lieutenant Parker, Thirteenth Infantry.

The one thing clearly demonstrated by this war is that the Negro soldier performed his duty as a true and loyal American, and did not hesitate, but went into the very thickest of the fight.

Sergeant David T. Brown, of Troop H, said:
During the war I was stationed with Lieutenant C. P. Johnson in the recruiting office in Atlanta, Georgia, and it made my heart swell with joy and pride when I learned that my regiment had taken such a noble stand and had become the firing pin of General Shafter's great army.

Sergeant William Payne, of Troop E, Tenth Cavalry, who was only sixteen years of age when he joined the army on February 4, 1892, tells the following very interesting story of the part he took in the war.
We left Fort Keogh, Montana, April 20, 1898, for Chickamauga Park, Georgia, arriving there on the 25th of the same month. It was some time before we were ordered to the front. I did not think that we would have a chance to fight. But on the 7th of June we boarded our transport Leona. We waited in Tampa Bay for seven days, and longed for the opportunity to meet the enemy. The water was very poor. I paid ten cents per quart for ice water and as high as twenty-five cents for a lemon.
Finally we received orders to sail. It was about the fourth day at sea that our transport lost sight of the fleet. About midnight, when we found that we were lost at sea, the first mate of the ship sailed the boat around, describing a circle, until morning.
During the time we were lost, some one remarked that we would have to surrender in case a Spanish man-of-war should attack us; but General Young said: "No! We will all go to the bottom before we surrender." Not a single man manifested any fear or weakness. The

UNDER FIRE. 221

various troops of the Tenth Cavalry were detailed to stand half-hour watch. We were armed with carbines only; but all felt that we could stand off any Spanish fleet until reinforcements came to our rescue. Luckily no ship of any kind came in sight until about 3 o'clock in the afternoon, when the United States gunboat Bancroft came back to guard us safely to the fleet.

On the evening of June 21st we came in sight of Morro Castle at Santiago de Cuba. About 6 A.M., June 22d, the gunboats and battleships commenced to bombard the towns of Siboney and Daiquiri in order to effect a landing of the troops. While the bombardment was in progress, the soldiers were landing in lifeboats. My regiment commenced to land in the afternoon. While landing, one of the lifeboats containing sixteen men of the Tenth Cavalry was caught between the tug boat Laura and a lighter, upsetting the lifeboat. Corporal Cobb and Private English were drowned.

The first American flag was raised on Cuban soil at 5:10 P.M., June 22d. Being the troop quartermaster's sergeant at that time, I was detailed to remain on board the ship with seventeen men to look after the troop's property.

June 23d we were detailed to go down the bay about thirty-five miles to get General Garcia's army of five thousand Cubans. Our transport brought six hundred of them. They were a hungry, ragged lot; some of them were almost famished. We landed them at Siboney June 25th. While there, I learned that my troop had been in an engagement, and that my dear friend, Corporal William White, had been killed, who was the only man killed during the engagement. I at once requested that I be sent to join my troop. This request was granted. I walked seven miles from Siboney to join my troop. When I was told about the battle I envied the boys who had taken part in the engagement.

I declared then and there that I would not be left in the next engagement—that I would be found in every set in the great ball given by Uncle Sam and Miss Spain. On the afternoon of June 30th we were ordered to the front. Then my heart leaped for joy to think that I would have a chance to participate in the battle for humanity. We marched until about midnight and went in camp for the rest of the night. Our supper consisted of hard-tack and raw bacon. We were not allowed to build a fire to make coffee, for we were in sight of the enemy's lines.

About 6 A.M., July 1st, the battle started. I remarked: "Boys, we are in for it." Later in the day we received orders to advance. As we did so we stopped for the balloon to pass; after it passed we again resumed the march. Just as the front troop crossed San Juan River the enemy opened fire on us and the balloon. We all threw off our blanket-rolls and knapsacks then, prepared for action. At this place Private Henry McCormick, of my troop, was wounded through the left leg and right foot.

We remained at San Juan River about three hours. Then came the advance for the bloody charge up San Juan Hill, which we did in good order. This was the second time we came to the rescue of the Rough Riders. After we drove the enemy from their stronghold we deployed our skirmish line on the hill and awaited orders to commence firing. During this time our brave commander, Captain Charles G. Ayres, had to be begged and finally ordered to kneel or lie down out of danger, for shot and shell were falling all around him. He is the coolest man I ever saw in action. Shortly afterward we were again ordered to the brow of the hill and the command was, at seven hundred yards, fire one volley. When the men fired that one volley it was all the officers could do to stop them from firing long enough to change the sights on their guns. We had been firing about a half hour this time, which was about 6:30 P.M. I was wounded in the left arm, causing a complete compound fracture. I tried to carry my gun from the line but could not, as I had to support the broken arm with the good one. Two men were detailed to go to the hospital with me, but I did not want them to go. However, they started with me and on the way to the hospital I met Lieutenant Willard of my regiment who asked me if he could have one of the men to help carry rations to the regiment. I gave my consent and left one of them with him. I had gone about half a mile when the American guard stopped me, took my belt and pistol, and ordered the man with me to return to his troop. This left me alone. While traveling alone I was fired at several times by Spanish sharpshooters. But none of them hit me. Finally, I reached the hospital about 12 o'clock midnight. The doctors set my arm and dressed it. I was then sent about two hundred yards from the hospital to sleep in the grass. I had nothing to lie on and only the sky for a cover; but I could not stay in the hospital for the sharpshooters fired on it all night.

The next morning, July 2d, being wet with my own blood and the heavy dew that fell during the night, I naturally felt miserable. I was quite anxious to be in another engagement to get my revenge.

About 8 A.M., July 2d, I left the brigade hospital for the general hospital at Siboney, a distance of nine miles, walking all the way. After reaching the hospital, I found that their accommodations were as poor as those at the front. I did not get a blanket to lie on. One of my comrades had one blanket and we shared it together. This one blanket was spread on the ground and both of us slept on it during the night. At least he did the sleeping; I could not sleep at all, as I was in too much agony. When I laid on my back I was helpless and could not get up again without assistance. To remedy this, I procured a small box to rest my back against during the night.

Every day while I was at this hospital wounded men were brought in by wagon loads. It was a distressing sight to look on. When I saw the condition of some of them, I considered myself lucky to get off so lightly. On July 8th I was ordered aboard the hospital ship Olivette, bound for Fortress Monroe, Virginia. We sailed July 9th. On our way to the United States I suffered greatly. We arrived at Fortress Monroe, July 15th. For some reason they refused to take us in the hospital at that place. We were then ordered to New York. We sailed for New York on the evening of July 15th, arriving there July 16th, late in the afternoon. We were admitted to the United States Marine Hospital, Staten Island, 11 P.M. July 16th.

After several days in this hospital I began to improve through the never tiring efforts of the surgeons in charge; and the citizens of New York have gained the love and respect of all who were in the hospital; for they did everything in their power to make it pleasant for the inmates. I left the hospital August 20, 1898. I was not entirely well, but could get along fairly well. I joined my troop again after an absence of one hundred and forty days. I would go to the front again just as cheerfully as I did this time. This war has indicated what the Negro can do.

On June 22, 1898, eight troops of the Tenth United

States Cavalry landed in Cuba, and the hostilities against the Spaniards had commenced. Of the eight troops, E, under my command, was one. June 24th this troop went into action at Las Guasimas at 7:45 A.M., taking position to the right of the Santiago road about eight or nine hundred yards from the Spaniards, and right in the open. The troop stood for an hour and a half under a terrible fire without firing a shot in return for fear of killing our own men in front, who were in the bushes. But for the fact that they were covered in part by a mound like a plow furrow, many would have been lost. On a piece of ground about forty feet square, of which square the troops formed one side, were picked up after the fight sixteen men killed and wounded, among the latter the gallant Bell of the First United States Cavalry.

Some idea can be formed from this of the intensity of the Spanish fire: they had the distance to our position measured. Nothing could have been finer than the cool gallantry of the men. Corporal White was killed. The position taken up by this troop was more exposed than any other, being, as stated, in the open. It was here that Privates Nelson, Neal, White and Walley gave evidence of conspicuous gallantry by coming to my assistance in carrying Major Bell, First Cavalry, to a place where he could receive the care of the doctor. The fire where he was lying was terrific. A post just in front of where he fell, which was about eight feet high and six inches wide, had nineteen bullet holes through it. After lying at Las Guasimas for a time, the troop, with the others, pushed on to Sevilla, and on the night of June 30th took up position near El Pozo, not far from Grimes' battery. At daylight when the sky was crimson as the earth was soon to be, a gun of the battery opened, and upon that fire being returned by the Spanish battery, the battle of San Juan had commenced. These batteries worked on each other for an hour, perhaps, when the skill of the gallant Grimes silenced his opponent and then the cavalry division swept like a flood down from the top of the El Pozo position up the road to Santiago, and the real business of killing men began in earnest.

"As we approached the San Juan Creek, Troop E (imperial guard) of the army was in the lead of the Tenth Cavalry. When we got to the creek the order was brought by the gallant Pershing, who was as cool as a bowl of cracked ice, for the troops to take cover along the creek and await further orders. Into the creek we went after the courteous Pershing, who was showing us where we were to go, and in a moment were right under the balloon, which had been carefully located to give the Spaniards the range. The troop stayed there about twenty minutes, awaiting under a heavy infantry and artillery fire, for orders. As none came, the troops then prepared for its part in the tragedy.

Striking the road it marched in column of file without a halt to fire over nine hundred yards in the open, straight for the center of San Juan Hill. Passing through crowds of infantry, among others the Seventy-first New York, who were armed with obsolete muskets, out of the brush into the open field, to the left of the pond, through the wire fence, heads up, carbines at right shoulder, a quick, tripping step like the French infantry of Napoleon, the men of this troop swept up the slope of San Juan, and when they approached to within about four hundred yards of the Spaniards the latter broke and up we went to the crest of the hill; then and not until then, the guard spoke to them in quick, rapid, deadly volleys. The troop struck the top of the hill about 12 o'clock, and stayed there until dark.

While on the crest the gallant Wint was hit while directing the fire of his men. When Troop E reached the crest of San Juan, there was nothing in front of it but the Spanish infantry. After a time others came and joined them.

At this place, to the left of where the Santiago road passes through the San Juan Hill, and while on the crest, I was requested by the Rough Riders, who were on the right of the road, to give them the range for their dynamite guns, which I did. After a time this gun hoisted a Spanish gun and squad right up near the housetops and we heard of them no more. That night, after the firing ceased, rifle pits were dug under my direction and then about daylight, the Tenth Cavalry moved by the right flank, Troop E on the right, and occupied the Spanish position all through the 2d of July; and although under a sharp dropping fire we did not return it.

In going from the San Juan Creek under the balloon to the top of San Juan Hill, nine hundred yards, the troop lost eleven men out of about forty-five. This all occurred July 1st. After dark July 2d, the regiment marched still further to the right and took up the position which it occupied until the surrender. Troop E was on the left at the highest point, immediately beside the Rough Riders.

It was here that the courteous and gallant Tiffany had his colt's rapid-firing guns. About 11 o'clock on the night of the 2d, while the moon was smiling upon us and while all was quiet, there rose as quick as lightning a terrific cannon and musketry fire; ten thousand men, apparently, on both sides, were firing as fast as they could, painting the sky red. Three troops of the Tenth

Cavalry lying just under the crest and a little to the right and near the Rough Riders' right flank, started to their feet and up to the crest of the hill, which would have brought them about forty yards in rear of Rough Riders' right. These troops as they were about to fire listened to my command, stopped, and laid down. Had they fired the result would have been terrible, for they would have fired into the back of the Rough Riders.

From the crest of the hill could be seen the most beautiful but terrific picture I ever imagined. The electric lights of the city—the tall, graceful palms with their white trunks, and in the midst of this scene of exquisite beauty the fire along the Spanish pits and our own, looking very like the fringe of the red Indian shawls.

The two lines worked on each other in this deadly fashion for about half or three-quarters of an hour, then the firing of the batteries and rifles of the troops ceased and we could hear the crickets again. Many gallant souls passed through the gates then into the presence of their Maker, and are comparing notes with the soldiers of the past. As this firing ceased a voice called me, asking: "What officer is that giving orders on that line?" Upon being told, the speaker requested me to come where he was, shook my hand and thanked me, asking me to help lay off and dig rifle pits, approaches and traverses for his regiment; which was done. This was Colonel Roosevelt.

Early on the morning of the 3d of July, before dawn, I was informed that Spanish riflemen had been seen in the moonlight climbing the white palm trunks. Some men of the troop which was in the pits were selected for the purpose, and when it got light enough to see they were directed to fire into the tops of the trees, while the other men tried to keep down the fire from the Spanish rifle pits.

While sitting on the edge of the rifle pits next to Tiffany's (colt) guns, and trying to locate the sharpshooters, Corporal, now Sergeant Hubert, Troop E, being by my side, a ball struck the top of the work between our heads, and from the gash it cut in the earth, I saw where it came from. Directing the corporal how to fire I made a rest for his carbine on my knee, fearing he would be hit if he stood up as the fire was very hot. He fired into a tree and a Spanish sharpshooter fell from it. In this manner the troop killed seven and went to breakfast. For his cool daring upon this occasion Corporal Hubert was made a sergeant. During all the fighting in Cuba, the men of Troop E were superb. Their devotion to me was perfect, whatever honor has come to me is theirs, won by their effort. I am perfectly satisfied that if they were called upon to march though the gates of Hades they would do so in the same jaunty manner in which they went up San Juan Hill. I am perfectly willing to stake my all on their dashing gallantry.

In conclusion—an example. During the afternoon of July 1st it became necessary to remove this troop to the rear for a short time. It was desired that they should drop below the enemy's fire for a little rest. The order to rise was given—it was obeyed. "About face" was given, which placed them with their backs to the enemy; then, "Forward, guide right, march!" Some of the men hurried in a manner unworthy the "imperial guard." The troop halted, a guide moved back several yards and then, "Right backward dress, front!" This, as stated, with their backs to the enemy on the crest of San Juan, under a terrific fire. After being dressed, the order "Forward, guide right, march!" and they passed below the enemy's fire, halted, faced about again and then rested. During this beautiful display of dare-devil courage, by God's gracious will, not one of the men was touched.

(Signed) CHARLES G. AYRES,
Captain Tenth Cavalry,
Commanding Troop E.

CHAPTER XV.

THRILLING STORY OF GALLANTRY.

Sergeant Presly Holliday, of Troop B, Tenth United States Cavalry, Tells What He Saw—Graphically Describes Ascent up San Juan Hill—Generals Wheeler and Young Leading the Way—Sergeant Douglass—Hospital Corps Complimented—Horrible Scenes on the Battlefield—Coincidences in the Lives of Lieutenants Wm. E. Shipp and Wm. H. Smith—Lieutenant H. C. Whitehead.

THE following very interesting narrative is contributed by Sergeant Presly Holliday, Troop B, Tenth Cavalry:

On the morning of the 24th of June, having come within close proximity to the enemy, having cracked many a joke among ourselves in the meantime, the command was halted and the order was passed along from the head of the column to fill our magazines. This order was received with much humor by myself and I believe by most of the old soldiers, but the order was executed and the march was resumed with Generals Wheeler and Young in the lead.

We were again and again cautioned against loud talking. The reason for so much caution was well understood when, a few minutes later, having made another short halt and again taken up the march, a volley was poured into the troop at the head of the column. The Tenth Cavalry was in a gorge so narrow that two men could hardly march abreast of each other, a position poorly suited to an attacking party, and my troop was sixth in column. We did not know what was going on at the front, but learned later that the halt was made to allow Captain Watson time to post his mountain guns.

When we heard the first volley every man, I believe, took cover with a single exception. That exception was Sergeant Douglass, who stood up and looked for the place from which the bullets came. That volley was the first thing that ever made me realize what an awful thing it is to be in actual battle.

About three volleys were fired by the enemy before we made a reply. After the third volley Captain Watson opened up with his battery which must have caused much discomfiture in the Spanish ranks as was shown thereafter by the irregularity of their fire. They fired quite rapidly wherever they saw any of our men, but our volleys, which were fired only by the First Cavalry, the Tenth having not yet been engaged, were more deliberate.

My heart nearly sank within me when I heard a call from the front for Hospital Corps. That gallant organization, which goes into battle without means of defense, dashed forward right into the enemy's fire and soon brought out on a litter a young man seriously wounded.

We had lain in our first position probably ten or fifteen minutes when I heard General Young give the order: "Send two troops of the Tenth Cavalry forward," and the command of our major, "B and I Troops forward!" There was a perceptible hesitancy among our raw recruits at first, but seeing the example of the older soldiers, they all dashed forward and in a few seconds were in a galling fire.

As we passed several correspondents, aids, staff

officers, etc., I remember hearing an adjutant-general sending a verbal message for reinforcements, saying that we had been heavily attacked and that General Wheeler expected a serious engagement and that the messenger should not spare the horse.

We lost three men in that deployment. While going into position the enemy kept up a deadly fire at us. Private James Russell, lying on our line of battle, attracted my attention by trying to call out. I looked at him and he was staring at me with blood streaming from his nose and blood on his face. I thought he had been killed and cried: "Oh, God, Russell is shot!" It was the first real sight of a man wounded in battle I had ever seen, and it sickened me. I reported him dead after the battle was over. He was alive, however, and is still living.

Our men were much demoralized in the deployment. as the enemy poured volleys into us incessantly, and there was a continued cry of "Go to the right." The right platoon went so far to the right that we found ourselves in a deep ditch thickly covered with bushes, with a wire fence just in front of it. The enemy saw us go into this place and they fired volley after volley over it for about half an hour.

After we had gone quite a distance to the right, Sergeant Douglass, seeing that we were disconnected with the rest of the command, informed me that I was the senior at present with the squad, Sergeant Bailey, contrary to my belief, having been left farther to the left. When he gave me this information I halted the squad, asked by whose orders they were going to the right and Sergeant Douglass told me they were simply obeying the orders of the troop commander, and thought the whole troop was following. I directed the men to remain where they were, went back and called Sergeant

Bailey, and having received an answer from him went back to my squad, had them crawl up a short distance and report to Sergeant Bailey, he then being the senior present. He told me all we could do was to lie there and await orders. The bullets were passing over us in a storm and it would have been instant death for a man to stand up. While lying there I sent Private John Gullion, who had gone into battle without a gun (having lost his while landing on the 2d) to get that of Private Morris, one of the first men wounded.

When Morris told me he was wounded bullets were coming so fast that to stand up and endeavor to take him to the rear would have been madness, so I instructed him to keep under cover and wait for a better opportunity to be taken to the hospital; but contrary to my instructions, when we had made another forward movement, he was with the command. After we got into this last position I volunteered to take him to the hospital if I could get assistance. Two privates, Gardner and Hockins, volunteered to assist me, and we went to the place where we last saw him, but were told by Sergeant Douglass that he had ordered him to the hospital as he said he could go there alone.

While lying there I repeatedly urged Sergeant Bailey to take us to the front, but as he heard the voice of Captain Ayres with the reserve cautioning his men to keep under cover, he decided it was best to remain where we were. As the firing sounded more in the distance and we heard American voices near us, I again urged him to move forward, with the same result. Exasperated at the idea that our comrades were fighting at the front, some of them dead and wounded, I asked permission to go and find out who the persons were we heard talking, which was granted.

Loading my carbine, I crawled cautiously toward

the voices and hallooed. "Hello!" came the answer. "Who is that?" "General Wheeler's headquarters. Who are you?" "A sergeant of the Tenth Cavalry." The officer called me to him. When I went up I saw General Wheeler, and, I believe, his adjutant-general, seated on the ground. Another sight struck me, too, which almost sickened me. Close by them lay a soldier of the First Cavalry whom they had partly undressed and who was severely wounded and literally covered with blood. I reported the situation to General Wheeler. He cautioned me to sit down while doing so, as I might be hit by a stray bullet, asked the name of my troop commander, directed me to send for a doctor and also to call my platoon up to him. When the platoon approached I was so chagrined that he did not see things as I did and give us orders to move forward that I left and went over and reported to the First Sergeant of Troop E, Tenth Cavalry, which was held in reserve.

I found Troop E as restive as a young horse at the bit, eager to go to the front, and I believe it was only prevented from doing so by the strict discipline to which the regulars are no strangers.

While relating my experience to the first sergeant of that troop, Major Norvell overheard me and called me to him, and I reported in substance what I had said to General Wheeler. He told me to remain with the troop, but later ordered me forward with others who had become separated from their commands.

It was in this battle that I became so filled with admiration for Captain J. W. Watson, who commanded a battery of hotchkiss guns, and whose coolness had done much toward driving the enemy from his works.

The battle was a complete victory for our arms. During the afternoon of June 30th we broke camp and marched to the heights above El Pozo, and went into camp about 9 P.M. right in the face of the enemy. We were up early the next morning and cooked and ate our breakfast and filled our canteens. We soon heard sounds of battle three or four miles to our right and could see the explosions of the shells from our guns, but could not see the lines of battle.

Captain Grimes' battery soon moved up to our position and threw shells at a blockhouse right in front of us on San Juan Hill. The enemy replied quite briskly and as our battery used black powder its position became quite warm. After awhile the enemy ceased to answer the shots from our battery and we moved down the hill and filed along a road leading to the hill which was shortly afterward made famous by the charge which was made to carry it. The road was jammed with soldiers and at times two regiments were moving forward on it side by side. As we neared our position and were seated on the roadside to let some of the regiments ahead of us get into theirs, I was struck with admiration by the great size and soldierly bearing of the men of the Seventy-first New York as they passed us.

We were soon ordered forward, and a volley was poured into our ranks, but I don't think a man was hit. Quickly halting and divesting ourselves of blanket-rolls and haversacks (getting in fighting trim as we call it), we were again on the march. Our line of march led us right over the Sixth Infantry, who were lying in position in the road. We then turned out of the road to the right, all this time under a heavy fire, and marched up a stream, taking shelter under its bank nearest the enemy.

A captive balloon had been hovering over us ever since we first took the road on leaving El Pozo, giving us the direction, and it led the command right into an ambuscade. The enemy made it so hot for the men drawing this balloon that they had to leave it and it descended right in rear of our position, the enemy firing shot and shell at it right over our heads in their attempt to render it useless.

Having remained in this position about half an hour, the advance was ordered and the command was formed in some four or five skirmish lines, one behind the other. We made several advances by rushes and then the charge was ordered and we charged a short distance with a yell, but halted and lay down again. This yell caused a storm of bullets to fall among us from the hill. The advance was continued by rushes, and I heard the constant commands—"B Troop, forward!" Thinking all the time that my troop was meant and not knowing that B of the First Cavalry as well as B of the Rough Riders were just ahead of me. I soon found that I had obeyed other officers' commands and was in the front rank with a troop of Rough Riders.

It was during the charge and this forward movement of mine that Troop B, my troop, went to the left, and I became completely separated from it. Our captain was also separated from the troop. We were soon ordered to fall back about twenty yards so as to be again in the underbrush and long grass, our position being too open. While making the second advance I came upon Captain Watson, who asked me where the troop was. I told him I did not know and was following him to the front when the idea struck me that I ought not to be behind my captain when he had no arms save a revolver and I had a carbine, so I rushed ahead of him and as he turned off we were soon separated again. I next came across Sergeant Bell of my troop, and together we went and reported to Captain Jones of Troop F, and asked permission to join his troop, which he granted, and we ascended San Juan Hill with Troop F.

There I again fell in with Captain Watson and we assembled a little squad of our men and moved up the hill, he ordering us into position to begin firing, but as the plateau just in front of us was full of our own men we did not fire. The Spaniards were just in front retreating. Our men pushed on in pursuit, highly elated at their victory. Captain Jones held F under admirable control, as in many instances discipline was thrown to the winds; indeed, in some cases there was no semblance of organization and the men that pursued the fleeing enemy till he was safe behind intrenchments were little else than howling mobs. Excitement ran high. I saw men so excited that they pointed their guns into the air and fired. Some wanted to fire right through our men in front into the enemy. Captain Jones drew his saber and had to almost take hold of some of the men to prevent them firing; some fired anyhow. About a hundred yards to my right a platoon of Rough Riders knelt in line and asked if there was no officer to give the commands of firing, as they saw some of the enemy far ahead. I ran to them, yelling at the top of my voice, and warned them those were our men just in front of them. They did not fire.

As the excitement cooled down Captain Watson continued his advance followed by eight or ten of us. He placed me in the rear to see that the men kept closed up. We soon reached a line which had been established by Colonel Roosevelt. Here we halted and opened fire. The time I judge must have been about 1 or 2 P.M. Our captain left us here and went back to look out for the rest of his troop.

Our position became so warm, several men having been either killed or wounded in a short time that we had to crawl back about one hundred yards under the brow of the hill.

We lay in this position all the afternoon. That afternoon and the next day were the most disagreeable I have ever spent. With bullets whizzing past one's head for hours at the time, now and then taking off a man, when one can't see a thing to fire at, gives the nerves one of the most severe strains I believe to which they can be subjected.

That night we had four hard-tacks and a slice of fat bacon (raw) for supper. We were wet to the skin, having waded a creek up to our waists in making the ascent of San Juan Hill, besides perspiring freely from our many exertions during the day, and it had rained a little on us as we lay on the heights overlooking the city. So we lay on the wet grass to pass a miserable night in our wet clothes without a thing to cover us. The misery of that night can never be described, and it will never be forgotten. A man could only take cat naps of about five or ten minutes' duration, and then awaken and find himself shivering. Early on the morning of the 2d I was awakened by the sound of horses' hoofs, and shortly afterward heard some one calling Colonel Roosevelt. I looked up and saw a staff officer. I was struck by the deliberation with which he repeated his message as though reading from a book, but was more struck by the message itself which said in substance that Capron's battery was coming and would open up the engagement on our left and that General Lawton with his division would march all night to reinforce us in the morning.

Intrenchments were dug during the night and once the working parties were driven in by the enemy's fire, but our men replied so hotly that they were glad to cease firing for the night.

The next morning bright and early the enemy opened the engagement by firing at our position, but we answered with deliberation as there was seldom anything seen to shoot at. They kept up a continuous rattle of musketry. Why more of us were not killed or wounded I can never tell.

Foraging about that morning, I got a few hardtacks and found a piece of fat bacon some one had thrown away the night before, and on this I made my breakfast. We cracked many a joke that day while under hot fires, and following the example of some of the other men I held my canteen to my head in such a manner as to turn aside any bullet which might strike it. None struck it, however, and soon tiring of this I laid it down. Once a bullet came "zip" past my head and I heard a comrade just beyond me cry "Oh!" The bullet had passed through his shoulder and he went to the rear. Just about the same time the enemy opened up at us with a battery, and about ten minutes later a shell passed so close to my face that had I not turned on my left side it would have carried my right shoulder away. The sparks from the burning fuse sputtered in my face and it exploded about fifteen feet beyond me and tore the head of a Rough Rider to pieces. It was under a hot fire here that Amos Reed, Troop I, and myself renewed our acquaintance. We had not seen each other before for about nine or ten years. He used to live at my home.

The chilly dew of the previous night and the hot rays of the sun were beginning to tell on the men, and numbers were being carried to the rear in a storm of bullets from the enemy. The men were first attacked by chills then severe fevers set in. As I lay on the damp ground that morning after the battle opened and shivered from the cold of the night, I would often strain

UNDER FIRE.   241

my muscles to stop shivering, fearing some of the men might think I was trembling from fear. Since the battle I have talked with others who were up there and they tell me they had the same experience.

Abut 12 M. that day Lieutenant Fleming gave me permission to go to the rear, and it was a run and a dodge for about three or four hundred yards going there and the same coming back, for as soon as one started either way he came in sight of the enemy and there would be a rain of bullets as long as he could be seen.

While at the rear I found the position of my troop, and a few hours later when the detachment of the Tenth Cavalry was ordered to leave that part of the line and join the regiment I had another run to the rear. When I had gotten out of danger I came upon a man of Troop I lying under a tree, who, like myself, had made a run to the rear. He was completely exhausted and lay on his back panting for dear life. I gave him some water from my canteen and fanned him until he had so far recovered as to tell me I had saved his life and to swear eternal friendship to me.

Having rested awhile I took up the march toward my troop and reported to my captain, almost too feeble to walk. My comrades from whom I had been separated for over twenty-four hours were as glad to see me as I was to see them (they heard that I had been killed), and they kindly gave me coffee, bacon, and roast beef, of which I cooked me a dinner fit for a king —I thought. It was here I first learned of the death of my long-time friend Steel, of the Twenty-fifth Infantry, and of Corporal Johnson, of my troop.

We held this position until dark and then marched farther to the front and took a position on the left of the First Cavalry.

That night I was sent into the intrenchments with

fourteen men to guard a working party. I had orders not to fire unless I got orders from some officer to do so.

We were there only a short time when an attempt was made to break through our lines, and volley after volley was fired at us. Having been fired upon, some of my men opened fire, but I quickly stopped this and told them all to get under cover in our trench. The whole camp was in a state of excitement. Our officers tried to stop the men from firing, while the officers of the Twelfth Infantry could be heard giving commands for firing by volleys. Colonel Roosevelt and Captain Ayers walked side by side, fair marks for the enemy's bullets and encouraged the men and ordered them not to fire. Finding the attack fruitless the enemy retired, and we were not again molested during the night. The next morning the enemy began the engagement again, but with more caution than heretofore. About 10 A.M. that day, July 3d, an armistice was declared, and my experience from that time on was similar to that of nearly every other soldier that was engaged in the siege that followed. PRESLY HOLLIDAY.

The brief but brilliant records of Lieutenants William E. Shipp and William H. Smith are so interwoven that the name of each recalls the other. The immediate circumstances surrounding their deaths are known to the world only through the records of the Tenth Cavalry. They illustrate that type of American soldiery, the contemplation of which makes mankind tingle, even as do the lives of Damon and Pythias. They left our historic nursery of arms on the Hudson together; at the same date they became officers of the Tenth Cavalry. They were one and inseparable, knew no pleasure that each did not share, felt no ambition that was not linked with their dual advancement; were accorded promotion

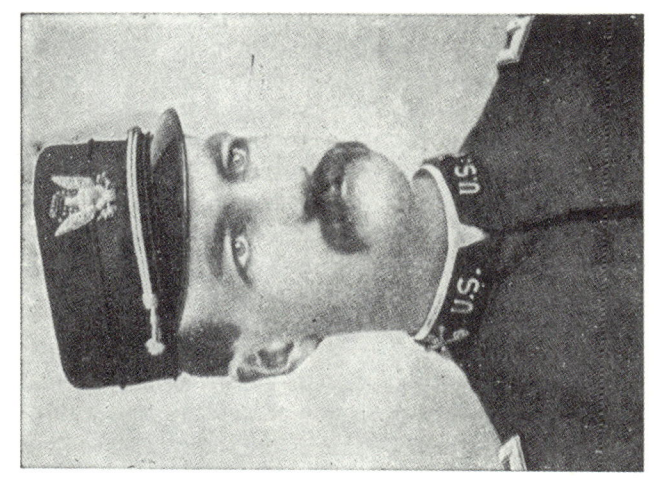

Lieutenant W. E. Shipp.
Buried on the Battlefield of San Juan.

Lieutenant Malvern Hill Barnum.

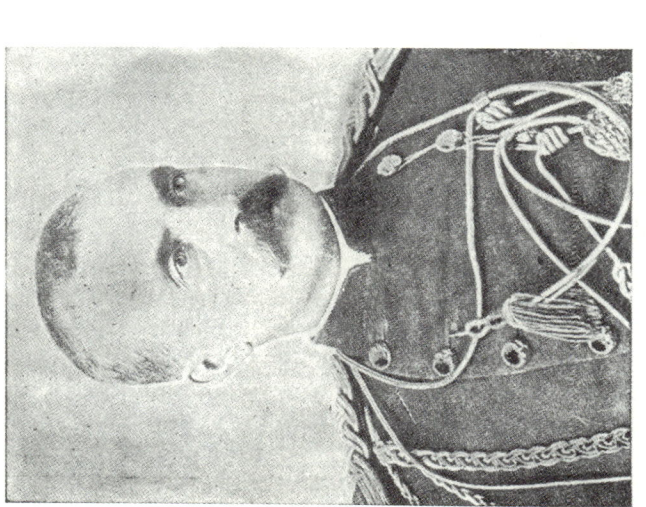

Lieutenant Wm. H. Smith.
Buried on the Battlefield of San Juan.

TENTH ON THE CREST, SAN JUAN.

from second to first lieutenant almost simultaneously and were well known by all their regiment for the unselfish fraternal love which each bore for the other. When the regiment left for Cuba there were none more eager to face the Spanish guns, and when Lieutenant Smith fell, it was almost at the same dread instant that the soul of Lieutenant Shipp took its flight. They lie buried together on the field of San Juan—comrades in death as in life.

Must they not be reunited where friends do not part? The lives of these two Southerners linked with the history of this Negro regiment are an inspiration.

Troops C and F were detached from the regiment and loaded on transport Alamo before leaving Port Tampa *en route* to Santiago de Cuba, consequently, in disembarking at Daiquiri, Cuba, we were the last of the regiment to go ashore. Four troops were already pushed to the front that night and with four troops of the First Regular Cavalry and eight troops of the First Volunteer Cavalry engaged the enemy at Las Guasimas on the site of which we bivouacked on the night of June 24th, having, by a forced march of fourteen or fifteen miles, arrived too late for the engagement by several hours.

From this time the troop did nothing out of the routine until arriving at El Pózo on June 30th, about 9 P.M. Captain T. W. Jones, commanding Troop F, then received instructions to advance about one thousand yards to the front and establish outposts connecting with the Cuban outposts on the left and with Troop G, Tenth Cavalry, on the right. Captain Jones conferred with Lieutenant Smith, commanding Troop G, and they established outposts accordingly. From what we had seen of the Cubans we decided that it was safer not to look for their outposts.

Everything was quiet during the night. Not a challenge was made except of our own patrols. We made no fires, our instructions being to see without being seen. Santiago lay in the valley not more than a mile and a half away, in plain view, but still as death.

The next morning, July 1st, we saw the artillery open on El Caney and watched the exploding shells with fieldglasses.

The adjutant-general of the Second Cavalry Brigade, now Colonel Mills, superintendent of the Military Academy at West Point, visited our outposts and told us that the right flank of the army was to take El Caney and swing toward Santiago on the left as a pivot. As El Caney was not taken until the center had been pierced and San Juan Hill taken, the plan of attack seems here, as in all history, not to have been carried out.

Not later than 9 o'clock we were withdrawn from the hill which we occupied as outposts, and with the regiment marched toward San Juan Hill from El Pozo until we were halted under the famous "war balloon," where, in Troop F, Sergeant Frank Rankin and Blacksmith Charles Robertson were wounded. Finally we took refuge in the creek, where we had some cover. We remained at this crossing for perhaps half an hour and advanced to the attack. We had just deployed when Sergeant Elliston was wounded. Later Corporal Allen Jones, Private John Watson and Isom Taylor received wounds which disabled them. I received a slight cut from a mauser bullet, just enough to make a mark and place my name on the list of wounded.

Before advancing far we came into the open, and then I found that I had got separated from Captain Jones with a part of the troop. He advanced between the road from El Pozo to Santiago and the right blockhouse,

TREE IN FRONT OF TENTH CAVALRY, SAN JUAN, SHOWING BULLET HOLES.

TENTH CAVALRY IN TRENCHES.

looking at the hill from the direction of our attack, and I went just to the right of the blockhouse and joined him soon after the hill was taken.

We held our positions under a heavy fire, which we returned only when the conditions were favorable in order to economize in ammunition until dark. Captain Jones, being the senior officer at this part of the line, took command, and that night we intrenched under his directions.

The next day, July 2d, we stayed in our trenches until late in the afternoon. We were withdrawn and joined the remainder of the regiment which had been across the El Pozo road from us and moved to the new position which the regiment occupied until the surrender. After this there were no individual troop operations, and regimental reports will show what was done by the regiment.

In Captain Jones' report, made on the field of battle, I remember he said that the conduct of the men in the troop had been uniformly all that could be desired, and then when all had done so well distinctions in individual recommendations could not be made for any without injustice to others. I have no copy of his report, but this is as I remember it. For this same reason I made no special recommendations when called upon a short time ago.

(Signed)   HENRY C. WHITEHEAD,
Second Lieutenant, Tenth Cavalry,
Commanding Troop F.

P.S. Before closing this report I must record the sad death of First Lieutenant W. E. Shipp, Troop F, Tenth Cavalry, who was shot and killed July 1, 1898, before Santiago. He was detached from the troop on duty as brigade quartermaster, and had with him as

Tenth Cavalry in Trenches.

SECOND LIEUTENANT JOHN C. PENDERGRASS.
Promoted for bravery at Santiago de Cuba to 10th U. S. Volunteer Infantry.
Late First Sergeant Troop A, 10th Cavalry

orderly, Private Henry Jackson, Troop F, from whom I get what we know of his death.

When the cavalry division engaged the enemy Lieutenant Shipp left Jackson to hold the mules they rode, saying that he would join his troop instead of remaining where there was no danger, in the capacity of brigade quartermaster. When next seen he was lying in the open in front of San Juan Hill dead, not more than one hundred yards from his bosom friend, Lieutenant Smith. He chose the only course for such a soldier, although it led him to the grave. Suitable tributes have been made by his regiment and by the American people. This is simply a record of events. Jackson was standing holding the mules when a shell burst near his head from which he is stone deaf in one ear, and was for months paralyzed, but has since recovered and is with his troop.

CHAPTER XVI.

EXULTANT SONGS OF PRAISE.

Corporals and Sergeants Relate Personal Experiences—The Negro's Heroism Clearly Demonstrated—Seven Days at Sea—Engagement of June 24th—Night Spent Digging Trenches—Camp Hamilton—Ironclad Determination of the Tenth to Win.

WHAT is here said by Corporal Walter W. Board, and Sergeants S. W. Douglass, Paschal Conley, James Murrell, George R. Taylor, Carter Smith and Augustus Wally, all members of the Tenth Cavalry, must be regarded as individual experiences, and while they may differ in some minor details, in the main they each state the same facts and these facts show that the Negro proved himself a soldier—that he appreciated the danger of the situation, the peril of both the geographical position and the treachery of the Spaniards; but he went to perform a duty which no element could furnish power enough to hinder, and he clearly demonstrated a heroism that is not common in any race.

Corporal Walter W. Board writes:

As Troop F, Tenth Cavalry, left Fort Assinniboine, Montana, April 19, 1898, few of us believed that we were soon to be engaged in battle. All hearts were gay and free from care. The cars in which we rode seemed to ring with national airs as we passed swiftly onward.

Arriving at Chickamauga Park, Georgia, April 27th, we began pitching camp, but only for a short stay. The end of three weeks found us again on our journey to the front.

After stopping at Lakeland, Florida, for a few weeks, we went on to Port Tampa, Florida, where we were to board the transports (June 7th) for Santiago de Cuba.

The delay in starting, after boarding the transports, was one to be remembered; the excessive heat was almost suffocating, and all the boys could do to pass the time away was to indulge in frequent sea baths. By and by we started and the whole troop felt gay again.

Seven days' travel brought us to the shores of Cuba, where the vessels laid off-shore until a safe place of landing could be ascertained. Finally Daiquiri and Siboney were selected. Immediately, preparations were made for the landing of our entire army.

In order to do this the bombardment of these towns was begun on June 22d. At the same time troops were landing under the fire from the battleships. On the 23d Troop F placed their feet upon Cuban soil, struck camp, and a part of us began to stroll about at leisure, taking in the many sights.

On the morning of the 24th, at the dawn of day, we broke camp and began on our first day's march toward Santiago. Troop F, in the second squadron, commanded by Major Wint, occupied the advance of this squadron, Captain T. W. Jones, commanding.

As we came in sight of Siboney we met a band of Cuban soldiers, bearing the body of a dead comrade, and in a few moments a courier rode up at full speed bearing orders for us to move quickly to Las Guasimas where our advance guard had encountered two thousand Spaniards who were intercepting our advance.

Our packs that had been thrown aside for a short rest, were quickly thrown across our shoulders and we rushed for the field. We came to the place of battle too late to take a part. Our advance, composed of one squadron of the Tenth Cavalry, one squadron of the First Cavalry, and one squadron of the Rough Riders, had completely driven them from the field, with a loss to us of about forty-nine men.

The American force numbered about nine hundred and fifty men. This engagement occurred June 24th.

We camped at Las Guasimas two days, then pushed our advance about seven miles nearer Santiago, where we camped until June 30th, then advanced to the battlefield of San Juan Hill under cover of night.

Our troop, on the night of June 30th, guarded the extreme left of the line until the battle opened at 7:15 o'clock, July 1st. Before we were ordered to the firing line, our light field artillery had been directing their fire at the enemy's fortifications without reply; all at once a shell came screaming ver from the Spanish line, singing its song of destruction which told too well that their artillery was about equal to ours.

As we proceeded toward the firing line, there came an interval of quiet, too soon to be changed into the rattling fire of mauser rifles, which could not be returned on account of not seeing anything to direct our fire, for the Spaniards were hidden in rifle pits, grass, and shrubbery. In order to save ourselves we had to seek cover, which we did. About that time the order was given by our captain, T. W. Jones, "By the right flank, march!" The order was quickly obeyed. By this time the cries of wounded comrades could be heard on every side, one of whom was our blacksmith, Charles Robertson, struck in the leg by a piece of an exploded shell. Shot was at that time coming so thickly that we had to seek cover under the banks of San Juan River; many were standing in the water waist-deep, and the humble writer was so deep in the water that it was no trouble for him to sip the water from that welcome stream without bending his body.

At that critical moment two white comrades came wading down the stream, both bearing wounds that were paining them greatly; but the order was soon given to move and we left them to their fate.

In a few moments "Old Whistling Dick" (a large Spanish gun so named by our boys), hurled over an eight inch shell which burst into atoms, inflicting a terrible wound in the back of Sergeant Frank Rankin, who was left in the care of one of our men while we marched nearer to the enemy.

In a few moments there came a lull in the conflict, and we halted for a short rest. It was short indeed, for in a few minutes the mausers began to crack again as if hundreds of children were popping corn, modified by the deaf crash of Spanish and American artillery.

Captain Jones then gave the command: "Troop F forward, as skirmishers, guide left, march!" The boys arose and advanced by rushes amid shot and shell with the ferocity of lions.

During our second rush a ball struck Private John H. Laws without doing him any injury, and hit Sergeant Amos Elliston, now our first sergeant, in the left hip, inflicting a very painful wound. He was sent to the rear by our captain and put in the care of Trumpeter Carey Lewers.

Only a hundred or so yards farther and we would be to the bottom of the hill, *i.e.*, the first hill, for we yet had to reach the one called San Juan. We soon gained all ground to the bottom of the first hill and could see the enemy moving about through loopholes in a stone wall, and in a blockhouse at the top of the hill.

The gatling guns immediately to our right began to

slay the Dons as they fled from their first defense; and at that time the "war-whoop" sounded from the throats of the men all along the line and we charged up the hill, and found a deserted blockhouse, but could see the Spaniards jumping in a stronger defense on the top of San Juan Hill. Here we had to come to a short standstill; but in an hour or so, we had them on the jump again. We charged over San Juan Hill, and very near to the outskirts of Santiago, where Corporal Allen Jones and Private Isom Taylor were wounded. We could get no farther that day for night brought an end to the conflict. Our boys were so tired they could lay down and sleep in almost any place.

We spent the night in digging intrenchments in order to hold what we had already gained. It was scarcely daylight on the morning of the second when the Spaniards opened fire upon us. They were quickly answered by the boys in blue.

We remained in the trenches all day without relief. The tropical sun almost scorched the brows of our brave boys, but they fought like heroes regardless of their surroundings. Water, too, was very scarce and thirst was a common thing.

The second day ended with little or no advantage to either side.

About 12 o'clock P.M., on the night of July 2, '98, the Dons saw they were hemmed in and sought a refuge by trying to break through our lines, but the fire was too hot and they had to retire to the city with an estimated loss of between five and seven hundred men.

On the morning of July 3d firing began early as usual, but was not so heavy as on the day previous, and at 12 o'clock the enemy hoisted a flag of truce, asking permission to bury their dead. It was granted and we got a few days rest for every time the truce ran out the Spaniards would ask a continuance. It was granted until 4 P.M., July 11th, when fire was opened upon them by the American artillery, which was fairly shaking the earth. The firing was kept up until Monday about noon, when they again asked for a truce. It was granted and continued until the 14th day of July when the city of Santiago surrendered to the American arms with twenty-one thousand prisoners of war, arms, ammunition and equipage.

A few days after the surrender, our regiment moved to a new camping-place, leaving the writer, and several men of Troop F sick in the old camp along the trenches, and he knew nothing more of the boys until he met them in September in his own native land.

CORPORAL WALTER W. BOARD,
Troop Clerk.

On the 22d of June Troop B, Tenth Cavalry, disembarked from the transport ship Leona, at Daiquiri, Cuba, about 1:30 P.M. and marched about one mile inland under the command of Major S. T. Norvell, then commanding the first squadron of the Tenth United States Cavalry, composed of the following troops: A, B, E, and I. We went into camp about 8 P.M. with orders that no fire should be started under any circumstances, not a match was to be struck on account of being in the enemy's country and with no knowledge as to their whereabouts. It was thought best not to give them any advantage. We remained all night in the heavy dew. Next morning we were up early. After breakfast we were ready for our day's march but the order did not come until late in the afternoon. We were soon in marching order, carrying three days' field rations with us.

We started cheerfully on our journey and passed regiment after regiment. That night we marched until about 10 o'clock. It began to rain, and caused many of us to take a severe cold. About 11 o'clock we went into camp with the first squadron of the First United States Cavalry. We were all wet through and through. The grass was tall and wet which caused us to have a very disagreeable night; however, there was no complaint made by any of our men. On June 24th we started the march about 3 A.M., and about 6 A.M. we arrived at Siboney. After a short rest we started again, only to be attacked by the Spaniards. On the march we passed groups of Cuban soldiers who warned us that the Spaniards were not very far ahead. About 7:45 we were ordered to fill our magazines. We then halted for a few minutes and while we were resting, I noticed that some one had been sitting under the small bushes, and after a more careful examination we found some cards and coins (eighteen pieces) that they perchance had left in their hurry in getting away.

We began our march and had not been marching five minutes when we discovered that we were within range of the Spaniards, who, taking the advantage of their position, began pouring volleys into our ranks. Captain J. W. Watson, of the Tenth, was in command of the hotchkiss gun. The enemy seemed to understand that these guns would do a great damage to them, so they tried to drive the gun crew from its station, but the detachment remained at its station until the Spaniards were out of our reach. The first squadron of the First Cavalry, was the first on the firing line, it being in advance of us. Before many minutes General Young called for two troops of the Tenth Cavalry to reinforce the First Cavalry. Major Norvell ordered troops B and I to advance. We were soon darting through the bushes to take our position on the firing

UNDER FIRE. 259

line—We were compelled to pass in the rear of the gun which was then being crossfired by the Spaniards.

It was at this point that Troop B sustained its greatest loss. Seven of our men were wounded in crossing the road. We reached our position on the right of the line which was a good one and we used it to a great advantage. We were soon on the top of the hill, flanking the Spaniards and driving them from their position, placing them between the firing of the Tenth Cavalry and the Rough Riders with the First United States Cavalry, driving them from their stronghold. At about 11 A.M. we were in command of the hill and the enemy's breastworks. This was a very short but hard day's work, and after it was over we were tired and hungry but had to remain until reinforcements came to relieve us.

We spent the time here, and saw regiments advancing on Santiago until the evening of June 30th, when the general call was sounded and we were all in line in ten minutes. The march was taken up and continued until about 9 o'clock, when we went noiselessly into camp and also without fire as the enemy was right in front of us.

The next morning, July 1st, we were up at 5 o'clock, made coffee and ate our breakfast. Soon we heard the artillery on the right followed by the small arms of the infantry, which told us that the battle had begun and that we were to have another hot day's work. A few minutes later a battery of artillery that was with us opened fire on the breastworks of the enemy and after firing several shots an answer came from the Spanish side which told us that they were there waiting and ready for anything that might happen. After a short time the Spaniards stopped their firing and a few minutes later our battery also stopped, then came the call for the Tenth to keep close to the First, which was on our right.

The march was taken for about three miles, when we halted. About this time the balloon was just over us, and was low enough for the officer in charge to give the following instruction: "There is a clear road to the right, but follow the left hand road and be ready for an attack at any time." The order was promptly obeyed and before we had marched one hundred yards we received a volley from the Spanish blockhouse that was on the hill and had a clear view of us. We continued the march under the heavy firing of the Spaniards and crossed the San Juan River under the artillery and small-arm firing of our enemy. Our deployment was quickly made and the battle of the day begun slowly. We moved forward, emerged from the heavy undergrowth and made for the top of the hill.

I, myself, was now separated from my troop and when I found myself I was in K Troop, First United States Volunteer Cavalry. Many more of my comrades were in the same fix. I assisted First Sergeant John Buck, Troop B, Tenth Cavalry, in getting the scattered men together and started to my troop, but was stopped by an aid of General Sumner's staff and was placed on the reserve line until late in the evening. The general himself came along and relieved us and ordered us to join our command. It was then about 5 P.M. The order came from division headquarters to hold the hill. As soon as the fighting ceased we begun to dig trenches to intrench ourselves.

I was on the first relief and worked until 2 o'clock next morning when I was relieved by First Sergeant John Buck. After a short sleep I was awakened by the cracking of a whip. The artillery was climbing the hill to plant their guns and be in readiness for the day's work. About 4 A.M., July 2d, the order came to change stations, and as soon as the march was taken

UNDER FIRE. 261

up the Spaniards opened fire on us. It was quickly returned by our artillery. We were then ordered to reinforce the trenches, where we remained until 4 o'clock that afternoon. We then received orders to get supper as soon as possible and be ready to change stations for the purpose of being with our brigade. At 6 o'clock we took our new station and were ordered to take the trench. We had hardly reached the trench when we heard very rapid firing to the right of us. The flash from the Spanish rifles told us too well that they were trying to break our line. We soon frustrated their little plan, for in less than a minute the whole line was firing into their line. Things got too warm for them; they soon retreated and that ended the day's work for July 2d.

I with my squad was near the place where a colt automatic rapid-fire gun was being mounted. I assisted during the night in this work and by morning it was completed. The sun rose clear and warm on the morning of July 3d. Very little firing was going on save from the sharpshooters, who were doing pretty fair work. Soon orders came for us to shoot only when we saw something to shoot at. Later an order was received that all firing should cease after 12 M. and that an officer under a flag of truce was going into the city of Santiago.

Nothing of great importance took place until July 10th, except repairing our trenches and building bomb proofs for our protection. On July 10th orders were published that at 4 o'clock firing would begin and that General Lawton's division would open the engagement from the right of the line. It was 4:30 when the first volley was fired, and this was the beginning and the end; for on July 11th we only fired at will and at any object we saw moving. At 10 o'clock orders came that firing would cease at 12 o'clock and that a flag of truce was going into Santiago at 1 o'clock. In the afternoon we received the news that the Spanish general would surrender the Province of Santiago to the American force.

The news was received with great joy, as our boys had begun to feel the effects of the climate. On the 17th of July we were ordered to Camp Hamilton, a mountain about five hundred feet above the level of the sea, where we camped until we embarked for the United States. S. W. DOUGLASS,
Sergeant Troop B, Tenth Cavalry.

I left Fort Assinniboine, Montana, with the regiment in April, '98, *en route* for Cuba. We stopped at Chickamauga for organization and equipment. For about two weeks I was with the Q. M. Department, when I was relieved and detailed in the regimental commissary where I remained until the first and second squadrons left for Cuba in early June, when these departments were discontinued. Our commissary officer had to leave with that part of the regiment bound for Cuba and his armful of papers bearing his transactions and responsibilities to our country was placed with me. In one week I closed these papers and forwarded duplicates to the commissary general at Washington. Of this work I feel proud, because it was an immense amount, difficult, and I had the pleasure of doing it for one who was absent. After this I was on duty as chief assistant to the quartermaster and ordnance officer left behind in Florida with the horses and other property of the regiment. Our principal duty was to clothe and equip the five hundred or more recruits who joined to fill the regiment to its war strength—twelve hundred men.

This was quite a task, made so by the fact that no requisition was ever filled entire, and it kept us making requisitions all the time. However, by persistent effort we were very well equipped and clothed when ordered North to Montauk Point, New York, about the middle of August. Owing to sickness and promotions of our Cuban heroes, I was detailed as acting sergeant major of the regiment. For about a month and a half I worked as hard as I ever did in my life, making up back returns, reports, current details and records. This business was fairly up when we arrived at Huntsville, Alabama, early in October. After the establishment of the camp and making reports of our arrival, etc., I was relieved as acting sergeant-major, when I took a fifteen days' furlough among relatives and friends, this being my home.

It is a pleasure to myself to feel that wherever placed, I have done the duty of one man and that to the best of my ability. It would not be amiss to state that I feel an especial pride in the work at Lakeland with the quartermaster and ordnance officer from the fact that we received and issued thousands of dollars worth of clothing and equipments and that when we left there for the North, every article issued was receipted for and properly charged. My office work was as complete and as perfect as could be; nothing that could be done had been left for the future and it stands to-day a credit to the regiment and I hope to myself.

Respectfully,   Paschal Conley,
Sergeant Troop N, Tenth Cavalry.

The battle of June 24th began at about 8 A.M. Troop A of the Tenth Cavalry was ordered up a ravine; it was here that I first experienced real service as a soldier. We were the advance guard. Upon leaving the ravine we marched up the hill to our right until we were in full view of the enemy. We came to a halt, and stood there on the summit of the hill where sudden death seemed to await us, and where our courage would have failed us were it not for the inspiring thought that we were fighting for the cause of humanity.

> " 'Twas July first, we seemed to know,
> It was the day for weal or woe;
> Two lieutenants—six privates dear
> Were killed, while we were charging near.
> To my sergeant's side I hear the call
> To bind the wound of a mauser ball.
> And this is the way the day was spent.
> And many a soul to judgment went."
> JAMES MURRELL, Troop A.

Leaving Lakeland, Florida, June 6th, for Tampa, Florida, for embarkation on one of the many transports that had been assembled there to receive the Fifth Army Corps and Cavalry Division *en route* to Tampa, June 14, 1898, we arrived off Cuba June 21, 1898.

The next day, the 22d inst., the regiment disembarked and went into camp on a knoll about three miles from the point of landing. The next day, the 23d, the remainder of the brigade (General Young's), landed. Immediately upon landing General Young was ordered by General Wheeler, to advance toward the interior of the country and drive the Spaniards from their position.

Taking with him the First Volunteer Cavalry (Rough Riders), first squadron, Tenth Cavalry, and first squadron First Cavalry, he moved out that evening about 4 o'clock and marched until 10 o'clock that evening in a drenching rain, moving out the next morning about 5:30, he marched until 7 A.M. when the command was fired upon by the Spaniards. The First Volunteer Cavalry had previously been sent to the left about five miles and the First Cavalry to the right, the Tenth Cavalry taking the center. Generals Wheeler and Young made their headquarters with the Tenth Cavalry. I was recommended by Captain Ayres, commanding troop E, Tenth Cavalry for a medal of honor, for helping to save, while under fire, Major Bell, First Cavalry, who was dangerously wounded. I remained on the firing line until 11 A.M., when the Spaniards retreated. I was in the engagements July 1st, 2d and 3d, in the charge of the San Juan Hill, and also in the night attack of July 2d, remaining with the regiment and troop until they were ordered to the United States, August 14, 1898.

AUGUSTUS WALLEY,
Private Troop E.

I was a participant in the Spanish-American war, and what I saw I am totally unable to even speak of. Nevertheless, I must acknowledge that we had a straight-up, hot time, especially during the terrible stubborn charge up San Juan heights. The regiments, officers and men, moved up the hill with an ironclad determination. Never in all my life have I had the pleasure of witnessing such a beautiful charge and hearing such sweet music as was then rendered by the American guns. The bass solos furnished by Sampson's fleet joined by the many different voices (carbines, artillery, hotchkiss guns, etc.) of our land forces, were just grand. I am now patiently waiting to again join this excellent choir and the command from our dear Uncle (Sam), "Forward!"

GEORGE R. TAYLOR,
Sergeant, Troop A, Tenth United States Cavalry.

It is wonderful to note how men will become enthused in battle and will charge upon the enemy when death seems certain. They seem to know no danger and have no fear. The young men of the regular army did excellent service. The volunteers, though untrained in military tactics, were prompt in action and did their duty. It was distressing to see comrades fall and beg for help when help was impossible. I noticed that both white and colored soldiers had a brotherly affection for each other while on the way to Cuba, in Cuba and on our way back to the United States. They got along nicely together. During the whole campaign I never heard a cross word passed between them. Why can't it be so at home? CARTER SMITH,
First Sergeant.

CHAPTER XVII.

SOME THRILLING EPISODES.

Corporal John Walker of D Troop, Tenth Cavalry, Gives Dramatic Account of Death of Lieutenant Ord—Captain Bigelow—Capture of Spaniards—The Death of a Hero—Sketch of one of Uncle Sam's Noted Musical Organizations, the Tenth Cavalry Band.

CORPORAL JOHN WALKER, of Troop D, writes the following dramatic account of the part played in the San Juan Hill tragedy by his troop and those officers commanding it:

Upon the 1st day of July, as the Tenth Cavalry went into battle at San Juan Hill against the Spanish forces, Troop D deployed to the left and joined General Hawkins' brigade in the charge, the Sixth Infantry becoming excited and retreating. They stampeded the entire line, making the charge. Lieutenant Jules G. Ord, of the Sixteenth Infantry, and Captain Bigelow of the Tenth Cavalry, endeavored to rally the American forces and succeeded by their timely and brave assurances that by standing their ground and continuing the charge up the hill, victory was in store for them. Immediately after which Lieutenant Ord walked down the line toward the road leading to the city of Santiago. Upon seeing the gatling gun detachment selecting a more advantageous position from which to play upon the Spanish lines, and becoming greatly encouraged at this, he hastily retraced his steps down the line, saying: "Men, for God's sake raise up and move forward, for our gatling guns are going to open up now." As the gatling gun opened fire upon the enemy's trenches, the Tenth Cavalry and the Sixteenth Infantry arose from their reclining position and charged forward, commanded by Captain Bigelow and Lieutenant Ord respectively. In the charge Captain Bigelow fell pierced by four bullets from the enemy's guns. Upon falling he implored the men thus: "Men, don't stop to bother with me, just keep up the charge until you get to the top of the hill."

Captain Bigelow's fall left Lieutenant Ord in command of the front forces in the charge as they ascended San Juan Hill. As we reached the Spanish trenches at the top of the hill, Lieutenant Ord with two privates of the Sixteenth Infantry and I being the first to reach the crest, and at that time the only ones there captured four Spaniards in their intrenchments, one of whom was armed with side arm (revolver) which I took from him. Lieutenant Ord said: "Give it to me as I have lost mine, and we will proceed to this blockhouse and capture the rest of the Spanish soldiers." Taking the revolver from my hand, he and I walked toward the blockhouse. Lieutenant Ord stopped, near a large tree, directing his attention to the firing which was coming from the Spaniards who had previously occupied the blockhouse fortification. Just as he tiptoed to see over the high grass Lieutenant Ord was shot through the throat by a Spanish soldier who lay concealed in the heavy underbrush at the foot of the tree by the side of which he paused to watch the Spanish firing. As Lieutenant Ord fell upon the spot, the Spaniard jumped up and ran toward the already retreating Spanish line. As he started to run I shot him twice in the small of the back, killing him; one bullet entering close to the other. I was by Lieutenant Ord's side when he re-

The Tenth Cavalry Band.

ceived the mortal wound, and he fell at my feet. Without moving out of my tracks I fired twice at the fleeing Spaniard while standing directly over Lieutenant Ord, and just before he gasped his last he muttered: "If the rest of the Tenth Cavalry were here we could capture this whole Spanish command."
        CORPORAL JOHN WALKER,
           Troop D.

  The pen of the historian has been used in such a manner as to almost exclude any reference to the service of Negro soldiers in the various wars in which these United States have been involved. None of the individual acts of unsurpassed bravery, courage, coolness and dash of the Negro regiments are recorded by those who have heretofore written our histories. Notwithstanding the fact that the sable sons of silent, wronged and magnificent Africa have born a conspicuous part in every war in which this country has engaged since the dark and gloomy days of the early part of the seventeenth century, before this "land of the free and home of the brave" had taken its stand among the powers of the earth.

  The Negro has shared in the glory of Trenton and his feet marked with blood the frozen banks of the Delaware. In the war of 1812 his dusky form was again seen in the ranks beneath the folds of "Old Glory." In the Mexican war he helped carry that banner to triumphant success. Of the late Civil War I need not speak, for the world knows the result of his manhood therein displayed. But it was in the memorable siege of Santiago and the never to be forgotten charge up San Juan Hill that he challenged the admiration of the American people and solicited the tumultuous applause of every liberty loving nation throughout the civilized world!

UNDER FIRE. 271

And not once in all this great drama of American warfare has there been a traitor found in black skin.

The question has been and is oftimes asked: "What part did the Tenth Cavalry band take in the war with Spain?" This question can be easily answered.

At the opening of the battle of San Juan Hill the Tenth Cavalry band was on the firing line between the troops F and D of the Tenth without any arms whatever save one Colt's revolver in possession of their sergeant, T. E. Janifer, a man of great daring and unquestioned bravery. Thus the bandmen were in the thickest of the fray. They were ordered to lay down their instruments, blanket rolls, etc., and remained with the hospital corps to help care for the sick, dead and wounded soldiers. It was Sergeant Janifer of the band who, when ten wounded American solders were deserted by their attending surgeon and a number of the men of the hospital corps, dared to summon the assistance of three of his fellow-bandmen together with two men of the hospital corps and removed these ten helpless creatures from beneath a hailstorm of Spanish bullets to a place of safety. On one occasion, while carrying a wounded comrade to the hospital on a litter the poor helpless creature was shot and killed by a Spanish sharpshooter, but nevertheless these brave heroes of the band pursued their course with the dead body to the place of landing which was about three-quarters of a mile distant.

From 6:30 A.M. July 1st until 4 P.M. the 2d inst. they were kept busily engaged in carrying sick and wounded soldiers from the field; besides, they dug trenches, built bomb proofs and threw up breastworks. All this time they were without food or drink. As the Spanish blockhouses were taken they took their shattered remains and built shelters for our sick and wounded soldiers.

John W. Campbell, chief trumpeter of the Tenth Regiment of cavalry, assisted on the 1st of July in carrying twenty-one wounded soldiers across the San Juan River to the general hospital, a distance of about four miles. Remember that this was done not only under a heavy fire from the enemy, but beneath a burning tropical sun.

On one occasion, after the first day's battle, Major Wood, chief surgeon of the general hospital, was moved to exclaim:

"If all the men here were as faithful to duty as the men of the Tenth Cavalry band there would have been many more lives saved."

So earnest and faithful were the chief trumpeter, John W. Campbell and others of the band, that they were ordered to relinquish their toil for awhile and go to some place and lie down and rest for fear that they might die from exhaustion.

On the afternoon of July 3d, a terrific storm ranged over the country which blew down a brush shed under which at least five hundred wounded American soldiers were sheltered. The men of the band who succeeded in removing the fallen brush and timber from off them, while the very heavens wept in torrents.

After the surrender of San Juan Hill they played "Hot Time in the Old Town To-night," which aroused the military enthusiasm of the American soldiery and seemed to foretell the surrender of Santiago. But when on the 4th of July they played the national air, it seemed as though the air from pure joy burst into blossom, and kindled in the breast of every American soldier present a white heat of patriotism and a more ardent desire to avenge the dishonored flag.

Long may they live to render such splendid service

to their country, and in the end may it be said to each of them:

"Well done, my good and faithful servant; thou hast been faithful over a few things, come and I will make thee ruler over many."

CHAPTER XVIII.

PORTFOLIO OF WAR POEMS.

Wheeler at Santiago—The Fighting Tenth—The Negro Soldier—The Rough Rider's Remarks—Sergeant George Berry Who Served His Country for Thirty years—Poem on Sergeant Berry, by Rev. B. A. Imes

WHEELER AT SANTIAGO.

INTO the thick of the fight he went, pallid and sick and wan.
Borne in an ambulance to the front, a ghostly wisp of a man;
But the fighting soul of a fighting man, approved in the long ago,
Went to the front in that ambulance and the body of Fighting Joe.

Out from the front they were coming back, smitten of Spanish shells—
Wounded boys from the Vermont hills and the Alabama dells;
"Put them into this ambulance; I'll ride to the front," he said;
And he climbed to the saddle and rode right on, that old ex-Confed.

From end to end of the long blue ranks rose up the ringing cheers,
And many a powder-blackened face was furrowed with sudden tears,

As with flashing eyes and gleaming sword, and hair
    and beard of snow,
Into the hell of shot and shell rode little old Fighting
    Joe!

Sick with fever and racked with pain, he could not stay
    away,
For he heard the song of the yester-years in the deep-
    mouthed cannon's bay —
He heard in the calling song of the guns there was work
    for him to do,
Where his country's best blood splashed and flowed
    'round the old Red, White and Blue.

Fevered body and hero heart! This Union's heart to
    you
Beats out in love and reverence—and to each dear boy
    in blue
Who stood or fell 'mid the shot and shell, and cheered
    in the face of the foe,
As, wan and white, to the heart of the fight rode little
    old Fighting Joe!
—*John Lindsay Gordon in New Orleans Times
Democrat.*

THE FIGHTING TENTH.

THERE wasn't any color line
    At San Juan that day;
They didn't look so very fine,
    It was their dogged way
Of going straight where duty led
    That made their record bright;
A nation cheered them when they said:
    "We're simply here to fight."

And many a happy man has grasped
    Again the sable hand
Whose rifle, resolutely clasped,
    Answered to each command.
And many a heart bereft would pine
    Were it not just to say
"There wasn't any color line
    At San Juan that day."

THE NEGRO SOLDIER.

WE used to think the Negro didn't count for very much—
Light fingered in the melon patch and chicken yard, and such;
Much mixed in point of morals and absurd in point of dress,
The butt of droll cartoonists and the target of the press;
But we've got to reconstruct our views on color, more or less,
    Now we know about the Tenth at Las Guasimas!

When a rain of shot was falling, with a song upon his lips,
In the horror where such gallant lives went out in death's eclipse.
Face to face with Spanish bullets, on the slope of San Juan,
The negro soldier showed himself another type of man;
Read the story of his courage coldly, carelessly, who can—
    The story of the Tenth at Las Guasimas!

We have heaped the Cuban soil above their bodies,
   black and white—
The strangely sorted comrades of that grand and glorious fight—
And many a fair-skinned volunteer goes whole and
   sound to-day
For the succor of the colored troops, the battle records
   say,
And the feud is done forever, of the blue coat and the
   gray—
   All honor to the Tenth at Las Guasimas!
           —*B. M. Channing.*

There is printed on this page to-day a war ballad—
"The Rough Rider Remarks"—which is worthy of the
war. Rough in rhythm, it is full of human sentiment
and sympathy of the kind that exalts and ennobles. Its
theme is the heroism of the Negro troops, and it is a
well-earned tribute, given as Bret Harte might give it,
and as John Hay did give it in "Banty Tim."
           World, Aug. 22, 1898.

THE ROUGH RIDER "REMARKS."

"I was raised way up in the Pecos Valley;
   They call me now the Texas lamb;
I was in Hell Caney in Roosevelt's rally,
   If I was not may I be dam,"
           Said the Rough Rider.

"I never had no use for a nigger,
  A yellow mulatto I didn't admire;
But I lay that day with finger on trigger
  And watched the colored cavalry fire,
And thought out loud, as we waited for orders,
  'If them there darkies should break on our right
'Twould be good-by to the first Rough Riders!'
  And I wished to God them niggers was white,"
    Said the Rough Rider.

"'Twas a red-hot time, and a dam tough place,
  That there same fight at the Hell Caney;
And the language we used wasn't saying grace—
  It doesn't matter what folks may say;
There was bullets from front, and rear, and flank,
  And nary other support in sight
Save them nigs of the Tenth, in single rank;
  And them there darkies they acted white!"
    Said the Rough Rider.

"Up the hill through bramble and briar,
  Leaving killed and wounded there in the brush,
They pushed straight ahead in the face of the fire,
  Then lined up true for the final rush;
Straight in front was the barb-wire fence;
  Over they went it, hellity split;
You should have seen the greasers git from thence;
  I swear, I reckon they're running yit,"
    Said the Rough Rider.

"All that was some days ago, but I haven't forgot;
  And here we are now on this cussed hill,
In just a similar kind of a spot;
  And there's them niggers, a fighting still,

Right in the nastiest part of the mess;
　　I swear, when it comes to a stand-up fight,
Or to stay by a comrade in distress,
　　You bet your sweet life them darkies is white!"
　　　　Said the Rough Rider.

"There is plenty of sand in troops that stand
　　Such a rain of bullets as comes this way;
In this kind of a game I'll fill my hand
　　With them black devils that fight for play.
For beauty they don't show up very much;
　　For color, they're off a little bit,
But the way they git there beats the Dutch;
　　They may lack beauty, but they don't lack grit,"
　　　　Said the Rough Rider.

"Here's a darkey now with an artery cut;
　　Say, doc, can't you put a compress on?
There ain't no time to be fooling about,
　　If you do the cuss will surely be gone.
I've seen such before; I'll grip that hole
　　And stop the blood as long as I can,
A nigger? Who says it? Blast my soul
　　If that there darky ain't a *man!*"
　　　　Said the Rough Rider.

"The cowboys always pay their debts;
　　Them darkies saved us at Hell Caney;
When we go back on the colored vets,
　　Count Texas Bill as out of the play,"
　　　　Said the Rough Rider.
　　　　　　—*W. A. B., Washington, D. C.*

TENTH U. S. CAVALRY REGIMENTAL FANFARE SONG.

WALTZ.

For Piano Solo, Orchestra, and Military Band. Introducing Cavalry Calls, and Field Trumpets in F. Respectfully Dedicated to the Officers and Enlisted Men of the Regiment as a Token of their Gallantry before Santiago de Cuba, in Conjunction with Colonel Roosevelt's Rough Riders, June 24, 1898. By Elbert Williams, Private 24th U. S. Infantry Band.

1.

LET all voices ring with this ode to thee,
Sounding praises due the Tenth Cavalry,
And their colonel brave who is known to be—
Filled with pride in lead to ride, his men to follow free.

CHORUS:

Put on your stable frock and overalls,
Water your horses, how plain the trumpet calls;
March to the stable and groom if you're able,
And feed your horses on corn, oats and hay—
Some to the white and some to the gray,
Some to the black and some to the bay—
March from the stable, repair to the table,
And eat and drink while you feel that way.

2.

Now and ever sing of this Cavalry,
And proclaim a fact now in history,
While the Stars and Stripes waved for liberty,
They fought with the Rough Riders to help set Cuba free.

CHO.—

3.

May this music keep fresh in memory
That their motto now as at El Caney,
Is to charge to win and shall ever be,
"Boots and Spurs" and loud huzzas and on to victory.
Cho.—

SERGEANT BERRY.

'Twas a sultry day on the Cuban coast,
   And the Spaniard guarding the San Juan Hill
Stood by his guns with a stern resolve,
   And the mauser rang out with a deadly will
Till the air was rife with the battle strife
   And from open wounds ebbed many a life.

Shall the brave assault be a failure now,
   Defeat and rout for the Stripes and Stars?
They halt—they tremble, and men by scores,
   Fall there in death, or to live with scars!
Shall the vanquished host with a battle lost
   But tell to the world of the fearful cost?

Are there men at hand who can take those heights—
   Can cover themselves with a worthy fame,
And win the day, tho' the terrible fight
   Shall many a hapless victim claim?
Ay, they rally there now on the hill's rough brow,
   And the foe shall soon to their valor bow.

And up o'r the fallen and tangled slopes
   Charge the Negro troop with defiant shout;
'Gainst storm of bullets their daring copes,
   And the Spaniard yields in total rout!
And Sergeant Berry—two flags in hand,
   Leads on in front of the charging band!

Sergeant George Berry of the Tenth, who planted the Colors of the Third and Tenth Cavalries on San Juan Hill.

Flag Sergeant Berry ahead!—He shouts:
  "Come on!" And the troopers press to his side,
The "Tenth's" own standard and flag of the "Third,"
  He holds, caught up, as it fallen, he'd spied;
And waving them there on the summer air
  He planted the colors with loyal care.

O'er brush and thorn and barb and trench,
  With steady fire and dauntless mein,
They carry the works where hundreds dead,
  And prisoners living make up the scene.
The foe in retreat give proof of defeat;
And the charge of the Tenth is with valor replete.

"Old Sergeant Berry," a veteran strong,
  And modest in manner as brave of will,
Henceforth shall be told in story and song,
  How you led in the fray on the San Juan Hill;
How with Titan-like tread the brave band you led
  Till your flag on the summit its folds outspread.

May you see the good day when no narrow scorn
  Of men, shall deny you a hero's own place—
When all with the spirit of patriots born
  Shall honor the manhood which honors a race;
And grateful in heart all justly shall tell
  How *"he carried the flag and carried it well!"*

And when Cuba a happier day shall know,
  And peace hath well banished the horrors of war,
Let the race and the nation then fail not to show
  Such tribute to merit as time may not mar.
All honor then pay with honest good will
  To Flag Sergeant Berry of San Juan hill!
        —*Rev. B. A. Imes, January, 1899.*

THE CONQUERORS.

THE BLACK TROOPS IN CUBA.

Round the wide earth from the red field your valor has
  won,
Blown with the breath of the far-speaking gun,
  Goes the word.
Bravely you spoke through the battlecloud heavy and
  dun—
Tossed, though the speech toward the mist-hidden sun,
  The world heard.

Hell would have shrunk from you seeking it fresh from
  the fray,
Grim with the dust of the battle, and gray
  From the fight.
Heaven would have crowned you with crowns not of
  gold but of bay
Owning you fit for the glory and peace of her day,
  Men of night.

Far through the cycle of years and of lives that shall
  come,
There shall speak voices long muffled and dumb
  Out of fear.
And through the noises of trade and the turbulent hum,
Truth shall rise over the militant drum
  Loud and clear.

Then on the cheek of the honester nation that grows,
All for their love of you, not for your woes,
  There shall lie
Tears that shall be to your souls as the dew to the rose:
Afterward, thanks that the present yet knows
  Not to ply!
            —*Paul Laurence Dunbar.*

UNDER FIRE.   285

CHAPTER XIX.

PERSONNEL OF OFFICERS AND MEN.

In order to preserve to the world in simple form the *personnel* of the dignified, chivalrous officers of the gallant, fearless, and invincible Tenth Regiment of Cavalry of the United States Army, because of the great value, both to contemporaries and to posterity, the following brief biographical sketches are here given.

GENERAL GUY V. HENRY was born at Fort Smith, Indian Territory, March 9, 1837. He was a cadet at the United States Military Academy trom 1856 to 1861; appointed Second Lieutenant First Artillery May 6, 1861; served during the rebellion of the seceding States 1861 to 1866; in drilling volunteers at Washington, D. C., May to July 1861; promoted first lieutenant First Artillery, May 14, 1861, on Brigadier-General McDowell's staff, taking part in battle of Bull Run, battle of Manassas, and figured conspicuously in most of the important campaigns in the Civil War. He entered the United States Army 1865, engaged in Indian campaigns of Big Horn and Yellowstone expeditions against Sitting Bull and the Sioux Indians; engaged at Tongue River—Rosebud Creek, Mont., where he made his famous charge and received a severe wound in the face. He commanded the Ninth Cavalry in Sioux campaign, 1890 and 1891; was assigned to Tenth United States Cavalry, June 1, 1897, Fort Assinniboine, Montana; accompanied regiment to Chickamauga Park, April 19,

1898, at which point he was appointed Brigadier-General, United States Volunteers; entered the Porto Rican campaign in action against the Spanish forces, July 1898; promoted major-general for gallantry, December 1898.

BRIGADIER-GENERAL T. A. BALDWIN was born in New Jersey. He was assigned to the Tenth Cavalry in 1870. He figured in Indian campaigns from 1870 to 1880, and was promoted to major of the Seventh Cavalry from captain of the Tenth, October 5, 1887. He was made lieutenant-colonel and assigned to the Tenth Cavalry, December 11, 1896. He assumed command of the regiment at Chickamauga Park, Georgia, in May 1898. He accompanied and commanded the regiment in Cuba and participated in the battles at Las Guasimas, June 24th, and before Santiago July 1st to 17th.

He commanded the second brigade, cavalry division, from July 22 to August 1, 1898. Promoted to Brigadier-General of United States Volunteers for gallantry.

During the Cuban campaign General Baldwin paid special attention to the comfort of the soldiers, and he is, to our knowledge, the only commanding officer who gave a regular military burial to any soldier during the campaign. When the Ninth and Tenth cavalries arrived at Montauk Point under his command, the inspecting surgeon said that these regiments as far as cleanliness and sickness were concerned, were in better condition than any other regiment that had arrived. It was General Baldwin who so proudly led the Tenth in review before the President of the United States at Washington, D. C., in October, 1898.

MAJOR JOHN J. PERSHING.
Formerly Military Instructor at West Point Military Academy.

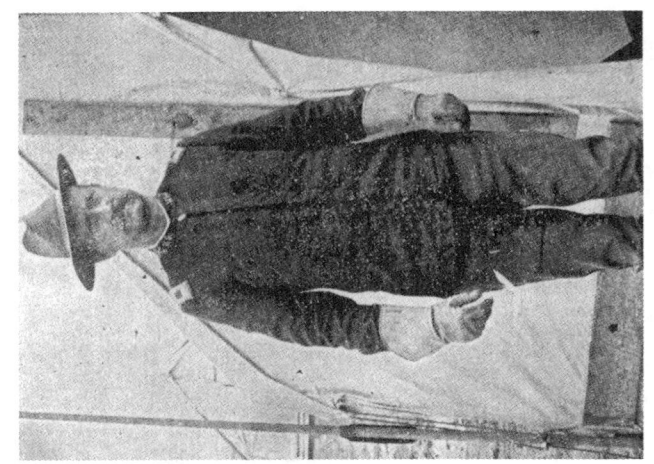
Captain Carlton.

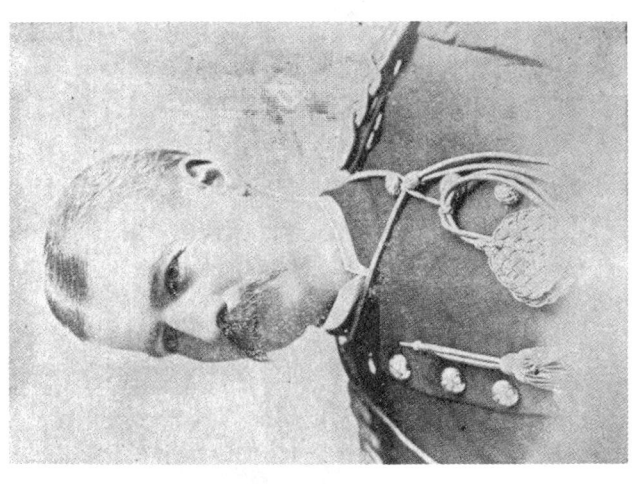
Major Theodore J. Wint.

Colonel Whitsides.

LIEUTENANT-COLONEL STEVENS T. NORVELL was born at Detroit, Mich, February 14, 1835. Assigned to Tenth Cavalry, June 10, 1868. Figured in Indian campaigns from Texas to Montana, has commanded Fort Grant, Fort Custer and Fort Keogh. Accompanied the regiment to Cuba in action with the Spanish troops at Las Guasimas, June 24, 1898, and before Santiago de Cuba, July 1 to 17, 1898. Mentioned in report of regimental commander for untiring energy and gallantry.

MAJOR THEODORE J. WINT was born March 6, 1845. He was appointed second lieutenant, November 25, 1865; promoted first lieutenant, May 9, 1866; promoted captain, April 21, 1872. Promoted major and assigned to Tenth United States Cavalry, May 6, 1892. Figured conspicuously in various campaigns against the Indians. Accompanied Tenth United States Cavalry to Cuba in action against Spanish forces, June 24th and around Santiago July 1st, where he received wounds and had to be borne from the field to the hospital. He was mentioned in report of regimental commander for gallantry and untiring energy.

MAJOR JOSEPH M. KELLEY. Born September 27, 1844, New York City. First lieutenant of infantry, March 7, 1867; assigned to the Tenth Cavalry February 1, 1871; promoted to captain April 15, 1875; promoted to major, April 15, 1893; June 1, 1898, ordered from detached service to Fort Assinniboine, Montana, to relieve Chaplain W. T. Anderson from command to enable him (Anderson) to join his regiment.

CHAPLAIN WILLIAM T. ANDERSON, Tenth United States Cavalry, was born at Saguin, Texas, August

20, 1859. He is a graduate of the Theological Department of Howard University, Washington, D. C., and of the Homeopathic College, Cleveland,

CHAPLAIN WILLIAM T. ANDERSON.

Ohio. He was appointed chaplain of the Tenth United States Cavalry August 16, 1897, on the retirement of Chaplain Weaver. He joined the regiment at

Fort Assinniboine, Montana, November 11, 1897. He was appointed post treasurer, librarian, and superintendent of the Post School. He was appointed quartermaster, commissary, signal and engineer ordnance, and exchange officer and commander of Fort Assinniboine from April 19 to June 28, 1898. He joined his regiment near Santiago de Cuba July 25, 1898.

The following communication is self explanatory:

"CAMP ALBERT G. FORSE, Alabama, Jan. 6, 1899.
"Adjutant, Tenth Cavalry.

"SIR: Having been asked at different times what duty Chaplain William T. Anderson performed during the war, I would state that when the regiment was ordered from Fort Assinniboine, Montana to Chickamauga, *en route* to Cuba, Chaplain Anderson was ordered to receipt for all quartermaster, commissary, signal and ordnance stores left at that post. Was also placed in charge of Exchange, which he continued to operate, and settling up all indebtedness which had occrued. During this time he commanded the post until he was relieved by Major Kelley, Tenth Cavalry, now retired. These responsibilities were entirely new to Chaplain Anderson, as he had been in the service but a few months and the fact that his several accounts have been examined and approved by the head of these departments, is evidence that he was equal to the responsibilities and the trusts reposed in him. After being relieved by Major Kelley, Chaplain Anderson on his own request was ordered to join his regiment in Cuba and on the 24th day of July reported for duty. He at once applied himself to assisting in the relief of the many fever patients then in the regiment by visiting and nursing the sick and cheering them by his Christian example and fortitude even after he was sick and suffering himself and effected much good. While Chaplain Anderson is not an applicant for promotion or brevet, I think it is but just that his services should be recognized and I believe that all of the officers of the regiment that served in Cuba will bear me out and to that end I would request that this communication be made a matter of record and that it be forwarded to the War Department to be placed upon file.

"Very respectfully,
(Signed) "T. A. BALDWIN,
"Lieutenant-Colonel Tenth Cavalry.
"Brigadier-General Volunteers."

SAMUEL LIPPINCOTT WOODWARD, was born in Burlington County, New Jersey, October 28, 1840. When the War of the Rebellion commenced he was living in Paducah, Kentucky, where he was severely persecuted, and his life threatened, on account of his sentiments of loyalty to the government. This becoming unbearable he left his home and enlisted as a private in Troop G, Sixth Illinois Cavalry, February 1, 1862. He was detailed as clerk in the office of the assistant adjutant general of Brigadier-General W. T. Sherman, commanding a division of the Army of the Tennessee, and while in this capacity, participated in the battle of Shiloh, the engagement at Russell House and all engagements of that division during the siege of Corinth, and the march to Memphis, Tennessee.

He was commissioned second lieutenant Sixth Illinois Cavalry, November 1, 1862, and assigned to duty as acting assistant adjutant general of an infantry brigade commanded by Colonel David Stuart, in the corps of General W. T. Sherman, where he served until about November 25, 1862, when he rejoined his regiment and took part in the operations of General Grant's Mississippi campaign, during which he was detailed as acting assistant adjutant general of a division of cavalry.

He was appointed post adjutant, signal and ordnance officer and commissary of subsistence, at Fort Davis, Texas, in which capacities he served from De cember 1, 1884 to March 31, 1885. He left Fort Davis, Texas, with his regiment April 1, 1885, and marched to Whipple Barracks, Arizona, arriving May 20, 1885, since which date he has been adjutant of this latter post.

Left Whipple Barracks, July 13, 1886, and marched with noncommissioned staff and band of the Tenth Cavalry, to Fort Grant, Arizona, arriving July 21, 1886. Was post adjutant and commissary of subsistence, from August 1 until November 30, 1886, when he was ordered to Santé Fe, New Mexico, as acting assistant adjutant general, District of New Mexico; assumed these duties December 1, 1886, and continued until September 30, 1887, when under the provisions of General Orders, No. 14 Headquarters of the Army, Series of 1887, it being necessary to replace him as regimental adjutant, by another officer, he was relieved as acting assistant adjutant general of the district, and assigned to Troop B, Tenth Cavalry. On October 5th he was promoted to the captaincy of Troop I.

During September, October, and November 1887, in addition to his other duties, he performed those of chief commissary of subsistence, of the district of New Mexico.

CAPTAIN LEVI P. HUNT was born August 7, 1845, at Bowling Green, Missouri; was a cadet, United States Military Academy; appointed second lieutenant and assigned to Tenth United States Cavalry, June 14, 1870; promoted first lieutenant, June 30, 1875. Promoted to captain, March 25, 1890. Took part in campaigns against the Indians. Transferred to Wentworth Military Academy, Lexington, Missouri, May 24, 1896. Was in command of the third squadron at Lakeland, Florida, during the war.

CAPT. WILLIAM H. BECK was born in Philadelphia, Pennsylvania, June 29, 1842. Assigned to the Tenth Cavalry June 18, 1867, as second lieutenant. Promoted to first lieutenant, December 11, 1867. Recommended for promotion to captain, 1882; also for acting quartermaster. Captain Beck has figured conspicuously in a number of engagements against the Indians. He joined the regiment as commander of Troop A, June 12, 1898, in Tampa Bay. Transport Leona commanding first squadron. Accompanied the regiment to Cuba, was conspicuous for gallantry during entire campaign in action with Spanish troops at Las Guasimas, June 24, 1898; also before Santiago de Cuba, July 1 to 17, 1898. Mentioned by brigade and regimental commanders for gallantry during campaign.

COL. THADDEUS W. JONES was born July 30, 1838, in Bumcomb County, North Carolina. Was a cadet in United States Military Academy from which he was appointed second lieutenant, June 14, 1872. Promoted first lieutenant November 20, 1879. Took conspicuous part in various campaigns against the hostile Indian. Was given special mention in report of department commander for bravery, energy and willingness. Promoted captain January 14, 1891. Accompanied regiment to Cuba in action against Spanish forces before Santiago de Cuba from July 1st to 13th. Recommended for gallantry in report of regimental commander. Promoted colonel volunteers and placed in command of Tenth United States Volunteers in July, 1898.

CAPT. CHARLES GREENLIEF AYRES, who has been recommended for the very highest possible rank in the

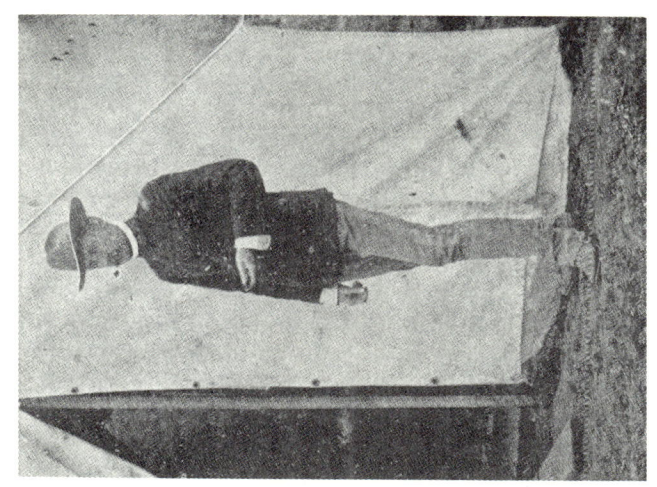
Captain J. W. Watson.

Captain Levi P. Hunt.

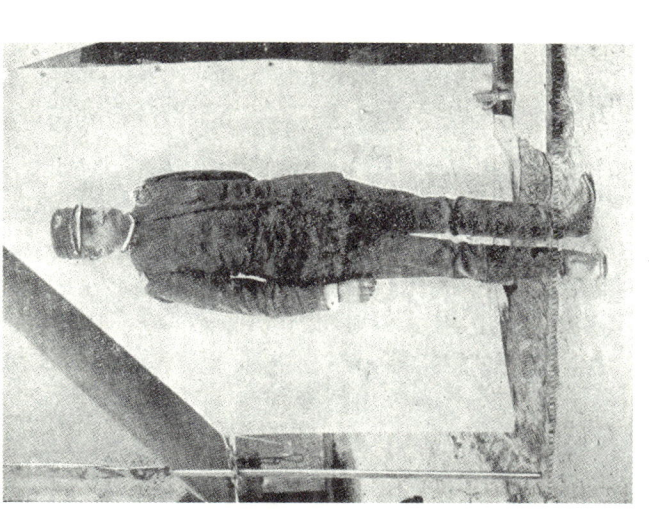
Captain S. L. Woodward.

Captain Robert D. Read, Jr.

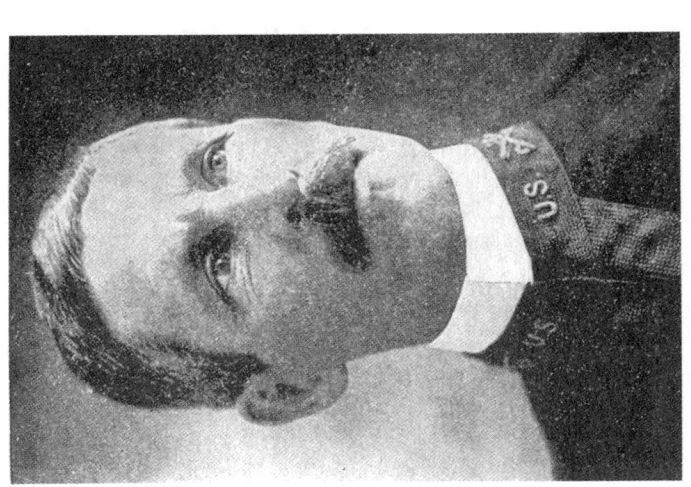

Captain John Bigelow.

Captain Charles G. Ayres.

army, on account of his indomitable courage and brilliant daring on the battlefields in Cuba, was born February 26, 1854, in New York City. He was commissioned from the line, October 31, 1874. Was transferred from the Twenty-fifth Infantry September 18, 1875, to Tenth United States Cavalry, as first lieutenant. He took a conspicuous part in twenty-four campaigns against the Indians. He was promoted to the captaincy January 1, 1892. He accompanied his regiment to Cuba. In action against the Spanish forces June 24, 1898, also before Santiago de Cuba from 1st to July 17, 1898. Captain Ayres is mentioned in report regimental and squadron commanders for conspicuous gallantry and bravery under fire.

CAPT. JOHN BIGELOW, JR., born May 12, 1854, New York City. Cadet United States Military Academy, 1877. Assigned to Tenth United States Cavalry, September, 1877, as second lieutenant. Promoted to first lieutenant, September 24, 1883. Took part in campaigns against the Indians. Promoted captain April 15, 1893. Was appointed regimental quartermaster, 1890; October 16, 1893, to August 20, 1894, college duty, Massachusetts Institute of Technology, Boston, Massachusetts. Joined regiment at Chickamauga Park and assumed command of Troop D with expedition to Cuba, in action with the Spanish troops at Santiago de Cuba. Severely wounded, (received four wounds), July 1, 1898. Mentioned in report of regimental commander for gallantry.

CAPT. ROBERT D. READ was born February 22, 1854, Clarksville, Tennessee. Cadet United States Military Academy. Appointed second lieutenant and assigned to Tenth United States Cavalry, 1877. Promoted to first lieutenant January 24, 1884. Promoted captain July

26, 1893. Took part in various campaigns against the hostile Indians. Was in charge of Troop K at Lakeland, Florida, during the Spanish-American war.

CAPT. CHARLES H. GRIERSON was born at Jacksonville, Illinois, August 11, 1855. Graduated United States Military Academy, June 12, 1879. Joined Tenth Cavalry October 13, 1879. Acted as post adjutant, regimental adjutant, ordnance and signal officer and regimental quartermaster. Figured in many Indian campaigns. On recruiting service, October 1, 1885, to July 19, 1887. Promoted first lieutenant July 6, 1886. Detached service as assistant acting adjutant-general, district of New Mexico, October 1, 1887. Promoted captain November 6, 1897. Accompanied regiment to Cuba. Left regiment June 27, 1898, and was appointed lieutenant-colonel and chief commissary, United States Volunteers.

CAPT. JAMES W. WATSON was born October 3, 1854, at Port Gibson, Mississippi. Cadet United States Military Academy. Appointed second lieutenant June 11, 1880. Promoted first lieutenant December 23, 1887. Promoted captain January 12, 1898. In action against hostile Indians in various campaigns. Accompanied regiment to Cuba, in action against Spanish forces at the battle of Las Guasimas, June 24, 1898; also before Santiago de Cuba from July 1st to 17th. Mentioned in report of regimental commander for gallantry. Mentioned in General Orders No. 191 for gallantry.

CAPT. GUY CARLTON. Born of English parentage at Austin, Texas, September 9, 1857. Appointed to Military Academy from Texas, 1877. Graduated June, 1881, and was assigned to Second Cavalry. Served with the regiment seventeen years in Montana, Idaho, Arizona, New Mexico, and Kansas, being regimental quartermaster, 1891 to 1895. Promoted captain, July 1, 1898, and assigned to Tenth Cavalry.

FIRST LIEUT. WILLIAM E. SHIPP was born August 23, 1861, at Asheville, North Carolina. Was a cadet in the United States Military Academy; from which he was appointed second lieutenant June 13, 1883. He joined the Tenth Cavalry September 30, 1883. He was promoted to first lieutenant December 25, 1889. He took part in engagements against the hostile Indians in 1886. He was recommended for a medal of honor for his gallantry January 11, 1886. He accompanied the regiment to Cuba and took part in the battles at Las Guasimas, June 24th, and before Santiago de Cuba in July, 1898. He was appointed chief commissary and quartermaster of second brigade cavalry division in May, 1898. Was killed on the battlefield before Santiago de Cuba. His grave has been marked.

FIRST LIEUT. WILLIAM H. SMITH was born January 13, 1860, at Harrisonville, Missouri. He was a cadet in the United States Military Academy and was recommended by the school staff for duty as assistant instructor of the departments of tactics and strategy at West Point. He joined the Tenth Cavalry, September 30, 1883. He was appoined second lieutenant June 13, 1883, promoted to first lieutenant March 25, 1890. He accompanied regiment to Cuba in action against Spanish forces at battle of Las Guasimas, also before Santiago de Cuba, July 1898. He was killed on the battlefield July, 1898. Buried on battlefield; grave marked.

FIRST LIEUT. CARTER P. JOHNSON. Born July,

1851, at Staunton, Virginia. Appointed from the ranks to second lieutenant, June 14, 1883. He joined Tenth Cavalry September 19, 1883. Won distinction as a private in pursuing hostile Indians; also after commission and appointment. Promoted first lieutenant, June 7, 1890. Ordered for special service to duty with Troop M, by Major-General Joe Wheeler, in Cuba, to join General Gomez's forces. The most important raid, however, in the department of Arizona was made by Lieutenant Carter P. Johnson, Tenth United States Cavalry.

FIRST LIEUT. ROBERT J. FLEMING. Born in Ireland. Appointed to United States Military Academy, June 16, 1887. Assigned Seventh United States Cavalry. Joined Tenth United States Cavalry, May 12, 1898, at Chickamauga Park, Georgia. Accompanied regiment to Cuba. In action with Spanish forces at Las Guasimas, June 24th; also in front of Santiago de Cuba, July 1 to 7, 1898. Taken sick in trenches and sent to hospital. Commanded Troop I through the whole expedition.

FIRST LIEUT. SAMUEL D. FREEMAN. Born December 23, 1858, Matthew Co., Virginia. Cadet, United States Military Academy. He was assigned to Tenth Cavalry, September 30, 1883. Appointed second lieutenant, June 1883. Promoted first lieutenant, August 20, 1889. Was appointed acting quartermaster and commissary officer, May 5, 1885, to 1886, at Fort Thomas. Was post adjutant, detached service at the military academy, West Point, New York, August 10, 1887. Quartermaster at Fort Custer. Was with third squadron at Lakeland, Florida, during the war.

Lieutenant Robert J. Fleming.

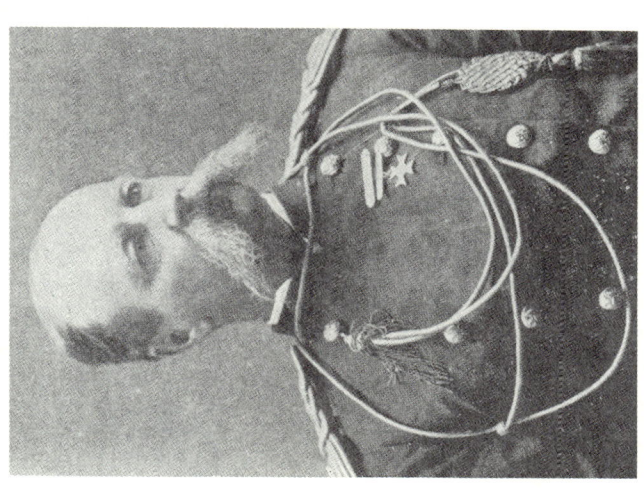
Lieutenant Carter P. Johnson.

Lieutenant H. C. Whitehead.

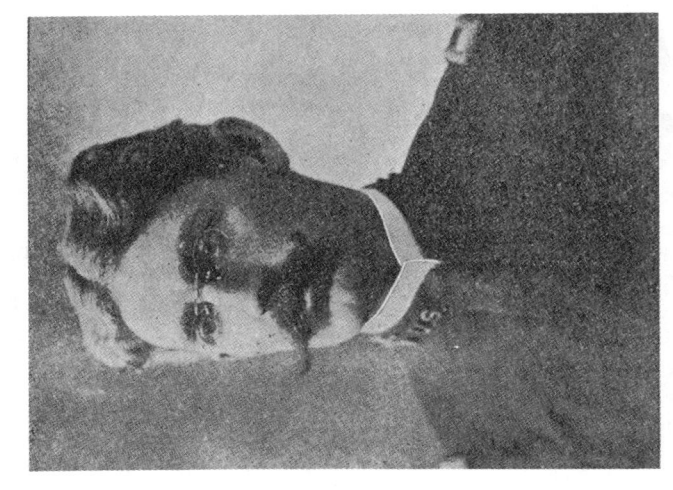

Lieutenant Robert G. Paxton.

Lieutenant James B. Hughes.

Lieutenant Samuel D. Freeman.

UNDER FIRE. 303

FIRST LIEUT. JAMES B. HUGHES. Born May 7, 1863, at Goldsboro, North Carolina. Cadet, United States Military Academy. Joined Tenth Cavalry, September 29, 1884. Appointed second lieutenant, June 15, 1884. Promoted first lieutentant April 23, 1891. Was appointed post adjutant, April 9, 1891, and regimental adjutant April 16, 1891. Commanded Hotchkiss battery manned by members of Tenth Cavalry. Accompanied regiment to Cuba; in action against Spanish force before Santiago de Cuba, July 1, to 17, 1898.

Recommended in report of regimental commander for gallantry and endurance.

FIRST LIEUT. E. D. ANDERSON. Born at Jasper, Tennessee, January 28, 1868. Cadet at United States Military Academy. Appointed second lieutenant, July 9, 1891, and assigned to Fourth United States Cavalry. Promoted first lieutenant and assigned to Tenth United States Cavalry November 6, 1897. Accompanied regiment to Cuba; in action against Spanish forces, July 1st to 17th. Wounded and mentioned in report of commanding officer of Troop F, also regimental commander, for bravery and gallantry.

FIRST LIEUT. RICHARD L. LIVERMORE. Born in Brooklyn, New York, October 22, 1869. Cadet United States Military Academy. Appointed second lieutenant and assigned to Eighth United States Cavalry, June 12, 1891. Accompanied regiment to Cuba; in action against Spanish troops at Santiago de Cuba, July 1 to 17, 1898. Mentioned in report of regimental commander for gallantry.

FIRST LIEUT. WILLIAM H. HAY. Born near Monticello, Jefferson Co., Florida, July 16, 1860. Cadet

United States Military Academy, July 1, 1882, to July 16, 1886. Appointed second lieutenant, Third Cavalry, July, 1886. Promoted first lieutenant, Tenth Cavalry, July 21, 1893. On detached service most of the time; infantry and cavalry school August 30, 1889, to June 19, 1891. Acted adjutant, quartermaster, commissary and exchange officer. Pennsylvania Military College, Chester, Pennsylvania, September 7, 1897.

FIRST LIEUT. ROBERT G. PAXTON. Born September 19, 1865, at Triford, Rockbridge Co., Virginia. Cadet at United States Military Academy. Graduated June 12, 1887. Assigned Tenth Cavalry, 1887, as second lieutenant. Promoted first lieutenant, October 16, 1894. Accompanied Sixth United States Cavalry to Chickamauga Park, where he received appointment as adjutant-general of United States Volunteers, Second Brigade, Second Division, Seventh Corps, May 25, 1898.

FIRST LIEUT. LETCHER HARDEMAN. Born near Acrum Rock, Salem Co., Missouri, April 30, 1864. Graduated from United States Military Academy and assigned to Fourth United States Cavalry. Promoted first lieutenant and assigned to Tenth United States Cavalry, April 15, 1893. Appointed regimental quartermaster, September 10, 1895. Relieved at his own request as regimental quartermaster, March 31, 1898. Detached service with National Guard of Missouri and mustering in of Missouri volunteers, at Jefferson Barracks, April 1, 1898. Granted leave of absence until further orders to accept major's commission in Second Missouri Volunteers.

LIEUT. SAMUEL D. ROCKENBACH was born at

Lynchburg, Virginia, January 27, 1869. Appointed second lieutenant, August 1, 1891. Appointed aid-de-camp to Brigadier-General Henry, United States Volunteers, May 10, 1898. Promoted to first lieutenant, October, 1898. Accompanied General G. V. Henry to Porto Rico. Was an expert manipulator of the hotchkiss gun; also regimental topographic artist. During the Spanish-American war he served as regimental quartermaster and commissary, Tenth Cavalry, from outbreak of war till May 12th, when he was appointed aid to Brigadier-General G. V. Henry, and served as such till he resigned, September 30, 1898. Landed at Siboney, Cuba, July 10th; remained in Cuba till the first Porto Rican expedition sailed; on duty in field throughout the campaign in Porto Rico and at close of hostilities on duty in Ponce, Porto Rico. Recommended for promotion to major and inspector United States Volunteers by corps and division commanders in June. For brevet captain in regular service for zeal and efficiency in the Santiago and Porto Rican campaigns at the close of hostilities. For promotion to captain on the reorganization of the army.

FIRST LIEUT. MALVERN-HILL BARNUM. Born at Syracuse, New York, September 3, 1863. Graduate of Military Academy, West Point, New York. Appointed second lieutenant and assigned to Third Cavalry, July 1, 1886. Detached service, Infantry and Cavalry School, August 28, 1891. D. S. Rock Island, Illinois, October 1, 1893, to October 7, 1894. Promoted first lieutenant Fifth Cavalry, April 7, 1893. Transferred to Tenth Cavalry, March 22, 1894. Assumed duties as adjutant in 1897. Accompanied regiment to Cuba, took part in battles before Santiago de Cuba,

July 1st and 2d, and received wound in the morning of July 2d. Carried from the field and placed on board hospital ship. Recommended in report of regimental commander for conspicuous gallantry and untiring energy in action, July 1, 1898.

MAJ. JOHN J. PERSHING. Born in Linn County, Missouri, September 13, 1860. Second lieutenant with Sixth Cavalry, July 1, 1886. Promoted first lieutenant Tenth Cavalry, October 20, 1892. Appointed regimental quartermaster, May 5th, at Chickamauga Park and Lakeland, Florida. Accompanied regiment to Cuba and took part in the terrific battles and siege of Santiago de Cuba, July 1st to 17th. In addition to other duties, he performed those of adjutant July 1st, and commanded Troop D from July 7th (in trenches) to July 17th. Mentioned in report of regimental commander for conspicuous gallantry. Promoted August, 1898, to major of volunteers, ordnance department.

FIRST LIEUT. J. G. HARBORD was born at Bloomington, Illinois, March 27, 1866, and was educated at the Kansas State Agricultural College, from which he was graduated June 9, 1886. He enlisted in the United States Army January 10, 1889. He was promoted to second lieutenant in cavalry and was immediately assigned to Fifth Regiment, July 31, 1891. He acted as major for the second United States Volunteer Cavalry, May 24, 1898 to October 24 1898 He was promoted to first lieutenant and assigned to the Tenth United States Cavalry July 1, 1898; joined the regiment, December 12, 1898, and appointed regimental quartermaster.

HENRY OSSIAN FLIPPER was born in Thomasville,

Thomas County, Georgia, March 21, 1856. He entered Atlanta University in 1869, and was a member of the Freshman Class of the Collegiate Department, when he

EX-LIEUTENANT HENRY O. FLIPPER.
First colored graduate from West Point Military Acadamy.

was appointed to enter West Point, the United States Military Academy. He graduated from West Point, June 14, 1877, and was appointed second lieutenant in the Tenth Cavalry, June 15, 1877. He joined the regiment in January, 1878, and left June 30, 1882. He was court-martialed, December 8, 1881. Mr. Flipper has a bill before Congress asking that the proceedings of the court-martial in his case be set aside and that he be restored to duty, grade, rank, pay, and status in the army to which he would have attained if he had remained in the service until this day.

MAJ. CHARLES YOUNG, United States Volunteers. Cadet at United States Military Academy. Born in Kentucky. Appointed additional second lieutenant to Tenth United States Cavalry, August 31, 1889, transferred to Twenty-fifth Infantry, October 4, 1889. Assigned to the Ninth United States Cavalry and appointed to first lieutenant, and assigned on detached service to Wilberforce military department. Promoted major of volunteers, May, 1898.

SECOND LIEUT. F. A. BARTON. Born at Washington, District of Columbia, July 23, 1869. Appointed to the regiment, June 1, 1892, from civil life. Has been in detached service most of the time. Detailed at United States Infantry and Cavalry School, September, 1897. Rejoined regiment at Chickamauga Park, Georgia, April 25, 1898; commanding Troop D to May 5th. Was in charge of regimental recruiting office in Tennessee during Cuban campaign.

SECOND LIEUT. A. E. KENNINGTON. Born at Camp Carlin, Wyoming, June 14, 1871. Cadet United States Military Academy. Appointed additional second lieutenant and assigned to Tenth United States Cavalry. Accompanied regiment to Cuba; in action against Spanish forces from July 1st to 7th, where he was taken sick with yellow fever and was sent to hospital.

SECOND LIEUT. HENRY C. WHITEHEAD. Born at Hemphill, Texas, March 22, 1873. Cadet at United States Military Academy. Appointed second lieutenant (additional) to Seventh United States Cavalry, and appointed second lieutenant and assigned to Tenth United States Cavalry, 1897. Accompanied regiment to Cuba and took part in action against Spanish forces from July 1st to 17th, before Santiago de Cuba. Received a slight wound, July 1, 1898. Mentioned in report of regimental commander for gallantry.

SECOND LIEUT. H. B. DIXON. Born in Grundy County, Iowa, January 10, 1872. Graduated from West Point, June 13, 1895. Assigned Tenth United States Cavalry. Joined regiment September 30, 1895. Exchange officer, April, 1898. Changed to Chickamauga Park, Georgia, and Lakeland, Florida. Commissary officer Second Brigade, Cavalry Division, June 7, 1898. Regimental commissary officer September, 1898.

SECOND LIEUT. ALEXANDER M. MILLER, JR. Born at West Point, New York, September 9, 1874. Cadet United States Military Academy, June, 1892, to June, 1896. Appointed second lieutenant and assigned to Tenth United States Cavalry, October 1, 1896. Accompanied regiment to Cuba; took part in action at Las Guasimas, June 24, 1898, and before Santiago, July 1 to 17, 1898. Recommended in report of regimental and troop commander for gallantry and acts of good judgment.

SECOND LIEUT. PAUL REISINGER. Born at Meadville, Pennsylvania, April 16, 1871. Entered United States Military Academy, June, 1892; was appointed second lieutenant Tenth United States Cavalry, August

LIEUTENANT H. B. DIXON.

LIEUTENANT J. G. HARBARD.

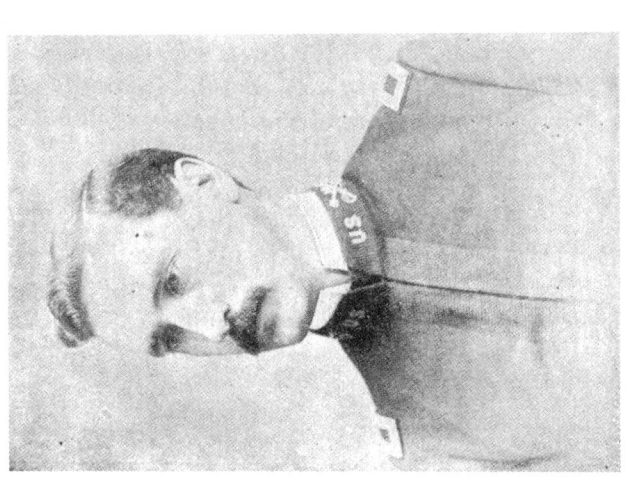

LIEUTENANT S. D. ROCKENBACK.

26, 1896. During the campaign in Cuba was acting quartermaster of the Tenth Cavalry and was stationed at Lakeland, Florida.

SECOND LIEUT. HARRY O. WILLIARD. Born at Brewer, Fairfield County, Ohio, September 1, 1871. He was a cadet in the United States Military Academy from June, 1892, to June, 1896. He was appointed additinal Second Lieutenant Tenth United States Cavalry, October 1, 1896. He accompanied the regiment to Cuba and was in action with Spanish troops at Las Guasimas, June 24, 1898; also in front of Santiago de Cuba, June 1 and 2, 1898. He was wounded July 2d, and borne from the field to the hospital. He was detailed to command Fort Assinniboine, and relieve Major J. M. Kelley, September, 1898.

SECOND LIEUT. GEORGE VIDMER. Born at Mobile, Alabama, August 16, 1871; was graduated from the Military Academy in 1894. He was assigned Second Lieutenant Tenth Infantry, June 12, 1894, and was transferred to Tenth United States Cavalry, October 31, 1894. Appointed signal officer and engineer officer, 1895; accompanied regiment to Cuba; in action with Spanish troops at Las Guasimas, Cuba, June 24, 1898, and again before Santiago de Cuba, July 1st to 17th. Recommended by troop and regimental commander for gallantry under fire.

SECOND LIEUT. THOMAS A. ROBERTS. Born in Springfield, Illinois. Was a cadet in United States Military Academy and was appointed additional second lieutenant and assigned to Second United States Cavalry, 1897, and appointed second lieutenant, April 22, 1898. He accompanied the regiment to Cuba and was in action against Spanish forces before Santiago de Cuba, July 1, 1898, where he was severely wounded.

SECOND LIEUTENANT JACOB C. SMITH,
of the 9th U. S. V. Infantry. Promoted for bravery at San Juan.
Late Sadler Sergeant 10th U. S. Cavalry.

SECOND LIEUT. FRANK R. MCCOY. Born in Lewistown, Pennsylvania. Cadet United States Military Academy. Appointed additional second lieutenant to Eighth Cavalry, June 11, 1897. Appointed second

Lieutenant A. M. Miller.

Lieutenant A. M. Ray.

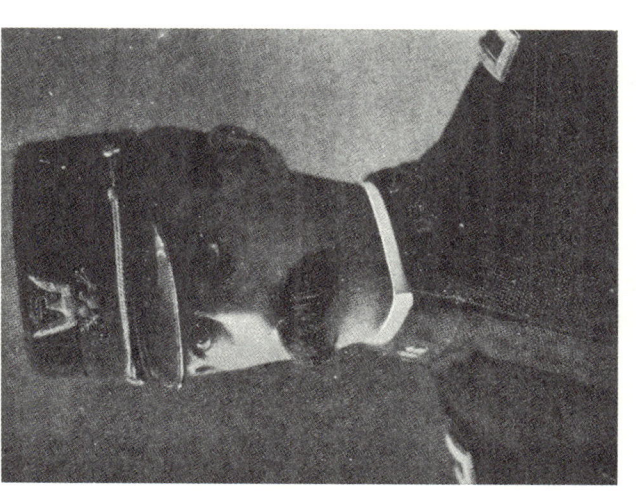

Lieutenant Harry O. Willard.

lieutenant and assigned to Seventh United States Cavalry. Transferred to Tenth United States Cavalry, May 4, 1898. Accompanied regiment to Cuba in action against Spanish forces, June 24, 1898, and before Santiago, July 1st, where he was severely wounded. He is mentioned in report of regimental commander for gallantry.

CHARLES BURRILL TURNER was born June 25, 1859, at Mineral Point, Wisconsin, and received his early training and primary education in Cincinnati, Ohio. When sixteen years of age he enlisted in the regular army at Indianapolis, Indiana, November 15, 1875. In May, 1876, he was assigned to Troop E, Tenth Cavalry, as troop clerk, joining the troop in July the same year on the Pecos River, Texas, the troop at that time being a part of Colonel Shafter's command operating against the Lipan Indians. From September, 1876, until June, 1879, he served on the Mexican border at San Felipe. In 1880 he was with his troop at the disarming of the Mescalaree Apache Indians in New Mexico, after which the troop took over two hundred captured ponies to Fort Stanton. In the latter part of 1880, he participated in the campaign against Victoria's band of renegades. November 14, 1880, he was discharged as a corporal; December 10, 1880, he re-enlisted, his warrant as corporal being continued from its original date (November 20, 1879). In July, 1881, he participated in the quieting of the Kiowas, and Comanches in the Indian Territory, returning to Texas in November same year. In the spring of 1885, the regiment moved to Arizona, where it took a very active part in the chasing and capture of Geronimo and his band of Chirrichucha's, under Generals Crook and Miles. In January, 1888, he passed a board of officers for the position of post quartermaster sergeant, but for some unknown cause the board did not

SERGEANT MAJOR CHARLES B. TURNER.

recommend his appointment. The regiment moved in 1892 to Montana. In August, 1892, he was examined,

passed and recommended by a board of officers for the position of commissary sergeant. He was a delegate to the National Regular Army and Navy Union Convention at St. Louis, Missouri, in 1893. Sergeant Turner was prevented from being with his troop in Cuba during the Spanish-American war by being on regimental recruiting duty in the State of Kentucky, under Lieutenant W. T. Johnston, who enlisted over three hundred and twenty-five recruits for the regiment in three months. Sergeant Turner is also a strong advocate of the principles of the grand United Order of Odd Fellows and the Masonic craft. November 6, 1898, he was appointed sergeant-major of the Tenth United States Cavalry.

JAMES E. TYNES, the first colored soldier to land in Cuba, was born in Smithfield, Virginia, May 22, 1872. He joined the army, May 25, 1896. Soon after he was detailed post school-teacher, then operator, which position he held until going to war. On arriving at Chickamauga, he was detailed as mail carrier, and it was in the performance of this duty that he was left by his regiment at Port Tampa, but reporting aboard the flagship Seguranca, on which General Shafter and his staff went to Cuba, landed three days before his regiment, and thinking his regiment had landed at another point, marched eighteen miles through Cuba, alone and without gun or belt.

FREDERICK FOSTER, Veterinary Surgeon, Tenth United States Cavalry. Born at Glasgow, Scotland, June 7, 1860, assigned to Tenth United States Cavalry, May 20, 1888. Accompanied M Troop on Indian campaign, 1889, in Arizona, against "The Kid." Was at Lakeland, Florida, during the war, as all the cavalry horses were left there.

UNDER FIRE. 317

DR. ARTHUR M. BROWN, Surgeon of the Tenth Cavalry, is one of the most skillful physicians and surgeons the Negro race has thus far produced in the United States. His efficiency has been thoroughly attested by the men of the Tenth, who are now singing his

VET.-SURGEON FRED FOSTER.

praise. He was born in Raleigh, North Carolina, where he attended the public school until he was fitted to enter Lincoln University, in Pennsylvania, from which institution he graduated in 1888. On leaving Lincoln he attended the medical department of the University of Michigan, at Ann Arbor, and was graduated with the degree of M.D. in 1891.

He immediately went to Alabama and located in Birmingham, where he conducted a large drug business beside having a lucrative practice in his profession.

FIRST LIEUTENANT EDWARD L. BAKER,
of the 10th U. S. V. Infantry.

When war was declared between the United States and Spain, Dr. Brown proceeded at once to organize a company of which he was made captain. This com-

UNDER FIRE.   319

pany waited patiently to be called into service after having notified the governor of the preparation it had made, etc. The company not being called into service,

SURGEON ARTHUR M. BROWN.
In Field Costume.

Dr. Brown determined to render his country the service due from every loyal, patriotic citizen and took steps to get on the battlefield to aid the sick and wounded. After communicating his strong determination to Dr.

A. M. Curtis, of Washington, District of Columbia, he was called to Washington by Surgeon-in-chief Sternberg, and was appointed a surgeon to be sta-

SECOND LIEUTENANT SANT FOSTER.
Of the 10th U. S. V. Infantry. Late Sergeant of the 10th U. S. Cavalry.

tioned with an immune regiment in Santiago de Cuba. On arriving in Cuba he found that the yellow fever had greatly abated and he was then ordered to the Tenth Cavalry. He was one of the most active surgeons on the battlefield in Cuba and was the only Negro surgeon who went to Cuba. He was in sole command of the entire regiment from August 12, to October 8, 1898. During that time perfect peace and harmony reigned in the regiment. Dr. Brown's services are highly appreciated by officers and men.

CHAPTER XX.

GENERAL MILES WARNS AGAINST ALCOHOL

Intoxicating Drinks a Dangerous Element in War—Booth, the Faithful Messenger Dog—How He Passed His Examination for Service in Cuba—Arthur Thompkins, the Regimental Mascot—"I Don't See What Them Spaniards Wanted to Shoot Me for, I Wasn't Doing Nothing to Them"—The Fighting Tenth in Philadelphia.

AT the instance of the army surgeons, General Miles issued an order presenting precautionary measures to those in charge of troops. He said:

"The history of other armies has demonstrated that in a hot climate abstinence from the use of intoxicating drinks is essential to continued health and efficiency. Commanding officers of all grades and officers of the medical staff should carefully note the effect of the use of such like beverages—wine and beer—as are permitted to be sold at the post and camp exchanges, and the commanders of all independent commands are enjoined to restrict or entirely prohibit the sale of such beverages if the welfare of the troops or the interests of the service require such action. In this most important hour of the nation's history it is due the government from all those in its service that they should not only render most earnest efforts for its honor and welfare, but that their full physical and intellectual force should be given to their public duties, uncontaminated by any indulgences that

Booth Guarding the Dead Body of Private Staughter.

shall dim, shall stultify, weaken or impair their faculties and strength in any particular. Officers of every grade, by example as well as by authority, will contribute to the enforcement of the order."

That a dog played an important part in the Spanish-American war need not be a matter of great surprise to those who are acquainted with first-class dogs.

The animal kingdom has furnished many examples which appeal to the humane feeling of men and women; especially in the dog, which arouses a sympathy in the human breast that is commendable and praiseworthy.

Booth, is the name of a dog belonging to Sergeant Horace W. Bivins, of the Tenth Regiment of Cavalry, that enjoys a wide celebrity. This dog is trustworthy, sympathetic and in every way reliable. He is, to Sergeant Bivins, a faithful messenger and agreeable companion.

Booth is a full-blooded Irish water spaniel, and when he was examined for service in the Spanish-American war was just three years of age. He was born in the West, and spent his early days of puppyhood around Fort Custer in Montana, where he received his first training in useful pursuits. He was instructed to do the service of a messenger on the battlefield near the Little Big Horn River. He proved himself an expert swimmer by going against the swift current of the river and bringing in geese and ducks which had fallen victims to his master's gun, while out hunting. He has accompanied the regiment on all of its practice and forced marches.

At the beginning of the war Booth's capabilities as a messenger was taken into consideration and he was regularly employed for the service in Cuba.

The test of Booth's ability was as follows: Captain Allyn Capron, who had charge of the transport on which the Tenth Regiment of cavalry were to sail at first decided that no dogs would be allowed on board of the boat. The dog's master stated that Booth could

ARTHUR THOMPKINS. "LAS GUASIMAS."
The 10th Cavalry Mascot.

render valuable service. "What can the dog do?" asked Captain Capron. "He will act as a messenger," answered Sergeant Bivins. "All right, you take him uptown, about five hundred yards away, and have him bring me a letter." Sergeant Bivins at once proceeded to carry out the order. He had the dog go with him up into the principal section of the city of Tampa and when he had gone about five hundred yards he gave the dog a letter addressed to Captain Capron. Booth immediately struck up a trot and did not stop until he had delivered the letter into the hands of the captain. This test was witnessed by five or six hundred men who were anxious to see the dog in the service. He displayed more intelligence than is common in the animal by guarding the remains of Private Slaughter who was killed in the charge up San Juan Hill, July 1, 1898. The dog was found lying across the dead soldier's breast, resembling the mastiff of "Excelsior" fame, having attracted the attention of passers-by by his mournful howls.

Booth has demonstrated his usefulness and so proud are the men of the Tenth of him that they would not suffer him to want for anything.

The subject of this sketch, whose photograph appears on the preceding page, is Arthur Thompkins, a lad fifteen years of age, born of menial parentage in the city of Chattanooga, Tennessee.

He, in putting into execution his desire to go to war with the Tenth Cavalry, displayed youthful courage and bravery of which few men can boast. Arthur became fascinated with army life at Chickamauga where he was initiated into the intricacies of a soldier's life, while earning a few dollars as laundryman in the troop streets. He went to Florida where the regiment was ordered preparatory to embarking for Cuba, boarded the steamer Leona and went to the scene of battle as a stowaway, fearing he would be discovered on board and ordered off the steamer. After the Leona had steamed well under way, he came from his hiding-place, and

TENTH CAVALRY HOSPITAL CORPS.

ARCH OF HONOR AT PEACE JUBILEE, PHILADELPHIA.

upon being seen aboard, he was employed by General S. B. M. Young who was in command of troops. Upon arriving at Daiquiri he disembarked, taking the same chance while so doing that old soldiers took, willingly and eagerly faced the same danger to health and peril to life which the brawny braves of the famous Tenth Cavalry faced who responded to arms at the first trumpet sound in obedience to a sense of duty and in defense of their country whose flag they so bravely bore and for whose honor they so nobly fought. Among the first to succumb at the battle of Las Guasimas, Arthur fell pierced in the right thigh by a ball from the wily sharpshooter, while standing some distance from the firing line, down in the thicket, holding an officer's horse. He was heard to remark between groans and sobs: "I don't see what them Spaniards wanted to shoot me for, I wasn't doing nothing to them. I was just standing there holding that horse." He was placed upon a Cuban pony and supported on each side by a soldier and taken to the rear where he received surgical aid. Upon his recovery he returned to the United States with General Young. Arthur remarked to the writer:

"The only thing I hated about this war was that General Young and I got sick and had to make our headquarters on one of the steamers, while the battle of July 1st, 2d and 3d was going on." Arthur Thompkins has made his permanent headquarters with the Tenth Cavalry and is one of the pet "mascots" of the regiment, having been nicknamed "Guasimas" in memory of the battle in which it was his misfortune to receive the wound which brought to an untimely end his career in the Hispano-American war.

It is worthy of notice that the citizens of Philadelphia

were especially anxious to have the Tenth Cavalry participate in their grand jubilee demonstration, and that they expended more money to have this famous regiment in the military parade than for any other regiment in the service.

The officers and men of the Tenth were highly honored by the patriotic citizens of Philadelphia, and on leaving, one of the leading journals of the city had the following to say concerning the Tenth United States Cavalry:

"With the departure of the Tenth United States Cavalry, at 4:30 o'clock yesterday afternoon, the last of the visiting regiments which participated in Thursday's military parade left the city. For more than twenty-four hours the officers of this regiment had been expecting orders to leave on a few hours' notice, and Friday night a report was current that they had left at 5 o'clock in the afternoon of that day; but, notwithstanding the fact that arrangements had been made for their departure at that hour, a countermanding order was received just as the men were making preparations to leave their quarters in the parish house of the Church of the Crucifixion.

"Upon learning that they would probably be compelled to remain all night in the city the officers, about 6 o'clock, granted the men permission to leave their quarters during the early part of the evening, but required them to report at stated intervals, and a few minutes later the colored heroes of the Cuban campaign were to be seen on all of the streets in the vicinity of their quarters.

"Despite the fact that all the visiting regiments, with one exception, proved by their good conduct that they were entitled to the respect and esteem of the citizens of Philadelphia, it is doubtful whether the members of any regiment who participated in the great military parade

Night View of Arch of Honor.

have been the recipients of so many encomiums as have the dusky warriors ot the valiant Tenth United States Cavalry. It mattered not whether they entered restaurants, saloons, the sacred edifice in which they were quartered, loitered on the streets, or accepted the invitations of local members of their race to visit them at their homes, their conduct was always the same—that of modest, well-behaving, self-respecting men.

"Every one, whether white or colored, who lives in the neighborhood of their quarters, gives them unstinted praise. Rev. H. L. Phillips, rector of the Church of the Crucifixion, said: "The conduct of the men was a revelation to me. When the proposal was made to me to allow them to be quartered in the parish house of my church I hesitated about giving my consent. I had been told that they had seen considerable service in the West, away from the refining influences of civilization, and that, notwithstanding their admirable record as soldiers, they were doubtless a rough lot, who were little likely to respect the sancity of their environments.

"It was only when the committee having the matter of quarters in charge assured me that the city would make good any damage that might be done to the church property that I at length gave my consent. But when I saw how well every one of them behaved my fears were at once allayed, and when I visited the parish house after the men had left this afternoon, I found everything precisely as it was when I visited the place a few minutes before their arrival.

"Orders were received by the officers of the regiment early yesterday to have their men in readiness to move in the afternoon, and a few minutes before 3 o'clock the men, numbering about two hundred, left the parish house and, amid the plaudits of the residents of the neighborhood, marched to Washington Avenue and

Broad Street. It was not until about 4:30 o'clock, however, that the train, consisting of five passenger coaches and a baggage car, began to move, and the heroic Tenth Cavalry was fairly on its way to Huntsville, Alabama.

CHURCH OF THE CRUCIFIXION, PHILADELPHIA, PA.

"In striking contrast with the behavior of the colored regulars was the conduct of the members of the Fifth Pennsylvania Regiment, who were quartered in the old Reading offices on Fourth Street below Walnut. These men, fancying that the food supplied to them was not

REV. HENRY L. PHILLIPS.
Rector Church of the Crucifixion, Philadelphia, Pa.

BETHEL A. M. E. CHURCH, PHILADELPHIA, PA.
Rev. L. J. Coppin, D.D., Pastor.

Rev. L. J. Coppin, D. D.,
Pastor Bethel A. M. E. Church, Philadelphia, Pa.

St. Thomas P. E. Church, Philadelphia, Pa.
Rev. E. G. Knight, Priest in charge.

Rev. E. G. Knight.
Priest in charge of St. Thomas P. E. Church, Philadelphia, Pa.

ALLEN A. M. E. CHAPEL, PHILADELPHIA, PA.

quite all that it ought to be, resolved to register their displeasure on the building.

"Accordingly, windows were broken, gas fixtures were wrenched out of place and all sorts of refuse was scattered about the place, instead of being consigned to the receptacles provided for its reception. The police were summoned and the ringleaders were arrested and locked up in the police station at Fourth and Union Streets. The regiment left Philadelphia on Friday night, and the men who were arrested were released yesterday morning to rejoin their regiment as best they might.

"Many of the men who failed to join their regiments before they left the city were forwarded to their respective camps yesterday. Other stragglers are still coming in, however, and though no less than fifty have thus far reported to the Jubilee Committee for the purpose of securing transportation, it is quite likely that many more will put in an appearance in the course of the next three or four days."

CHAPTER XXI.

THE OFFICIAL ROLL OF HONOR.

The True Aim of the American Soldier, Service, Not Gain—Roll of Honor from Each Troop of the Tenth United States Cavalry—Troops A, B, C, D, E, F, G, H, I, K, L, M—Full List of Names.

NOT gain, but service, is the object of the soldier's life. This appears to be especially true of the members of the Tenth United States Cavalry; for they are striving to render such service as will reflect credit upon themselves and their officers. Of those only we would speak who actually went to Cuba and took part in the campaign. We give their names in the list below, and this roll of honor shall live for all time to come.

There are many soldiers in the various regiments who would impress people in civil life that they were in Cuba and took part in the Cuban campaign. The following list will verify the claims of all those who were connected with the Tenth Cavalry at the time, and who did go, and will be a perpetual testimony against all those who make the claim but did not go.

ROSTER.

Lieutenant-Colonel T. A. Baldwin, Commanding.

Major Stevens T. Norville, Commanding First Squadron.

Major Theodore J. Wint, Commanding Second Squadron.

Lieutenant M. H. Barnum, Adjutant.

Lieutenant John J. Pershing, Quartermaster.

Captain William T. Anderson, Chaplain.
Lieutenant L. A. Fuller, A. A. Surgeon.
Lieutenant A. M. Brown, A. A. Surgeon.

The roll of the Tenth United States Cavalry; Commissioned and Non-Commissioned Officers and Privates, who were in Cuba during the campaign.

Troop A.

Captain, William H. Beck; First Lieutenant, Richard L. Livermore; Second Lieutenant, Frank R. McCoy; First Sergeant, John C. Pendergrass; Quartermaster Sergeant, Carter Smith; Sergeant, Smith Johnson; Sergeant, James T. Cole; Sergeant, George R. Taylor; Sergeant, James H. Williams; Sergeant, William M. Jackson; Corporal, John Anderson; Corporal, Joseph G. Mitchell; Corporal, Turner Jackson; Corporal, Issac W. Bailey; Trumpeter, Nathan Wyatt, Trumpeter, Ossie O. Bourroughs, Blacksmith, Lafayette Hall; Saddler, Nimrod Adams, Farrier, John W. Fields.

Wiley Hipsher, William Queener, William Anderson, Daniel Blue, Frank Brinkley, William H. Brown, James Buchanan, Robert Carter, William A. Cooper, George Delaney, Reuben Easly, Luther D. Gould, Benjamin Franklin, Hamilton Green, Robert F. Harvey, William Hawkins, Conley Holmes, Grant Hughes, Richard James, Edward Janes, James Johnson, William Lawson, Robert E. Lee, Solomon Motley, James Murrell, James Peters, William Richardson, Virgil Rowlett, Daniel Smith, John E. Smith, Thomas Smith, Henry Taylor, Abraham Temple, William Frontman, Israel Washington, William Washington, Cupid Willis, Percy T. Wilson.

UNDER FIRE. 337

Wounded in action, July 1, 1898—Sergeant Smith Johnson, Corporal Joseph G. Mitchel. Privates, William A. Cooper, Benjamin Franklin, Wiley Hipsher, Robert E. Lee, Richard James.

Killed, July 1, 1898—Private John H. Smoot

Died, October 2, 1898—Richard C. Parker.

Reserves of Troop A in United States during the war

Sergeant Hoyle Marshal, Corporal William D. Edwards, Farrier Samuel Alexander.

Ayers Robert, George Bassett, Otis Beaird, Arthur Boon, Samuel Brown, Jr., Willis Coats, Walter Collins, William Davis, John A. Davidson, Samuel Dobyns, Harvey Fields, Benjamin Franklin, George W. Gaines, Isaac Green, James C. Hayes, James B. Hall, William Hayden, William Jarrett, Cornelius Jasper, Napoleon Johnson, William Johnson, Lee A. Jones, Charles Lewis, Walter Marsengale, William McBride, John Marland, Ned Oneal, Virgil H. Parks, William Perrin, Henry Ralls, Less Roberts, John Henry Robinson, Berry H. Runell, Elijah Smith, Richard Smith, Robert V. Smith, William G. Stewart, Byron Thompson, Walter Thompson, John W. H. Twyman, William Washington, Lee White, William Wilson.

TROOP B.

Captain, J. W. Watson; First Lieutenant, James B. Hughes; Second Lieutenant, H. O. Willard; First Sergeant, John Buck; Sergeant Isaac Baily; Quartermaster-Sergeant, James W. Ford; Sergeant, James Thompson; Sergeant, Presly Holliday; Sergeant, Samuel W. Douglass; Sergeant, William Bell; Sergeant, Arthur C. Watson; Corporal, William F. Johnson; Corporal, William Dixon; Corporal, Burges Ware; Corporal, William Broaden; Corporal, Robert Anderson; Corporal, Edward F. Cobb; Corporal,

Lloyd Preston; Corporal, John M. Lane; Trumpeter, William Stanily; Trumpeter, Eugene S. Fennell; Farrier, Robert McDonald; Blacksmith, John Steward; Saddler, John Eubanks; Wagoner, Rand Harris.

James H. Austin, John Ayres, Thomas M. Berry, Leonard R. Blackburne, George E. Braxton, Harry Butler, William M. Bunn, Richard Combs, Richard F. Doyle, George English, Mosley Gaines, Seymour Gardner, William M. Gregory, Theodore Grice, George W. Gullion, John Gullion, Arthur Hamilton, Major Hockins, Lewis W. Holloway, William Jackson, Bradey Jewell, Thomas Mason, Frank A. Miller, James H. Miller, Edward Mitchell, Marion W. Murphy, Edward W. Page, John Prim, James Russell, Peter Saunders, Henry Sawyer, Frederick Sheffield, Johnie Stewart, Jesse W. Walker, Arthur G. Wheeler, Edward N. Whitson, Willie Wilson, John Morris. Total, sixty.

Names of those left behind: Privates John H. Bowman, Jefferson Lucas, Courtney Matthews.

Corporal William F. Johnson, killed in action July, 1898.

Corporal Edward T. Cobb, drowned June 22, 1898.

Private George English, drowned June 22, 1898.

Sergeant Arthur C. Watson, died of typhoid fever, Brooklyn, New York, October 3, 1898.

Corporal Robert Anderson, died of yellow fever near Santiago, August 14, 1898.

Private Mosley Gaines, died of typhoid fever near Santiago, August 19, 1898.

Private Henry Sawyer, died of typhoid fever in General Hospital, Montauk Point, Long Island, New York, September 4, 1898.

Wounded in action: Second Lieutenant Harry O. Williard; Privates Thomas M. Berry, George E. Braxton, Mosley Gaines, William M. Gregory, Theodore

Grice, William Jackson, Frank A. Miller. John Prim, James Russell, Peter Saunders, Arthur G. Wheeler, John Morris.

Reserves of Troop B in United States during the war:

Sergeant, John H. Bowman; Corporal, Joseph H. Green.

William Adams, William Adkins, Henry Birt, John Bowman, Major Bryant, William Bullet, James B. Bratcher, Jasper A. Cherry, James S. Conway, Eddie Cook, Allen Cooper, Peyton Craig, Albert Currant, Isaac Embra, Owen Evans, James D. Fuller, Jesse Gay, William H. Gray, Robert T. Green, John G. Gregory, Henry Hawkins, Samuel Hughes, Frank Jackson, William M. Jones, Charles A. Lee, Walter F. Locks, Charles Martin, James E. Miller, Cornelius Mitchell, William Myla, Will Palmer, William Pettie, Budd Pollard, John Rash, Sylvester L. Richardson, Henry Robinson, Fred Searcy, Isaac Shellington, Joseph J. Stevens, Blair Stout, David. Timberlake, Colvin C. Thomas, James Tucker, Thomas Taylor, Edward Wallace, Spencer White, James H. Wicks, William Winn.

TROOP C.

Men who were in Cuba during campaign of Troop C, Tenth United States Cavalry:

First Sergeant, Adam Houston; Sergeant, Henry Robertson; Sergeant, Thomas Griffin; Sergeant, Edward Lane; Sergeant, William Ancrum; Sergeant, Vodrey Henry; Sergeant, Walker Johnson; Sergeant, Tony Williams; Corporal, Thomas Dooms; Corporal, Edward Jones; Corporal, Samuel Covington; Corporal, Thompson Murry; Corporal, James M. Watkins; Corporal, Benjamin Gaskins; Trumpeter, Alexander Sulder; Trumpeter, WilliamYoung; Farrier, Samuel Holden; Blacksmith, Joshua Cook; Saddler, Benjamin Smith.

David W. Barts, Norwood Branch, John Brown William H. Brown, Benjamin F. Bryant, Robert Bush, James H. Camper, Edward C. Chelf, William H. Collins, Joseph S. Edwards, Alfred E. Griffith, William H. Johnson, Samuel M. Jones, Sidney Kirtley, Louis Marshall, William Matthews, Edward Nicholson, John H. Payne, Robert Ransom, Frank Ridgley, Forrest Robinson, Emory Salter, Charles Scott, Oscar Scott, Charles C. Senters, Roy Smith, William Street, Benjamin F. Tyler, Alfred Welch, Henry White, Thomas Woods, Otho J. Woodward, Charles Young.

Reserves of Troop C in United States during the war:

Walter Arnold, William Barks, Ether Beattie, Peter Bigstaff, Isaac Bright, Augustus Brown, William Bryant, Louis Carr, William L. Carter, Walter Chenault, Sidney Clay, John Davis, Charles E. Ellis, Robert French, Henry Graham, James Gunter, Benjamin Hawkins, George L. Heyman, Sims Holmes, McHenry Hudson, Claude Jackson, James Jackson, Charles Johnson, John Johnson, Henry Vineyard, William Wagner, Samuel Wallace, Lesley White, Matthew White, Henry Wilson, Arnold Winslow, Willie Woods, John Wright, William H. Johnson (2), Charles Jones, James C. Lewis, Prince Mosley, William Palmer, George Rankins, Joseph Seals, Robert T. Shobe, John W. Smith, John J. Streater, James Stockton, McCulloh Talley, William Turner.

TROOP D.

Officers and men who were in the Cuban campaign of Troop D, Tenth United States Cavalry: Captain John Bigelow, Second Lieutentant, A. E. Kennington.

First Sergeant, W. H. Givens; Sergeant, James.

UNDER FIRE. 341

Elliot; Quartermaster Sergeant, Edward Johnson; Sergeant, J. H. Stratton; Sergeant, W. H. Hamilton; Sergeant, A. C. Winburn; Sergeant, George Lewis, Corporal, John Walker; Corporal, Meredieth Arnold; Corporal, Bud Arnett; Corporal, John Thornton; Trumpeter, Sprague Sims; Trumpeter, Purcell Wiley; Farrier, Silas Johnson; Sergeant, Willis Hatcher; Sergeant, W. H. Bailey; Corporal, Robert Flynt; Corporal, Andrew Cooper; Corporal, James Wormley; Corporal, Luchious Smith; Saddler, Benjamin Brooks.

J. H. Campbell, James Clay, Clarence Hall, James Moss, Fred Owens, George Starkey, Harry Swan, Eston Thomas, Wade Bledsoe, Charles Boyd, William Brown, Isaac James, Thomas Mason, Fred Shockley. Charles Arnold, William Alexander, Lewis Boarman. Harry Brooks, William Cannon, William Campbell, Henry Fearn, Jefferson Jones, William Johnson, George Kellum, Benjamin Robinson, Alexander Schockley, Harry Sturgis, J. F. Taylor, William Tyler, Charles White.

Reserves in the United States during the campaign:

Samuel Bruden, Lawn Carroll, Standley Clauders, William Cissell, Edward Drivers, C. V. Ervine, William Hill, Enoch Johnson, William Miller, Charles Toliver, Scott Worrior, William Lee, H. C. Raymond, Neil Roper, Edward Brown, William Downs, F. E. Kelley, George Ramsey, J. T. Simpson, James Sutton, Evans Taylor, Otto True, J. C. Washington, Porter Whiesnant, J. B. Anderson, Mat Bell, Henry Bell, A. M. Berry, Robert C. Brown, Jr., Ennis Clark, Ezekiel Ficklin, Garfield Green, Edward Johnson, William Majors, W. H. Roberts, J. H. Sanders, Robert Wallace, Will Wright, George Brookins, Arons Clay, Samuel Childers, Albert Dade, Thomas Taylor, George Teble, Blacksmith, Pleas Cooper.

TROOP E.

Following officers and men of Troop E, Tenth Cavalry, were in Cuba:

Captain, Charles G. Ayres; Second Lieutenant, George Vidmer; First Sergeant, Peter McCown; Sergeant, John Graham; Sergeant, Benjamin Fassitt; Sergeant, William C. Beckett; Quartermaster-Sergeant, William Payne; Quartermaster-Sergeant, Ozrow Gathe; Corporal, Thomas H. Herbert; Corporal, John Hughes; Corporal, John Biggs; Corporal, John R. Swan; Corporal, John H. Henderson; Corporal Henry McComack; Corporal, William Collins; Corporal, Emmet Preston; Corporal, William L. White; Farrier, B. F. Johnson; Blacksmith, Lewis S. Anderson; Saddler, Edward Barr; Wagoner, Burr Neal; Trumpeter, William H. Johnson; Trumpeter, Joseph White.

Joe B. Anderson, Joseph S. Allen, John L. Anderson, John H. Brown, Charles Carver, Felix J. Cole, James A. Dyson, Isaac G. Eighmie, Harry V. Evans, William H. Fall, Murry Gibson, Gilmore Givens, Oscar Gurnell, William N. Henderson, Douglass Harris, William H. Mitchell, William R. Nelson, Freeman E. Pender, Willie Phillips, Charles Reddic, James S. Simpson, Isaac Singleton, John Smith (1) John Smith (2), Wilson M. Thomas, Burt Vandeburg, Augustus Wally, Hillie Brown, A. C. White, E. Wilson, William L. White.

Killed: William L. White.

Wounded: Quartermaster-Sergeant William Payne, Sergeant John L. Taylor, Blacksmith Lewis L. Anderson, Privates Gilmore Givens, Henry McCormick, Allen C. White, Hillie Brown.

Reserves in the United States during the campaign in Cuba:

First Lieutenant, Samuel D. Freeman; Sergeant

Charles B. Turner; Corporal, Josiah G. Tubeman; Corporal William B. Hill; Corporal, Fountain Howard; Trumpeter, Willie Taylor.

George Price, George W. Peck, Tillman Rowlett, Robert Scott, Dillard Lee, Edward Smith, Arthur Taylor, Charles Tudor, Gus Tudor, James Turner, Albert Thompson, John Vandyke, Frank Vanhorn, Clarence West, Charles R. West, James E. Wilson, Henry H. Williams, Henry Williams, Robert Ash, Stephen Ashe, Charles Bailey, Richard Bailey, George Bardison, Charley Beard, Hays Brown, James Brown, Cæsar B. Brown, Clarence Burbridge, Simon Benn, William Carter, Lewis Clark, Eugene Curry, John Cosy, Henry Freeman, Frank Fry, John H. Garrett, William Johnson, Oscar Johnson, William B. Kennedy, John Kellis, Edward Long, Julius C. McIntosh, Iscar Mason, Silas Pitman.

Troop F.

List of officers and men who were in campaign in Cuba in Troop F, Tenth Cavalry: Captain T. W. Jones and Second Lieutenant H. C. Whitehead.

First Sergeant, Amos Elliston; Quartermaster Sergeant, Harrison Porter; Sergeant, Alfred M. Ray; Sergeant, Walker S. Rollins; Sergeant, Samuel H. Alexander; Sergeant, William Barnes; Sergeant, Frank Rankin; Corporal, William H. Mitchem; Corporal, Absom Hicks; Corporal, Alonzo Bowens; Corporal, John Watson; Corporal, Willie Bolling; Corporal, John H. Anderson; Corporal, James K. Lee; Corporal, Allen Jones; Trumpeter, Carey Lewers; Trumpeter, Richard Cicell; Farrier, Charles Taper; Saddler, William H. Daniels; Blacksmith, Charles Robertson; Wagoner, William McCauley; Cook, James C. Sanders.

Walter W. Board, Garfield Brown, Tracy F. Brown,

James H. Catlett, John H. Cole, Paul Crittenden, John R. Creighton, Grant Curtis, Hugh Dickerson, Fred Fisher, Albert Gaskins, Edward Gray, John Grover, Frank Hanks, Lindsey P. Holt, Henry Jackson, George Jackson, Thomas Jordan, Thomas Kinslow, John H. Laws, William Lee, Edward W. Manley, Walter Smith, Isom Taylor, Julius Taylor, Walter Tolbert, Silas N. Wade, John Waters, Benjamin West, John Whiting, Charley Wilson, John W. H. Young, Jesse James, John Watson, Ernest Johnson, George Mayo, James P. Twisby.

List of men of Troop F, Tenth Cavalry, who were not in Cuba:

Wiley Foster, William Glover, Frank Howard, Roy Long, David Merriman, Archie McElroy, George Pickins, Sherman Robinson, Clarence Wells.

Wounded: First Sergeant Amos Elliston, Blacksmith Charles Robertson. Privates Henry Jackson, Isom Taylor, John Watson.

Killed at Montauk Point, Long Island, James P. Twisby, by Lindsey P. Holt.

Number of deaths by fever: Sergeant Frank Rankin, Ernest Johnson, George Mayo, Allen Jones.

Those who have been discharged that were in Cuba: Sergeant, Abraham W. Davis; Saddler, Albion Denney; Trumpeter, Albert H. Squires; Privates Cornelius Martin, Seth Williams, Jerry Norris.

TROOP G.

Troop G officers and men who were in Cuban campaign:

First Lieutenant, W. H. Smith; Second Lieutenant, T. A. Roberts; First Sergeant, Saint Foster; Sergeant, George Berry; Sergeant, Horace W. Bivins; Sergeant, Charles A. Dorsey; Sergeant, William Thacker; Sergeant, Charles Cliffoid; Sergeant, Ernest S. Washington; Sergeant, John Henderson; Sergeant, Richard Hopkins; Corporal, Albert Davis; Corporal, Frederick D. Boyd; Corporal, Marcellous Weight; Corporal, William T. Wells; Corporal, John I. Ray; Corporal, Charles E. Parker; Corporal, Washington H. Racks; Corporal, Joseph Williams; Trumpeter, James H. Cooper; Trumpeter, Zachariah Steward; Blacksmith, John Duff; Saddler, Charles Copelle; Farrier, Harry Williams; Wagoner, George Thrasher; Cook, Silas Goldwaite.

William Alexander, John Arnold, Charles Arthur, James Bell, Joseph Bird, Clarence L. Bluford, Emmitt L. Bluford, James Brantly, William Brown (1), John Brooks, William J. Davis, J. W. B. Dauglash, Jr., George DeMore, Herbert Earley, Richard Finney, Joseph Gates, John Henderson, William H. Jackson, Willie Johnson, Samuel T. Minor, William H. Quickley, William E. Snowden, Hamilton O. Spriddles, Cliff Thornton, Maryland Thompson, John Wells, Irioin Whitson.

Killed in action: First Lieutenant W. H. Smith; Privates William H. Slaughter, John Brooks (?).

Wounded: Second Lieutenant T. A. Roberts; Sergeant Earnest S. Washington; Corporal Marcellous Wright; Privates John Arnold, John Brooks, Charles Authur, Richard Hopkins, Samuel T. Minor, and Joseph Williams.

Reserves of Troop G in the United States during the campaign:

John Armfield, George Beeler, Sim D. Brantley, William Brown (2), Henry Buckner, Albert Searight, James Taylor, William Thomas, Garfield Thompson, Albert H. Turley, Clifford Chambers, Lige Chester, Robert I. Drake, Charles English, William Gale,

Charles Ganson, Albert Gilbert, Perry Grayson, Andrew Hankins, Nelson Harris, John Holmes, William H. Holland, Henry P. Houston, William F. James, William Johnson, John H. Lee, Samuel J. Leonard, Edgar Loyd, William F. Lytle, Charles Manning, Edward Washington, Masons A. White, Thomas White, Arbet Nilson, William Withers, Charles F. Wood, Buford Young, Robert Young, George A. Nielsen, Marshell Louis, Albert McKay, Thomas L. Mosley, Martin Nolan, Clarence E. O'Neal, John Redd, John Roberts, Henry Scott, Hughes F. Shobe, George Smith.

TROOP H.

Troop H officers and men left in United States as reserves:

Captain, Levi P. Hunt; Second Lieutenant, Paul Reisinger; First Sergeant, Shelvin Shropshire; Sergeant Charles Faulkner; Sergeant, David T. Brown; Sergeant, Lucelius Drane; Sergeant, James H. Alexander; Sergeant, Edward H. Braxton; Sergeant, Robert Lang; Sergeant, James Hopper; Corporal, Daniel Garrett; Corporal, James Ecton; Corporal, Andrew J. Jennings; Corporal, George H. Turner; Corporal, Joseph Wooden; Corporal, Edward Hartsfield; Corporal, James Branch; Corporal, John E. Lewis; Cook, Mack Harris; Trumpeter, William Plumo; Trumpeter, Thomas Bunch; Farrier, George H. Washington; Blacksmith, William C. Ewell; Wagoner, James S. Barnes.

Frank Carroll, Earnest Cherry, Matthew R. C. Clark, Rufus E. Cobb, Albert Collier, Thurston G. Derrett, Frank K. Dickerson, Edward Dosier, Robert Edwards, Henry P. Gaines, William H. Gaston, William Graves, Edward Gynn, Thomas Hames, Augustus Hargrove, Oscar Hoffman, Lyman Holdman, Charles Holland, **William Hose, Moses W. Hull, John Hurt, Abraham**

UNDER FIRE. 347

Jackson, Dudley Anderson, Authur Bell, Samuel Bergeon, Eddie J. Berryman, James Black, Frank Boyle, John R. Brooks, William Brown, John Bueford, Nathaniel Bullock, Henry T. Galloway, James Norris, George R. Ratcliffe, Clifford A. Sandridge, George H. Smith, William M. Strayhorn, John Timbers, Edward Ward, Walter Wilson, William Patterson, Frank Robinson, Robert L. Shell, William Smith, John Strickland, Joseph Thomas, John White, Joseph Stevens, William Jackson, Isaac Jernigan, Lewis Johnson, Richard Johnson, Edward Jones, Walter S. Jones, Joseph Kemp, Charles Lann, Martin C. McBride, Charles McGee, Simon Mothow, William Neal, Ollie Rodgers, Charles Schawtz, Max Kwtz Steel, Charles I. Taylor, John Wallace, John E. N. Westfall, George A. Garfield.

Men who went to Cuba with Lieutenant Carter P. Johnson:

Charles S. Allen, William Harris, Thomas Mitchem, Dennis Bell, Frank C. Henry, William K. Porter, Nathaniel Bullock, Lelwood Loving, John S. Williams.

TROOP I.

Officers and men of Troop I who were in Cuba:

First Lieutenant, R. J. Fleming; Second Lieutenant, A. M. Miller; First Sergeant, Robert Millbrown; Sergeant, Benjamin F. Potts; Sergeant, Ananias Lumkins; Sergeant, John Dunton; Sergeant, Ulysses G. Gunter; Sergeant, Barry Hanson; Sergeant, Major H. Peter; Corporal, Miller Reed; Corporal, Charles Dade; Corporal, George Smith; Corporal, George H. Racks; Corporal, Joseph Thompson; Corporal, Elsie Simms; Trumpeter, John Nuble; Trumpeter, Oscar N. Oden; Saddler, Amos K. Edwards; Farrier, Sherman Harris; Wagoner, John Boland; Blacksmith, Calvin C. Burns.

Frank D. Bennett, Tazwell Brigs, Thornton Burkley,

John F. Chevin, Jr., William H. Cook, Stephen H. Duboise, Robert Glover, Morris Green, Charles Howard, John A. Humphrey, Wesley Jones, Elsie Jones, Kelley Maberry, Victor L. Marshell, Frank Murry, Robert A. Payne, Ross Pendleton, Leonidus Piersaul, Lee Pryor, William Queen, Amos B. Reed, Samuel Redd, Houston Riddell, William H. Shoecraft, John W. Simms, James Steward, Frank Thomas, Robert Wells, John Wilson, George Wilson, Wills Groves, Clarence Hall, Thomas S. Hardy, Henry Hardaway, William Harrington, George J. Henson, Lewis Henderson.

Troop I men and officers left in United States:

Captain, S. L. Woodward; Sergeant, Phillip Roberts; Corporal, James E. Marshell; Corporal, Benjamin Mayo; Corporal, Joe Williams.

Alphonso Alexander, James Barnes, Loyd Bell, William Berry, Albert Bruin, Gilbert Bryant, Matt Campbell, Wiley Cordle, Gardner Coleman, George Dabney, Edward Decker. Robert Dorsey, Luther Drake, Theodore Durdin, Thomas Evans, Daniel Fant, John W. Frazier, James Green, John Graham, Richard Hardin, Forrest Hampton, Hugh Hayes, George Metcalf, Elbridge Moore, Moses L. Murphey, William H. Jackson, George McReynolds, John Norman, Jesse Patton, William Richardson, James Recketts, Elsie Simms, George C. Singleton, Alex. Sivel, John Tell, John T. Thompson, Daniel Walker, Harry Porter, Will Haughton, James Johnson, John Kaholokula, George H. Kellar, Saint Leavell, Edward Lewis, Luther Lockery, Frank Hayes, Jr.

TROOP K.

Troop K officers and men left as reserves in United States during the campaign:

UNDER FIRE. 349

Captain, Robert D. Read, Jr.; First Lieutenant, R. G. Paxton; Second Lieutenant, H. B. Dixon; First Sergeant, Walter Green; Quartermaster Sergeant, Philip Letcher; Sergeant, Robert Johnson; Sergeant, Thomas Young; Sergeant, Eugene P. Frierson; Sergeant, William H. Hill; Sergeant, William Winrow; Corporal, William Turner; Corporal, Ezekiel Green; Corporal, Thomas W. Murdock; Corporal, Willie A. Peterson; Corporal, Watts Frierson; Corporal, Edward A. Dorsey; Corporal, Lowery Holowell; Corporal, Robert E. Williams; Corporal, Beverly F. Thornton; Farrier, Ned Axom; Saddler, Archie Mills; Wagoner, Richard E. Robinson; Trumpeter, John Brown; Trumpeter, John S. Rhea.

Benjamin F. Alexander, George Allen, John A. Anderson, Louis Anderson, David Bell, Jesse Benn, Caleb Benson, Henry Bolden, Tillman Bonner, King C. Boykin, Farleigh Broadey, James W. Campbell, Wilson Carey, Fletcher Carter, Abraham Champ, Willie Coakgee, James Collins, Stephen W. Collins, James Crook, William H. Crosby, Walter C. Davidson, John Davis, William L. Dawson, Albert L. Diggs, James H. Dodd, Robert Donson, Howard P. Dunn, Ernest Finley, Charles H. Ford, George Fultz, Rubie Gibson, Will Gleaves, James Grace, Virgil Hammonds, Nathaniel Harris, Preston Hayes, William Hayes, John T Hopings, George Hudnell, Bernard A. Jackson, John A. Johnson, Harry R. Jones, Jackson Kendall, George Lapsley, Wade H. Leigh, William Lindsey, James E. Logan, Lewis Lloyd, Robert McAdoo, Robert B. Moore, Rufus Moore, Lindsey Morgan, Edward Nelson, Otis Obanion, James W. Peniston, Lonnie Pitts, Isaac C. Reddie, Robert Reynolds, Oscar G. Robinson, Julius B. Rucker, Archie M. Smith, Julius Stacy, James Stanton, Percy Standfield, Anderson F. Stewart,

Albert Tate, Willie Wiley, Daniel Williams, Willie A. Williams, Frederick Willis, George B. Willis, William H. Winger, Lee Woodson.

Men who went to Cuba and took part in the campaign:

George Fultz, Abraham Champ, Bernard A. Jackson, Isaac Lewis, Otis Obanion, Julius B. Rucker, James W. Penniston.

Troop L.

Troop L reserves in the United States during campaign.

Had no regular officers commanding.

First Sergeant, Charles Perry; Sergeant, Alexander Nadell; Sergeant, Jefferson Dowling; Sergeant, William Johnson; Sergeant, William Lacy; Sergeant, George Taylor; Sergeant, Clarence L. Proctor; Sergeant, William H. Pennean; Corporal, Noah Ridgley; Corporal, James C. Myers; Corporal, George Christian; Corporal, Harvey Berry; Corporal, Charles W. Robertson; Corporal, James Oden; Corporal, Lucius H. O'Neal; Trumpeter, Edward Green; Farrier, Washington Scott; Saddler, Ruben Dearing.

Martin Barnes, Charles Berry, Edward Berry, Samuel Britton, Charles Butler (1), Charles Butler (2), Richard Buckner, Robert Chanley, Robert Chenault, Stephen Clark, William A. Cleveland, Frank Calhoun, Harry Crocket, James Crutchen, Hayes Daniels, Robert Dean, Richard Moore, Henry Monroe, George C. Mullin, William Noland, Henry C. Noland, Richard C. Parham, George Patterson, Edward B. Porter, William Preyer, Joseph A. Priestly, George Randell, Charles Robinson, Wilbarn Robinson, Ramie Rollins, Alfred Rollar, Willie Dixon, Hall Duff, Fred Fowler, William Gilyard, James Greggs, William Harper, Isaiah F. Harris,

UNDER FIRE. 351

Monroe Head, Charles H. Henderson, John Holmes, Squire Hudson, Walter Huff, Isaac Hunter, Mark Jackson, James Jackson, James Jones, A. H. Jones, George W. Jones, H. M. Jones, William Johnson (1), William Johnson (2), Edward Johnson, Scott Johnson, George Layne, William H. Lander, John B. Lucus, Clarence M. Lenard, Gid Long, George Martin, Stephen Meeks, William McMichael, Edward C. McDowell, Samuel McClung, Edward W. Moore, Jack Shannan, Isaiah Sanders, James N. Shaw, William Skelton, Albert Smith, Charles Smith, William Stafford, Joseph Starr, Alexander Taylor, John Talbot, Luther T. Thornton, William E. Walton, Joseph Watts, George Washington, John Weight, John Lotterberry.

TROOP M.

Troop M reserves in the United States during the campaign:

Troop was without regular officers.

Sergeant, Paschol Conley; Sergeant, Edward W. Nimms; Corporal, George W. Newman; Corporal, James C. Williams; Corporal, John T. Crane; Corporal, Clarence Page; Cook, Boston Clay; Farrier, Bob Roberts.

John R. Acklin, George Bates, John Brewer, Robert Buckner, Albert G. Calloway, Charles Carter, James Chapman, Joseph Cheatham, Marion Cochran, Albert T. Cowings, Levi Cunningham, Charles A. DeHenderson, John Dickerson, Will Dixon, Clarence Dry, William Dunlap, Pike Eaves, Albert Ferguson, Stertes Ganson, Herbert J. Gaston, James Gleedon, John Glover, James D. Hale, Cæsar Hendricks, Samuel Hite, David Hughes, James N. C. Hughes, Willie Johnson, Walter Johnson, William Jones, Henry Jordan, Charles H. Kniffley, Thomas D. Lancaster, Fritz

Lee, Frank Logan, Luke Merriweather, Henry Miller, James B. Montgomery, Mose Murry, Ferdinand C. Newton, Emery Nothington, Thomas O'Neal, Clarence H. Owens, Jefferson Parker, Dorsie Peters, John Pierce, Loyd T. Porter, George Prince, Robert Price, Eddie Ratcliffe, McClellen Redd, Jesse Russel, Jeremiah A. Sheridan, Richard Simpson, Harry Smith, Lawson Smith, Thomas Smith, Edward Staley, William Stefy, Charles Tyler, Edward Wallace, William Walker, Jesse Ware, James White, Preston F. W. Wickliff, Lucius Winchester, Thomas Yancy, James Young.

Troop M men who went to Cuba with Lieutenant Carter P. Johnson and joined General Gomez's command:

First Sergeant, Louis M. Smith; Sergeant, Robert J, Noal; Sergeant, Robert J. Johnson; Sergeant, James L. Minor; Sergeant, James B. Jelkes; Sergeant, Thomas Travillion; Corporal, George H. Wanton; Corporal, William H. White; Corporal, William Watts; Trumpeter, McCallin Green; Trumpeter, George Smith; Saddler, Thomas Boyd; Blacksmith, William Kelley.

Grant Burrus, James Crolly, John Henry, James H. Lawson, Benjamin F. Offutt, Amos Roberts, Joseph Rodgers, Edward Williams.

BAND.

The members of Tenth Cavalry band who were in Cuba:

Sergeant-Major, Edward L. Baker, Jr.; Quartermaster Sergeant, B. A. Anderson; Saddler Sergeant, J. C. Smith; chief musician, Washington Darrow; Chief Trumpeter, J. W. Campbell; Sergeant, T. E. Jenifer; Corporal, John Harris.

Thomas Bruff, William L. Chester, John B. Drew,

LIEUT. JOHN BUCK.
Late Sergeant 10th Cavalry. Promoted for bravery in action.

LIEUT. J. H. HILL,
Late Sergeant 24th Infantry. Promoted for bravery in action at Santiago.

LIEUT. JOS. M. MOORE.

LIEUT. JOHN C. PROCTOR.
Eighth U. S. Volunteer Infantry.   Late Sergeant 9th U. S. Cavalry.

LIEUT. WILLIAM WASHINGTON.
Eighth U. S. Volunteer Infantry.   Late Sergeant 9th U. S. Cavalry.

Surgeon A. M. Brown.

E. R. Dolby, Albert Gaston, T. C. Hammond, John Hopkins, J. F. Hendricks, Peter Hambright, H. C. Jones, G. M. Jones, A. S. Lowe, Clifford Lowe, Harry R. Pleasant, William Whitlock, Solomon Williams, William White, John Wiggins.

Deaths from Cuban fever: Chief Musician, Washington Darrow; Thomas Bruff.

Chief Musician George F. Tyrell has been appointed to take charge of the band.

Left in the United States: George Johnson.

Noncommissioned officers of the Tenth United States Cavalry who were promoted in the United States Volunteers as commissioned officers for gallantry in the Cuban campaign:

To first lieutenancy, Edward L. Baker, Jr., Alfred M. Ray.

To second lieutenancy, W. H. Givins, Saint Foster, John C. Pendergrass, Jacob C. Smith.

The following officers were wounded in the battles in Cuba: Major Theo. J. Wint; Captain John Bigelow, Jr.; First Lieutenants, M. H. Barnum; E. D. Anderson; R. L. Livermore; Second Lieutenants, Harry O. Williard; Frank R. McCoy; T. A. Roberts; H. C. Whitehead.

Complete list of colored soldiers of the regular army promoted to commissioned officers:

Seventh United States Volunteer Infantry:

Second Lieutenants: First Sergeant, Peter McCown, Troop E, Tenth Cavalry; First Sergeant, John Buck, Troop B, Tenth Cavlary; Sergeant, William H. Brown, Troop L, Ninth Cavalry.

Eighth United States Volunteer Infantry:

First Lieutenants: Sergeant Joseph Moore, Troop A, Ninth Cavalry; First Sergeant, William Washington,

Troop F, Ninth Cavalry; First Sergeant John C. Proctor, Troop A, Ninth Cavalry; Sergeant William McBryar, Co. H, Twenty-fifth U. S. Infantry.

Second Lieutenants: Sergeant Wyatt Huffman, Co. G, Twenty-fifth U. S. Infantry; Sergeant Macon Russell, Co. H, Twenty-fifth U. S. Infantry; Sergeant Andrew J. Smith, Co. B, Twenty-fifth U. S. Infantry.

Ninth United States Volunteer Infantry:

First Lieutenants: Sergeant, John G. Beckham, Co. F, Twenty-fourth U. S. Infantry; First Sergeant William H. Franklin, Co. E, Twenty-fourth U. S. Infantry; First Sergeant, Alexander Richardson, Co. A., Twenty-fourth U. S. Infantry; First Sergeant Alexander Williams, Co. A, Twenty-fourth U. S. Infantry; First Sergeant, Edward Williams, Co. C, Twenty-fourth U. S. Infantry; Sergeant, William Wilkes, Co. F. Twenty-fourth U. S. Infantry; Sergeant Benjamin F. Sayre, Co. C, Twenty-fourth U. S. Infantry.

Second Lieutenants: First Sergeant, Robert G. Woods, Co. G, Twenty-fourth U. S. Infantry; Private, Thomas C. Butler, Co. H, Twenty-fifth U. S. Infantry; Sadler Sergeant, Jacob C. Smith, Tenth U. S. Cavalry; Sadler Sergeant, John W. Brown, Ninth U. S. Cavalry; Sergeant, Stephen Starr, Co. D, Twenty-fourth U. S. Infantry; Quartermaster-Sergeant, Joseph L. Jones, Twenty-fourth U. S. Infantry.

Tenth United States Volunteer Infantry:

First Lieutenants: Sergeant-Major, Edward L. Baker, Tenth U. S. Cavalry; Sergeant-Major, John H. Anderson, Ninth U. S. Cavalry; Quartermaster-Sergeant, Alfred M. Ray, Troop F, Tenth Cavalry.

Second Lieutenants: First Sergeant, John C. Pendergrass, Troop A, Tenth U. S. Cavalry; First Sergeant, William H. Givens, Troop D, Tenth U. S. Cavalry; First Sergeant, Saint Foster, Troop G, Tenth U. S. Cavalry; Sergeant Elisha Jackson, Troop H, Ninth U. S. Cavalry.